The Judicial Construction of Europe

7 Day Loan

The Judicial Construction of Europe

Alec Stone Sweet

*Chair of Law, Politics, and International Studies,
The Yale Law School and the Department
of Political Science, Yale University.
Offical Fellow, and Chair of Comparative Government,
Nuffield College, Oxford.*

OXFORD
UNIVERSITY PRESS

OXFORD
UNIVERSITY PRESS

Great Clarendon Street, Oxford OX2 6DP

Oxford University Press is a department of the University of Oxford.
It furthers the University's objective of excellence in research, scholarship,
and education by publishing worldwide in

Oxford New York

Auckland Cape Town Dar es Salaam Hong Kong Karachi
Kuala Lumpur Madrid Melbourne Mexico City Nairobi
New Delhi Shanghai Taipei Toronto

With offices in

Argentina Austria Brazil Chile Czech Republic France Greece
Guatemala Hungary Italy Japan South Korea Poland Portugal
Singapore Switzerland Thailand Turkey Ukraine Vietnam

Oxford is a registered trade mark of Oxford University Press
in the UK and in certain other countries

Published in the United States
by Oxford University Press Inc., New York

British Library Cataloguing in Publication Data
Data available

Library of Congress Cataloging in Publication Data
Data available

ISBN 978- 0–19–927553–3 (pbk.)

Typeset by Newgen Imaging Systems (P) Ltd., Chennai, India
Printed in Great Britain
on acid-free paper by
the MPG Books Group

For Harry Eckstein—mentor in exile

Acknowledgments

This book is the culmination of research begun nearly ten years ago. I am grateful to many institutions and individuals who supported it along the way.

Data collection was made possible by two substantial US National Science Foundation awards: SBR 9412531 (1994–7), and SBR 9710963 (1997–2000). These funds were supplemented with grants from the University of California-Berkeley Center for European Studies (1994, 1995–7, and 1998–2000), the University of California-Irvine Global Peace and Conflict Studies Program (1996, 1997–9), the University of California-San Diego Institute on Global Conflict and Cooperation (1994–5), and the US Council for European Studies (1995–7). I am particularly indebted to Russell Dalton for spurring me to write the grants in the first place; to Wayne Sandholtz for continuous, unfailing partnership in administrating them; and to Neil Fligstein for being the right kind of sociologist at the right time.

I have benefited from the kindness and generosity of many good people. Jacqueline Souter, of the Research and Documentation Division of the European Court of Justice, devoted precious staff resources to help me compile data from the Court's archives. Yves Mény, then Director of the Robert Schuman Centre, the European University Institute, gave me friendship, office space, and institutional support over many years. William Schonfeld, longtime Dean of the School of Social Science, the University of California-Irvine, cheerfully approved my innumerable, and increasingly unreasonable, requests for leave. Nuffield College, Oxford, my present academic home, encourages productive research in an unusually effective way: freeing its Official Fellows of formal teaching duties. I have been fortunate to be at Nuffield under Tony Atkinson's benevolent Wardenship. Sir Anthony is the paradigm of what economists ought to be: interested in the economy.

A number of graduate students worked on the project: gathering, coding, and helping to analyze the data. I owe special thanks to Thomas Brunell (now Professor), Rachel Cichowski (now Professor), Margaret McCown (Ph.D. student at Nuffield College), and Markus Gehring (Ph.D. student at the Yale Law School). They are co-authors of Chapters 2, 3, 4, and 5, respectively. I hasten to add that, in every possible instance, I alone am responsible for the book's errors.

Christine Mahoney (Ph.D. student at Penn State) worked on the manuscript in its final stages, making it (almost) possible to meet my deadlines. I am deeply grateful for her extraordinary patience and professionalism in managing the manuscript, and me.

Wayne Sandholtz, Martin Shapiro, and Joseph Jupille read the penultimate drafts of the book and gave me helpful feedback.

This book is embedded in two long-running research projects published, respectively, as *European Integration and Supranational Governance* (Sandholtz and Stone Sweet (eds.) 1998), and *The Institutionalization of Europe* (Stone Sweet, Fligstein, and Sandholtz (eds.) 2001). Some of the finest moments of my intellectual life were passed at the Hotel Laguna, on the glorious California coast, with wonderful people: Tom Brunell, David Cameron, Jim Caporaso, Rachel Cichowski, Russ Dalton, Neil Fligstein, Patrick Le Galès, Adrienne Héritier, Sonia Mazey, Kate McNamara, Andy Moravcsik, Paul Pierson, Mark Pollack, Martin Rhodes, Jeremy Richardson, Wayne Sandholtz, Alberta Sbragia, Martin Shapiro, Michael Smith, and Penny Turnbull.

All ideas are collective goods, if they are any good at all.

I also learned a great deal from conversations with Paul Craig, Louis Favoreu, Dolores O'Reilly, Ron Jepperson, Sally Kenney, John Parr, Otto Pfersmann, Miguel Poiares-Maduro, Walter Mattli, Yves Mény, Anne-Marie Slaughter, Mark Thatcher, Joseph Weiler, and Ola Wiklund. Each gave me more good ideas than I have been able to assimilate. The law faculty of the European University Institute (then Renaud Dehousse, Francis Snyder, Carol Harlow, Luis Diez-Picazo, and Massimo La Torre) and participants of the Yale Legal Theory Workshop and the Yale Law School Faculty Workshop gave guidance at crucial moments.

My fellow traveler and navigator-in-chief, Martha Lewis, made the cover art, inspired by the first paragraph of Stein (1981), whose "fairytale," castle-on-the-hill imagery was later adopted by Judge Mancini (1991).

This is my sixth book with Oxford University Press, and my fifth under the stewardship of my senior editor, Dominic Byatt: blessings on his head. I also thank Amanda Watkins and Claire Croft for shepherding the project from proposal to publication.

Most important, I am indebted to three truly great men who passed away before this book could appear.

Professor Federico Mancini—Advocate General and Judge of the Court of Justice—arranged access to the Court. This book attempts to chronicle the political impact of a long line of judges who shared a common commitment to building Europe through law. Adjudication of European law is, at least formally, anonymous business. Federico's presence, however, was a powerful one: his legacy will animate the life of the Court for decades to come.

Professor Ernst Haas, whom I met in person only once, provided insight and inspiration. Curiously, we corresponded regularly on a wide range of topics, over many years. It would seem that Wayne Sandholtz (one of Haas' students) and I are the last avowed neofunctionalists in the world of integration studies. Ernie claimed that my insistence on paying homage to his early work, now more than forty years old, pained him. He considered our "modified" version of the theory to be significantly different from the original, enough so that even he could be persuaded to reinvest in the project. In my view, Ernie was too modest: he got the big things right, as present obsessions—with "European" culture, identity, and constitutionalism—indicate, if only to those (few) who take the trouble to read him.

I have noted Professor Harry Eckstein's seminal influence on this project in *On Law, Politics, and Judicialization* (Shapiro and Stone Sweet 2002: ch. 4). When I joined the School of Social Sciences at Irvine, as an untenured assistant professor, Harry insisted that my office would be next to his. That simple arrangement changed my life.

Alec Stone Sweet

Oxford and Paris
March 2004

Contents

List of Figures

List of Tables

The European Court and Integration

European legal integration, provoked by the European Court of Justice (ECJ) and sustained by private litigants and national judges, has gradually but inexorably "transformed" (Weiler 1991) the European Community (EC). The "constitutionalization of the treaty system" not only displaced the traditional, state-centric, "international regime" of the diplomat and the international relations scholar (Stein 1981; Weiler 1981, 1994; Burley and Mattli 1993; Stone 1994). It has progressively enhanced the supranational elements of the EC, while undermining its intergovernmental aspects, federalizing the polity in all but name (Lenaerts 1990). And it has altered, within a very wide zone in Western Europe, how individuals and firms pursue their interests, how judges resolve disputes, and how policy is made at both the national and supranational levels of government (Stone Sweet and Brunell 1998a). Today, the ECJ has no rival as the most effective supranational judicial body in the history of the world, comparing favorably with the most powerful constitutional courts anywhere.

Formerly the purview of specialists, interdisciplinary research on the European legal system has exploded into prominence. Law journals, once concerned exclusively with national law, now routinely document the creeping reach of EC law into formerly autonomous domains. Journals devoted to European law and the ECJ have appeared,[1] and new treatises and perspectives on the Court's burgeoning case law are proliferating (Craig and De Burca (eds.) 1999; Craig and De Burca 2003). In the past decade, American political scientists, including those working in the fields of international relations, comparative politics, and law and courts, have published more articles on the ECJ than they have on any other court, excepting the US Supreme Court. Recent dissertations (also Nyikos 2000; Cichowski 2002) have begat new books (Alter 2001; Conant 2002), and the field of judicial politics in the EU is regularly surveyed (e.g. Mattli and

---

[1] The *European Law Journal*, for example, explicitly supports interdisciplinary approaches.

Slaughter 1998). Perhaps most importantly, legal scholars and social scientists now collaborate (Slaughter, Stone Sweet, and Weiler (eds.) 1998) and speak to one another (Börzel and Cichowski (eds.) 2003); and it is no longer uncommon for social scientists who do not normally study courts to notice and analyze the impact of the ECJ on discrete policymaking episodes (Mazey 1998; Pierson 1998; Sandholtz 1998; Sbragia 1998; Héritier 1999, 2001).

This book is partly an effort to explain why all of this has happened. It is also part of a larger research project, which I will briefly discuss in order to clarify the book's purposes and methods.

I was attracted to the topic of legal integration for reasons unrelated to existing scholarship on the Court. The project began as a means of testing theory about how a particular type of social system—a rule of law polity—emerges and evolves, with what political consequences. The theory was developed without reference to the European Union (EU). In an initial set of papers, I identified key variables, deduced causal relationships among them, and then used the theory to help explain the *judicialization* of the GATT-WTO and the French Fifth Republic (Stone Sweet 1997, 1999). By judicialization, I mean the process through which judicial authority over the institutional evolution of a society is constructed. I then derived a series of hypotheses about how new legal systems would evolve, and began searching for appropriate empirical settings in which to test these propositions.

The EU provided an attractive case, as a new, and indeed novel, legal system.[2] The system had a clear beginning point; data were, in principle, available; and no systematic social science on how it had developed existed. In 1995, four graduate assistants—my present coauthors—and I began to collect comprehensive data on process associated with integration, including trading, litigating, judging, and legislating in the EC. These data were later supplemented with further information, compiled by Neil Fligstein, on EC lobbying. We then developed a series of tests of our propositions, using both quantitative and qualitative methods; and we considered our findings in the light of current scholarly debates about how to explain the course of European integration (Stone Sweet and Brunell 1998*a*; Stone Sweet and Caporaso 1998*b*). This second set of papers served as the basis for the elaboration and testing of a more general macro theory of integration (Fligstein and Stone Sweet 2002).[3] Finally, in a third part of this research (see also

---

[2] This book focuses almost exclusively on the EC, the first pillar of the EU.

[3] See also Sandholtz and Stone Sweet (eds.) (1998); Stone Sweet and Sandholtz (1999); Stone Sweet, Sandholtz, and Fligstein (eds.) (2001).

Slaughter, Stone Sweet, and Weiler (eds.) 1998), we examined interactions between private litigants, national judges, and the European Court, and assessed the impact of these relationships on doctrinal, constitutional, and legislative outcomes (Cichowski 1998, 2001, 2002; Stone Sweet and Brunell 1998*b*, 2001; Stone Sweet 2000: ch. 6). This book extends and completes the project.

I Orientations

The generic question posed by this book is how a particular mode of governance, the judicial mode, is consolidated as a stable set of practices. By governance, I mean the mechanisms through which the rule structures in place in any community are adapted, on an ongoing basis, to the needs and purposes of those who live under them (Stone Sweet 1999). Such mechanisms are required for any social system to reproduce itself, given changing circumstances and the forces favoring social anomie (Eckstein 1988; Stone Sweet, Fligstein, and Sandholtz 2001: 4–16). In modernity, as markets and territorial units have expanded, as societies have become more secular, differentiated, and complex in other ways, the social demand for law (Durkheim 1947), and for formal, "rationalized," government (Weber 1978), has steadily increased (Schlucter 2003). At the same time, the organizational forms that governance actually takes have standardized and diffused (Jepperson 2001).

The book is guided by materials developed in two prior papers. The first, *Judicialization and the Construction of Governance* (Stone Sweet 1999), elaborates a deductive theory of third-party dispute resolution (TDR), including adjudication, focusing on the development of specific causal relationships between three factors: social exchange, or contracting; triadic dispute resolution, or judging; and rules—institutions, norms, law. The model shows how two sets of processes become linked to one another to produce an expansive, self-sustaining, system of governance. These processes can be expressed as testable propositions. The first set of claims concerns the relationship between dyadic contracting, or social exchange, and TDR. As social exchange grows and communities become more complex and differentiated, so will the demand for TDR; given certain conditions, TDR will be increasingly activated and thereby implicated in governance. The second set of claims concerns the underlying dynamics of judicial rulemaking—the clarification, modification, or creation of rules through TDR. Critical to the theory is the enormous social pressure placed on the judge to announce reasons to justify his or her decisions. The more the judge does so, the more likely he or she will be to insist that those with whom he or she interacts also defend their behavior with reasons. The paper sets out the conditions under which argumentation, deliberation, and justification not only become basic to how all actors in the system pursue their underlying interests, but also to how the rule system evolves. Judicialization is a feedback effect, observable as the impact of triadic rulemaking on how individuals take decisions and interact with one another (see Stone 1989, 1992; Stone Sweet 2000: chs. 3, 7).

The second paper, *Path Dependence, Precedent, and Judicial Power* (Shapiro and Stone Sweet 2002: ch. 2), seeks to explain why judicial modes of governance tend to be both incremental and *path dependent*. Legal institutions can be said to be path dependent to the extent that how litigation and judicial rulemaking proceed, in any given area of the law at any given point in time, is fundamentally conditioned by how earlier disputes have been sequenced and resolved. The paper develops a model of adjudication in which legal norms and reasoning are brought to bear on strategic action and decisionmaking through the propagation of discursive choice-settings, doctrinal structures called "argumentation frameworks" (following Sartor 1994; Stone Sweet and McCown 2002). Such frameworks are formalized analogies, assembled from materials found in past decisions, on related cases. Judges self-consciously curate precedents in order to organize their environments in ways that make judicial governance possible. Argumentation frameworks give some measure of determinacy to legal norms, and thus help to legitimize judicial lawmaking. They also help lawyers and judges build "litigation markets," enabling legal actors to achieve effective communication and coordination with one another (Shapiro and Stone Sweet 2002: 96, 294), even when they are widely dispersed in space and time. As discussed further below, certain characteristic features of how courts operate favor the path dependence of legal systems, and reinforce the centrality of argumentation frameworks.

At a more meta-theoretical level, these papers seek to resolve certain tensions between "utility-rationalist" and "sociological-constructivist" approaches to institutions and change. They do so through dividing the overall process of normative development into discrete stages, deducing the separate logics that govern each stage, and then demonstrating how and why institutional change depends critically on the co-constitutional or symbiotic properties of strategic behavior and normative deliberation. TDR and argumentation frameworks, the argument goes, constitute paradigmatic social mechanisms for coordinating institutions and purposive action, structure and agency, given changing circumstances (see also March and Olsen 1989; North 1990). Both papers, and this book, express a strong dissatisfaction with static, functionalist accounts of institutions and governance.[4] In a judicialized world, TDR will manage institutional change, reconstituting the world in ways that are both unintended and impossible to predict beforehand, at any *ex ante* moment, even by those who created or regularly make use of the system.

As should by now be clear, I view law, courts, and judging as instances of more generic social phenomena and activities. The law is conceived not as a *sui generis* matter, the esoteric stuff of lawyers, but as one type of institution, or normative structure, that interacts with other rule systems (e.g. culture, social norms) to shape outcomes. Legal reasoning is regarded as a formalized species of analogical reasoning. Doctrine and precedent are analyzed as argumentation frameworks, meso-level cognitive structures that enable lawyers and judges to perform their roles and maximize their effectiveness. Courts are just one type of governance structure in that they adapt rules (the macro setting of politics) to fact contexts (the micro setting), on an ongoing basis. At the micro level, the domain of decisionmaking and action, I assume that people are rational in the sense of being purposeful and goal-oriented. But I also assume that rational action is *skilled action* (see Fligstein 2001), which means that people define and pursue their interests in light of the social environments in which they find themselves. Institutions and organizations give structure to the social world. They provide logics and opportunities for action, but they also constrain it, through certifying actors, fixing roles and expectations, and authorizing certain forms of activity, while prohibiting others (David 1994; Jepperson 2001).

To this point, I have described my approach to the study of law and courts in relatively abstract terms. For the purposes of this book, the approach combines three strains of theory: on judicialization and governance; on

---

[4] Economics and political science, at least, are currently dominated by approaches to institutions and organizations that myopically focus on the functional needs of those who design them. These approaches typically deny, at least implicitly, that institutions meaningfully evolve through use (endogenously). In political science, examples include research on "international regimes" in the international relations subfield (especially since Keohane 1984), on "constitutional political economy" (e.g. Brennan and Buchanan 1985), and on legislative delegation to agencies (Kiewet and McCubbins 1991; Epstein and O'Halloran 1999). None of this work has produced satisfactory accounts of institutional change.

courts as commitment devices; and on the dynamics of judicial rulemaking and precedent. I will briefly introduce each in turn.

DYADS, TRIADS, GOVERNANCE

In *Courts* (1981), Shapiro elaborated a simple, reductive, but general theory of courts capable of organizing comparative research across time and space. At its core is an insight first made by anthropologists, namely, that the social demand for TDR is so basic, intensive, and universal that one can find no human community that fails to supply it in some form. Shapiro focused on the deeply *political* aspects of moving from dyadic conflict to triadic dispute resolution. When two parties in dispute ask a third party to help them, they build, through a consensual act of delegation, a node of social authority, or mode of governance (Shapiro and Stone Sweet 2002: ch. 4). This mode of governance, the triad, contains a fundamental tension that threatens to destroy it. The dispute resolver knows that her social legitimacy rests in part on the consent of the parties, and thus on the perception that she is neutral vis-à-vis the dispute. Yet if she declares a winner and a loser, she creates a two-against-one situation, which will erode that perception. Consequently, mediators and arbitrators have developed a host of techniques to settle conflicts without neatly declaring a loser.

Old-fashioned legal anthropology (Collier 1973) and new-fangled law and economics (Ellickson 1991) have both shown that consensual TDR in close-knit societies functions more to reassert preexisting norms than to evolve new ones (see also Hart 1994: ch. 2). In social settings characterized by rising levels of interdependence (i.e. increased social differentiation and division of labor), in which transaction costs are relatively high, and in which the disputants are strangers to one another in some significant way (e.g. culturally), the functional demand for TDR overlaps a rising demand for rule adaptation. In such situations, consensual TDR, with its emphasis on settling conflict and the (re)enactment of existing social norms, is often insufficient to sustain increasing levels of social exchange. More formal commitment devices—law and adjudication—are needed. If litigation is sustained, adjudication necessarily becomes governance (Stone Sweet 1999: 159–163). As important, "judicial" and "legislative" authority become increasingly interdependent, even interchangeable.

Adjudication, of course, is institutionalized, compulsory, triadic *government*. The triad is permanently constituted by jurisdiction, and coercion and office substitute for consent. Once activated, judges normally must make a ruling. Judges are agents of the state, or of the law; and when they invoke legal norms they bring a governmental interest to bear on the parties. All of this means that, in moving from consent to compulsion, "the problem of perceived two-against-one is aggravated" (Shapiro and Stone Sweet 2002: 212). Largely for this reason, courts exist in a quasi-permanent "crisis of legitimacy." In response, judges often seek to avoid, or to mitigate, the effects of declaring a loser, through the development of settlement regimes, splitting the costs of a decision among the parties, processing appeals, and so on. As important, they also generate a rhetoric of normative justification for their decisions.

One of the peculiarities of a robust judicial politics is that the capacity of judges to control political outcomes flows from what is essentially defensive behavior. Because adjudication marries dispute resolution and lawmaking, courts face the problem of how to rationalize the latter. The standard solution to the problem is for courts to justify their lawmaking with reasons, that is, with a formal interpretation of how the law is to be applied to resolve the dispute. Yet, giving reasons is also lawmaking: judges are telling people how they should have behaved in the first place and, if some conception of precedent exists, how they ought to behave in the future. Thus, to the extent that litigating becomes routine in any policy domain, those who inhabit that domain will have an interest in paying attention to the reasons that attach to judicial rulemaking. Judicialization is a variable (Stone 1994; Stone Sweet 2000: ch. 3): the decisionmaking of nonjudicial actors is *more or less* governed by the rules developed through adjudication. In heavily judicialized political settings, the evolution of the "rules of the game" governing policymaking is recorded in case law and registered in the decisionmaking of nonjudicial actors.

One purpose of this book is to track judicialization in the Community.

DELEGATION AND COMMITMENT

The logic of precommitment, or self-binding, has always lurked behind arguments for constitutional review, especially within federal arrangements (Shapiro and Stone Sweet 2002: ch. 3). Federations are cartels, and cartels are unstable. One classic rationale for federalism has been to build larger and more open markets (Mattli 1999). Assume that the members of the cartel have chosen to pursue their collective interest in liberalizing trade across borders by adopting rules to govern such exchange. The resulting situation is typically modeled as a prisoner's dilemma, since any cartel member can gain advantage, vis-à-vis the other members, if it chooses to ignore obligations to open markets while the others obey them. We have good reason to expect that the outcome will be that no cartel member complies fully with the agreement, and that the federation's collective ambitions will be thwarted. One means of stabilizing incentives to cooperate is to build a system capable of effectively monitoring and enforcing the cartel's rules. Courts constitute such a system.

Federal polities sustained through effective judicial review tend to evolve in ways that centralize power. The result hinges in part on the extent to which the court performs its assigned role, and in part on dynamics within the federation itself. If the joint gains of cooperation are important enough, each given member of the cartel has an interest in ensuring that all other members obey the rules of the federation, and thus has an interest in supporting the court, even if some judicial decisions will go against it. The logic of long-range reciprocity comes to govern the arrangement, reducing debilitating concerns about short-term relative gains and losses, and legitimizing judicial authority.

More generally, contracting generates a functional demand for judicial discretion; and certain forms of constitutional contracting—the establishment of federalism and rights, for example—imply the need for an effective mechanism of constitutional judicial review. The link between (*a*) the problems of imperfect commitment and incomplete contracting and (*b*) the extent of political power, or discretion, delegated to the constitutional judge should be obvious (Stone Sweet 2000: ch. 2, 2002). Constitutional obligations are typically expressed in quite general, even vague, language, not least because vagueness can facilitate the reaching of agreement in the first place. As Shapiro notes (1999: 323), "the more general the text, the more discretion to the interpreter." Constitutions are often more difficult to amend than other forms of public law, reflecting the fact that the underlying commitment problem is often more acute. Obviously, the harder it is for nonjudicial authority to nullify the effects of the judiciary's decision-making, the more authority the judiciary is likely to exercise over the polity's normative development.

This last point can be formalized. The strategic "zone of discretion" enjoyed by any court is determined by (*a*) the sum of powers delegated to the court, or possessed by the court as a result of its own accreted rulemaking, minus (*b*) the sum of control instruments available for use by nonjudicial authority to shape (constrain) or annul (reverse) outcomes that emerge as the result of the court's performance of its delegated tasks

(Stone Sweet 2002). Constitutional courts—including the ECJ—operate in an unusually permissive strategic environment: their zones of discretion are close to unlimited. I will return to the question of judicial discretion shortly.

Functional logics can help us understand why political rulers might delegate power to courts. Yet when it comes to how systems of adjudication actually operate, purely functional perspectives—viewing law and courts as solutions to the problem of making commitments credible—are woefully inadequate as explanatory theory. The dynamics of judicial interpretation and lawmaking subvert efforts to predict what will happen from the preferences of those who delegated to judges in the first place, or from the details of institutional design. A robust system of constitutional judicial review, for example, will work to define the paths along which the polity develops by clarifying, supplementing, or amending outright the constitutional law, on an ongoing basis. Where there is a steady case load, where judges justify their decisions with constitutional reasons, and where the constitutional text can be amended only with great difficulty or, in practice, hardly at all, we expect judges to dominate the overall process of constitutional development.

Put differently, the extent to which those who delegate are in fact able to rein in or otherwise shape the use of such authority should not be presumed, but rather constitutes a crucial empirical question for the social scientist (Moe 1987; Pierson 1998; Stone Sweet and Caporaso 1998a; Thatcher and Stone Sweet (eds.) 2002). The issue is a central preoccupation of this book.

NORMATIVE INDETERMINACY AND JUDICIAL LAWMAKING

The notion that the law is fundamentally indeterminate, at least from the perspective of those who litigate and judge, pervades the book's approach to law and courts. Indeterminacy constitutes a rationale for delegating to judges; it motivates litigation and it serves to justify judicial discretion and lawmaking, to the extent that both may serve to reduce indeterminacy. Further along, I will argue that, under certain conditions, the law can be expected to develop in path dependent ways. At this point, I will discuss only two aspects of the relationship between indeterminacy and lawmaking: precedent and balancing.

Precedent

Practices associated with precedent can be understood as a response to the basic existential crisis that judges continuously face. The judge is expected to resolve legal disputes with reference to the law. However, the law, being a social abstraction, cannot be applied to any concrete dispute or situation or set of facts, without adaptation. Normative indeterminacy—that is, uncertainty in how a rule governs a particular fact context—generates a second-order social demand, this time for judicial discretion and governance. The crisis blooms when judges actually do their jobs, in that they reveal that judicial lawmaking inheres in dispute resolution (norm application); judicial lawmaking, in turn, reveals that the disputants could not have known the precise scope of the applicable norms at the time their conflict erupted.

Courts typically respond to this crisis by propagating an overarching principle of governance, which, for simplicity's sake, I will simply call *precedent*. Supported by positivist legal theory (MacCormick 1978; Hart 1994), courts portray precedent as an inherently legal constraint on discretion and lawmaking. In its idealized form, governance through precedent proceeds incrementally, through formal exercises in normative deliberation and analogic reasoning. A court that does not actually or always proceed in this way nonetheless typically claims that it has. Judges package decisions in ways that make their rulings appear to be self-evident, redundant, deductive extensions of pre-existing law (Shapiro and Stone Sweet 2002: ch. 2). Precedent camouflages lawmaking, while enabling it. More broadly, the crisis engendered by judicial lawmaking generates mountains of legal materials—judicial decisions, commentaries, and treatises—whose purpose is to reassert the underlying stability and permanence of the law, and therefore the legitimacy of courts, with reference to precedent and settled canons of interpretation and reasoning.

Precedent-based judicial lawmaking also serves a related, defensive purpose. Adjudication typically comprises a relatively non-hierarchical, decentralized mode of governance. Courts therefore seek to structure their environments in ways that will reduce "noise" from below, and enhance systemic coherence from above. Practices associated with precedent allow judges to do both. Lawyers counsel clients and develop litigation strategies from cues given in existing case law, and these cues would have little meaning without some conception of precedent and coordination—horizontal and vertical—between courts (Shapiro and Stone Sweet: ch. 2).

Balancing

In balancing situations, judges are most clearly exposed as policymakers. In pure constitutional balancing situations (that is, when a court is faced with resolving a dispute in which each of the parties pleads a legitimate constitutional right or interest or value), it is the judges' reading of the situation—rather than the law, per se—that determines the outcome. In developing balancing tests, judges exploit the social logic of long-term reciprocity among potential litigants (society), and construct the law as a flexible instrument of dispute resolution (Stone Sweet 2000: 97–9, 142). Balancing makes it clear: that each litigant's legal interest is a legitimate one; that the court nonetheless must take a decision, by weighing each side's interest against the other; and that future cases pitting the same two legal interests against one another may well be decided differently, depending on the facts. Balancing standards hold sway precisely where the law is (*a*) most indeterminate and (*b*) most in danger of being constructed in a partisan way. Such tests constitute normative tools for managing this indeterminacy over time; they also enable the judges to maintain their own room to maneuver in cases likely to come before them in the future.

When it comes to balancing rights claims against a constitutionally-derived public interest pursued by government, we can expect that a steady stream of such cases will lead judges to develop a highly intrusive form of review: "proportionality," a form of "least-means" testing. The microfoundations of this prediction are to be found in the dynamics of "giving reasons" (see Shapiro 2001; Shapiro and Stone Sweet 2002: ch. 4). Sustained litigation drives courts to perfect a very particular technique of judicial governance: judges require public authorities to defend their actions with reasons. Under certain conditions, the following sequence ensues: (*a*) the rule that those being controlled must provide a reason to justify an action gives way to (*b*) the rule that only a good or sensible reason can be justified, which in turn develops into (*c*) the rule that the best possible reason will be strictly scrutinized, and even then may not be enough to prevail in court. Proportionality, or a strict least-means balancing standard, requires the judge to ask if government could not have proceeded in ways that would have caused less harm, say, to the rights of individuals. If the answer is yes, then the government's interest must be outweighed by the latter. If, in balancing, courts necessarily become legislators and administrators, the reverse is also true: in enforcing least-means tests, courts push lawmakers and administrators into a judicial mode, requiring them to reason as the judge will, that is, to consider the proportionality of their own activities (Stone Sweet 2000: ch. 7).

One of the purposes of this book is to trace if and how proportionality tests develop in the EC, and the consequences of such balancing on the exercise of legislative authority.

Summary

It should be obvious how these three sets of ideas can be combined. We have good a priori reasons to expect that the pace and scope of judicialization will be partly determined by the size of the zone of discretion enjoyed by the court. A court that operates in a relatively large zone of discretion is far more likely to gain decisive influence over the institutional evolution of a polity than one that operates in a relatively restrictive environment. For judicialization to proceed, however, a steady caseload is required, to which judges respond by building a precedent-based case law. Yet again, the greater the zone of discretion, the more likely it is that the specific modes of reasoning and decisionmaking developed by judges—such as those associated with balancing—will consolidate and diffuse as general modes of governance within the system. Judicialization will not proceed if judges produce capricious decisions, with no concern for the coherence of their own jurisprudence.

TESTING

Conceptualizing legal systems in more abstract, deductive, and generic terms is prerequisite to building and testing a comparative social science of law and courts (Shapiro and Stone Sweet 2002: ch. 4). Of course, every legal system is in some sense unique, with its own particularities; and organic differences between legal systems often help to determine the variance in how they evolve. Yet it is the very fact that systems vary that makes comparison possible and testing useful. Further, there are always important and subsidiary questions of theoretical import that can only be addressed by undertaking detailed, historically oriented, case study and analysis. Whenever possible, such questions ought to be restated as testable propositions capable of guiding qualitative research.

Three points about method deserve emphasis upfront. First, causal propositions are necessarily stated as perfect, immutable laws. Hypotheses simplify the world, by focusing analysis on particular relationships among a finite number of variables. Variables are abstract constructs, products of the theoretical imagination, for which direct indicators may not exist. One can hope to use the data that best represent—or operationalize—the variables; but unfortunately we often settle for the best measures we can get.[5] Testing hypotheses in an empirical setting as rich and complex as, say, an

---

[5] Given constraints of time and resources, and the possibility that the best data are not available.

evolving, multilevel legal system, means destroying the "social vacuum" that the theorist imagined when articulating the theory. Testing opens the door to factors that are theoretically extraneous, allowing relationships and processes left untheorized to sweep in. For these and other reasons, it typically reduces to assessing the proposed law in terms of measures of "fit" between the causal claim and a set of relevant observations. The absolute law will find, at best, only probabilistic expression in the world. In this project, my collaborators and I used multiple methods to test a series of hypotheses about how the legal system has evolved, and the kind of outcomes it has produced.

Second, in prior papers, we employed econometric and other statistical methods as first-stage testing devices, which we supplemented by "process tracing": case studies that are structured by explicit causal propositions. The major purpose of process tracing is to crosscheck previous findings or to elucidate causal mechanisms. In this book, we build on previous quantitative analyses, without fully reproducing them. Our broad purpose is to evaluate the impact of adjudication on the institutional evolution of the EC. We blend aggregate data analysis with comprehensive case studies of the operation of the legal system, at the domain level, across the entire life of the Community. We do so in order to (a) crosscheck results; (b) explore theorized relationships among variables in a diversity of contexts; and (c) evaluate propositions about the importance of sequencing to outcomes. I see no reason to think that quantitative methods comprise, a priori, stronger or weaker means of testing hypotheses than do qualitative methods, and I see every reason to combine them whenever possible (Goldthorpe (ed.) 1997).

Third, there exists an imposing mass of scholarship on topics relevant to the European legal system. Much of this work is worthy of more discussion than it will in fact receive. I focus on existing research that either makes testable claims about how the legal system has developed or operates, or makes arguments that are sufficiently developed to allow me to derive testable claims. That is, the book organizes the assessment of hypotheses. It does not organize a contest among research frameworks, or "isms," which I see as fruitless. If I would characterize my approach as being broadly institutionalist, I see no point in declaring it to be more "sociological" than, say, "rationalist."[6] It is possible for a properly specified hypothesis to be expressed in multiple ways, in vocabularies developed within diverse or

---

[6] For these distinctions, see Hall and Taylor (1996).

even contentious frameworks. In the next section, I note that aspects of my theory are congruent with some elements of Haas' "neofunctionalism," and that my arguments necessarily conflict with claims made or implied by "intergovernmentalist" theory. But my aim is to assess these arguments against evidence, as part of the effort to understand the dynamics of legal integration. It is not to validate some form of institutionalism, to champion Haas, or to defeat intergovernmentalism.

II European Integration and the Legal System

This book expands on previous efforts to elaborate and test a theory of European integration, as summarized in Chapter 2. In the culmination of this project, Fligstein and Stone Sweet (2002) demonstrated that the activities of market actors, lobbyists, legislators, litigators, and judges had become connected to one another in important ways. These linkages, in turn, produced a self-reinforcing, causal system that has driven integration and given the EU its fundamentally expansionary character. We recognized certain necessary but not sufficient conditions for such a causal system to emerge, the most important being the constitutionalization of the Treaty of Rome. In our analysis of period effects, we also found that two parameter shifts—whereby important qualitative events generate quantitatively significant transformations in the relationships among variables—had occurred in the development of the EU. The first shift began roughly around 1970; the second in the mid-1980s. The EU's developing legal system was implicated in both transitions, first, through constitutionalization, and, then, through the development of effective judicial controls of Member State compliance with EU law, especially with regard to rules governing the common market.

Constitutionalization (Chapter 2) refers to the impact of the diffusion of the ECJ's doctrines of supremacy and direct effect within national legal orders. The doctrine of direct effect, among other things, enables private actors to plead rights found in EU law before national courts; and the doctrine of supremacy requires national judges to resolve such litigation not only with reference to EU law, but also by giving priority to it. Litigation of EU law in national courts occurs under the supervision of the ECJ, whose authority stems from the procedures established by Art. 234 of the Rome Treaty. According to Art. 234, when EU law is material to the settlement of a legal dispute being heard in a national court, the presiding judge may (and some judges must) refer the matter to the ECJ. This referral, called a *preliminary question*, asks the ECJ for an authoritative interpretation of EU law. The ECJ responds with an interpretation of that law, an act called a *preliminary ruling*. The judge of referral is then expected to apply the ruling to resolve the case. By the 1970s, supremacy and direct effect had combined with Art. 234 to constitute a decentralized means of monitoring and enforcing EU law and, much the same thing, to constitute both the ECJ and the national courts as important sites of legislative and constitutional innovation.

This research also explored the impact of adjudicating EU law on legislating and treaty-revision. It emphasized two basic motivations for litigating EU law in national courts. First, actors engaged in transnational economic exchange would ask national judges to remove national laws and administrative practices that obstruct their activities, in order to expand their markets, and to fix market rules in their favor. As transnational activity increases, the pool of potential litigants expands, as does the number and diversity of situations likely to give rise to conflicts between traders and states. Second, private individuals and groups *not* directly engaged in cross-border economic activity—such as those seeking to enhance women's rights or the protection of the environment—would use the courts to destabilize or reform national rules and practices they find disadvantageous, and to enhance the effectiveness of EU law within national systems. As the corpus of EU law (including both secondary legislation and the Court's case law) becomes more dense and articulated, so would the grounds for pursuing such interests at national bar. We tested a series of propositions concerning (*a*) the determinants of litigating EU law; (*b*) the nature of the constraints facing the ECJ and national judges; and (*c*) legal outcomes (who wins and loses). The system worked steadily to expand the supranational character of the EU, to push the integration project much further than Member States' governments would have been prepared to go on their own, and to structure intergovernmental bargaining and the decisionmaking of the EU's legislative organs.[7]

---

[7] I do not mean to imply that our research was the first to suggest that European integration was heavily determined by the course of legal integration. Academic lawyers, especially Stein (1981) and Weiler (1981, 1991, 1999a), using quite different methods for different purposes, had shown as much in a series of papers produced over two decades. Burley and Mattli (1993), in an article of seminal importance, helped to place the topic of legal integration on the social science agenda. And others, including Alter and Meunier (1994); Berlin (1992); Cappelletti, Seccombe, and Weiler (eds.) 1986; Dehousse (1994); Mancini (1991); and Shapiro (1992), usefully blended law and social science perspectives in their explorations of the ECJ's impact on the evolution of the Treaty system and secondary legislation.

These findings bear on certain long-standing concerns of EU studies. First, they provide broad support for some of the core claims of "neofunctionalist," regional integration theory, originally developed by Haas (1958, 1961; also Burley and Mattli 1993), as modified more recently (e.g. Stone Sweet and Sandholtz 1997, 1999). Haas and his followers argued, among other things, that economic interdependence and the growth of transnational society would push the EC's organizations (primarily the Commission and the Court of Justice) to work creatively to facilitate further integration, while raising the costs of intergovernmental inaction. In drawing connections between Haas' neofunctionalism and this research, I mean to emphasize commonalities that become apparent at a relatively abstract theoretical level. Haas (1961) focused on relationships between (*a*) European rules; (*b*) supranational organizations (especially organizational capacity to resolve disputes); and (*c*) the behavior and dispositions of those political and economic actors relevant to integration. In Europe, he theorized, these three elements could evolve symbiotically, through positive feedback loops that would, under certain conditions, push steadily for deeper integration. What I find important in this formulation is Haas' emphasis on how integration could develop an "expansive logic," as the activities of an increasing number of actors, operating in otherwise separate arenas of action, became linked. Haas labeled this logic "spillover." This point accepted, we reconceptualized the notion of spillover, departing from Haas' formulation in crucial respects (see Stone Sweet and Sandholtz 1998, 1999; and Chapters 2 and 3 of this book).

Our results conflict with strong versions of intergovernmentalist integration theory. With the abandonment of neofunctionalism in the 1970s,[8] the field of European integration was robbed of its theoretical aims and vitality. Research on the EU, post-Haas, proceeded on a piecemeal basis, mainly through describing specific episodes of treaty-making, legislating, and litigating. There was little development of causal theory on the dynamics of integration, virtually no systematic data collection, and efforts to develop and test causal propositions dropped off. Sandholtz and Zysman (1989) revived the field, in a widely read paper whose arguments echoed Haas in important respects. In the 1990s, the claims of intergovernmentalists, especially those of Garrett (1992, 1995) and Moravcsik (1991, 1993, 1995), dominated theoretical debate, if not without challenge (Sandholtz 1992, 1993, 1996; Burley and Mattli 1993).

---

[8] Not least by Haas (1975) himself.

Although the nature of the arguments kept changing, the central claim of strong intergovernmentalism was that the executives of the Member States, or of a consortium of the most powerful ones, effectively regulated the pace and scope of integration, through their control of treaty-revision and the legislative process. Moravcsik (1991: 75) argued that "the primary source of integration lies in the interests of states themselves and the relative power each brings to Brussels," whereas private actors and the EU's organizations *never* play more than a secondary role. Among other things, he proposed that intergovernmental modes of governance typically produce outcomes that reflect the "minimum common denominator of large state [France, Germany, the UK] interests," given their "relative power positions" and the EC's unanimity decision rules. Although Moravcsik ignored the legal system entirely, Garrett (1992: 556–9) bluntly declared that: "Decisions of the European Court are consistent with the preferences of France and Germany." If it were otherwise, the Member States would have punished the Court, and moved to reconstruct the legal system.

The fatal flaw in strong intergovernmentalism was its failure to consider the institutional bases of the powers of the EU's organizations, not least, vis-à-vis the governments themselves. As discussed further below, the Treaty of Rome effectively insulates the ECJ from Member State controls: when it interprets the Treaty, the ECJ exercises the fiduciary powers of a powerful trustee court. Legal integration, a process that has been sustained for some four decades now, is just one of the many important outcomes produced through the dominance of the European Court over constitutional inter-pretation. The 1958 Treaty of Rome is, by definition, an interstate bargain; but strong intergovernmentalists treated the evolving system as if it had always remained nothing but that. They could do so only by ignoring the fact that the capacity of the Member States, as the contracting parties, to control the development of the Treaty system was heavily conditioned by restrictive decisionmaking rules (unanimity of the Member States, plus national ratification). In fact, the EU proved to be "functional"[9] not only for

---

[9] There are at least three meanings of functionalism that are currently being used in EU studies. First, Mitrany (1947, 1966) used the word "function" to denote an organizational competence to perform specific technical tasks, and his theory was labeled "functionalism." Haas (1958) took up the language (see Caporaso and Keeler 1995), adding a concern for societal demands and the interface between "political" and "technical" decisionmaking. Second, there exists an older, deeper meaning for social scientists, one developed in anthropology (Hobhouse 1906; Malinowski 1932) and systematized in sociology (Parsons and Shils 1951). For any society to reproduce itself on an ongoing basis, it must develop stable "structures" to perform certain necessary "functions." The family of theories these ideas produced is usually called "structural-functionalism," variants of which continue to inform integration theory, even

governments, but for economic actors, interests groups, and others who had, over time, invested heavily in making Europe work for them. Of course, the decisionmaking of officials who comprise or represent the executives of the Member States are often crucial to certain kinds of outcomes. Indeed, spillover exists, in my view, only to the extent that governments ratify or otherwise adapt to it. Intergovernmental decisionmaking is typically embedded in, and provoked by, larger processes going on around and between what governments do (Sandholtz and Stone Sweet (eds.) 1998; Caporaso and Stone Sweet 2001).

Not surprisingly, strong intergovernmentalism has been abandoned. The theory could not explain the steady expansion of supranational governance within the interstices of treaty-making, or the impact of the Commission and the Court on thousands of discrete policy outcomes. Moravcsik (1998) retreated into a far weaker brand of intergovernmentalism, grafting a simple principal–agent (P–A) account of delegation onto his basic framework, in order to link the major episodes of state-to-state bargaining with the ongoing, day-to-day, processes of supranational governance. He now stresses that the Member States designed, and continuously redesign, European institutions and organizations to help them resolve certain commitment problems. States confer on EU organizations powers to act against the short-term preferences of some governments in order to help them achieve their more basic, long-range, and collective objectives. In this way, "state purposes" infuse the system, animating supranational governance and encapsulating its evolution.

This strategy raises critical theoretical issues. Most important, the use of delegation theory cannot, in and of itself, distinguish Moravcsik's "weak intergovernmentalism" from other theories of integration, including my own (see also Pollack 1998, 2003; Tallberg 2002). After all, the heirs of Haas and others explicitly invoked P–A logics in their critique of strong intergovernmentalism (e.g. Pierson 1998; Sandholtz and Stone Sweet (eds.) 1998; Stone Sweet and Caporaso 1998a). What remains distinctive about Moravcsik's approach, apart from the narrow empirical focus on state-to-state bargains,[10]

today (Etzioni 2001). Third, economists and rational choice political scientists use the word "functional" to capture the utility that any given institution or organization has for those who created or use it. An institution is "functional" for—"in the interest of"—actors to the extent that the institution serves their interests. In international relations (Keohane 1984), we find "functionalist regime theory," of which Moravcsik's various brands of intergovernmentalism are variants (see Sandholtz 1996).

[10] Ernst Haas (2001, note 4) only addressed this issue on one occasion:

Andrew Moravcsik is the most visible defender of the continuing centrality of the nation-state and its government as the engine of integration. . . . I find it at least very curious that are two claims. Although the key exogenous, independent variable in the theory is increasing economic interdependence—just as it is in neofunctionalism—Moravcsik denies that "transnational" society or interests exist. Instead, private interests, and society, can only be "domestic." He also insists (e.g. 1998: ch. 7) that the EU's organizations have done nothing to "influence the distribution of gains," or the configuration of economic interests, in ways that could help to determine the preferences of governments. This second claim is, at least in principle, testable.

A final issue concerns the relationship between negative and positive integration. It is commonly asserted (e.g. Scharpf 1999: ch. 2) that "negative integration" (the process through which barriers to cross-border economic activity within Europe are removed) and "positive integration" (the process through which common, supranational public policies are made and enforced) are governed by separate social logics. Negative integration, because it enables the Member States to reap large and diffuse joint gains, moves forward relatively smoothly. Positive integration, in contrast, regularly pits these same governments against one another, to the extent that deciding on one form of regulation or intervention as opposed to another will have distributive consequences for identifiable national constituencies, given restrictive decision rules (Moravcsik 1993). It is further alleged that, as a result, the "market" has been constituted without adequate governmental capacity to regulate it or to counter its excesses (Scharpf 1996; see also Schmitter and Streeck 1991; Streeck 1995). In contrast, we found, and this book further reports, evidence in support of the view that negative and positive integration are in fact connected in important ways (they are meaningfully endogenous to one another).

THE EUROPEAN COURT AND THE NATIONAL COURTS

Beyond the founding of the EC itself, the single most important institutional innovation in the history of European integration has been the constitutionalization of the Treaty of Rome. The ECJ, in complicity with national judges and private litigants, constructed the legal system on the basis of a sustained commitment to making EC law effective within national legal orders. The outcome depended critically on the development

despite great similarities in both ontological and epistemological assumptions my treatment and Moravcsik's turn out to be so different. His ontology is described in detail as "liberalism" [yet] its core assumptions are identical with those of NF [neofunctionalism] and seem quite compatible with certain kinds of constructivism as well. It is difficult to understand why he makes such extraordinary efforts to distinguish his work from these sources.

of a working partnership between the ECJ and the national courts. This relationship has been the subject of a great deal of scholarly debate, the best of which combines doctrinal analysis with a concern for the strategic context in which the ECJ and the national judges find themselves. Some scholars have focused primarily on the logics of cooperation between the European Court and national judges, others on conflict. Those involved in the debate recognize that the relationship has been extremely complex and fluid, and that—in the absence of more systematic data and analysis—our attempts to understand its underlying features and dynamics are, at best, stylized simplifications of reality.

Cooperation received the earliest attention, as a puzzle to be explained theoretically. In most national jurisdictions, accepting supremacy meant abandoning deeply entrenched, constitutive principles, such as the prohibition against judicial review of legislation; direct effect required many judges to set aside traditional rules of standing and recognition, and to evolve new ones. Supremacy forbade the use of the standard dualist solutions to conflicts between national and international law, such as the *lex posteriori* doctrine and other corollaries of parliamentary sovereignty. Direct effect enables private actors to sue Member States' governments for noncompliance with EC law, including failure to implement EC secondary legislation; such suits potentially pit judges against governments and the parliaments they control. Accepting supremacy thus entailed significant, nonincremental adaptation on the part of national legal orders. Given vast potential for conflict, how was it that constitutionalization nonetheless proceeded steadily, even dramatically?

A first approach to solving the puzzle proceeds on the assumption that judges seek to empower themselves: given the opportunity, judges will work to enhance their own authority to control legal and, therefore, policy outcomes, and to reduce the control of other institutional actors, such as national executives, parliament, and other judges. As Chapter 2 shows, the Court's supremacy doctrine, combined with the procedures established by Art. 234, provided such an opportunity. Two academic lawyers (Stein 1981; Weiler 1981, 1991, 1994) pioneered thinking on the strategic choice-contexts facing European judges, and Weiler's own ingenious solution to the puzzle became the standard point of departure for others. Weiler argued that (*a*) constitutionalization of the Treaty and (*b*) the incentive structure in place for national judges pushed in the same expansive, integrative direction. National judges could acquire, many for the first time, the power to control state acts previously beyond their reach, such as statutes. Art. 234 not only legitimized what would become a complicit relationship between the ECJ and the national courts; it also afforded both judicial levels a good deal of protection from potential political fallout. The European Court responds to preliminary questions, as the Treaty requires, but the ECJ does not apply EC law within the national legal order; the national courts provide the ECJ with case load, but only "implement" the Court's preliminary rulings, as the Treaty requires. Thus, at critical moments, each court can claim to be responding to the requirements of the law, and the demands of the other court. Once national judges understood that they were advantaged by participating in the construction of EC law, the delicate mixture of the active and the passive in this new legal system flowed naturally, gluing the two levels together.

A second set of approaches (Burley and Mattli 1993; Stone Sweet and Brunell 1998a) emphasizes the role of transnational and other private actors in activating and sustaining European legal integration; the ECJ and at least some national judges are assumed to have an interest in expanding transnational society and in expanding the domain of supranational governance. Litigants and their interests are understood to be fueling a machine operated by judges. In this view, legal integration develops a self-sustaining logic. In announcing the doctrines of supremacy and direct effect, the ECJ opened up the European legal system to private parties, undermined certain constitutional orthodoxies in place in Continental legal systems, and radically enhanced the potential effectiveness of EC law within the Member States. Private actors, motivated by their own interests, provided a steady supply of litigation capable of provoking Art. 234 activity. Preliminary references generated the context for judicial empowerment, which proceeded in the form of a nuanced, intra-judicial dialogue between the ECJ and national judges on how best to accommodate one another. And, as the domain of EU law expanded, this dialogue intensified, socializing more and more actors—private litigants, judges, and politicians—into the system, encouraging still more use. Stated in this general way, the approach is broadly consistent with contemporary revisions of neofunctionalist theory (Stone Sweet and Sandholtz 1997, 1999), and with the theory of judicialization that underlies this book.

That said, my own variation on this approach does not rely on judicial empowerment (Stone Sweet and Brunell 1998b). The core claim is that judges who handle relatively more litigation in which EC law is material will be more active consumers of EC law, and more active producers of preliminary rulings, than would those judges who are asked to resolve such disputes less frequently. This formulation assumes that national judges seek to do their jobs well and effectively, that is, they would like to leave their courts at the end of their week having resolved more, rather than fewer, work-related problems. As the percentage of cases involving EC law rises, so do judicial incentives to master the tools that are most appropriate for the job, and those tools have been supplied by the European Court. Judges that need these tools less will be slower or more reticent to master them, and they will have less reason to be concerned with helping to guarantee the effectiveness of EC law. The approach helps us to explain some of the temporal variation we find within Member States, between autonomous court systems. We know, for example, that across the EC civil law jurisdictions typically accepted supremacy more quickly and with fewer reservations than did, say, administrative law courts, and they produced far more references. As the scope of EC law gradually expanded into more areas, so did the willingness of national judges to make use of it.

It is important to stress that those who focused on intra-judicial cooperation and empowerment did not ignore intra-judicial friction, but took friction for granted as the *expected* state of affairs. The trick, then, was to explain why the legal system had nonetheless taken off. It is obvious that legal integration must be read partly as a narrative of how tensions have or have not been resolved (Weiler 1994; Stone Sweet 2000: ch. 6). Some of the most important achievements of legal integration—such as the progressive construction of a charter of rights for the EU—are rooted in deep, as yet unresolved doctrinal conflicts between the ECJ and national courts. It is also clear that positive incentives "to play the Eurolaw game" do not apply to all judges, and that logics of empowerment can work in non-integrative ways (Stone Sweet 1998*a*). National constitutional courts have good reasons to resist the development of a European "constitutional" order that might subsume the national order (Chapter 2). Other judges could foresee that the ECJ's case law might evolve in ways that would undermine their own carefully curated case law, autonomy, or relations with other national governmental bodies, and they might choose to ignore the Court's pronouncements. Further, the development of EU law would, in effect, expand the "menu of policy choices" available to litigants and judges, and judges might exploit this development creatively, if not always in pro-integrative directions. In a recent book, Alter (2001) examines more systematically the reception of supremacy by French and German judges, paying full attention to the dynamics of intra-judicial conflict.[11] She shows that there were multiple, overlapping, and ever-changing reasons for how national judges chose either to make use of EC law or to ignore it. The point accepted, the general trend has been clear: over time, national judges have been more not less willing to participate constructively in the construction of the legal system.

This book's primary focus is on the impact of adjudicating EC law on the institutional evolution of the EU, rather than on the impact of EU law on (or the *Europeanization* of) national legal systems. How and to what effect national judges use EU law in their work remains a vast, largely unexplored area of research. Such questions are nonetheless addressed in each chapter.

III Determinants of Judicial Discretion in the EU

How has the European Court been able to have such an impact on the course of integration and on the work of national courts? Although the book responds to this question in multiple ways, my starting point is a focus on judicial discretion: the authority of judges to interpret and apply legal rules to situations, in order to resolve disputes.

I propose a simple model of judicial discretion and power, built of three elements, or determinants. Each determinant possesses its own independent logic, yet each also conditions how the other two determinants operate. Given a continuous stream of cases, these three factors will combine, dynamically, to determine the scope of the power of judges to control legal outcomes, generally within the system, and specifically within any line of case law. Although the approach can be used to study judicial discretion in any legal system, the focus here is on the system founded by the Treaty of Rome.

The first factor concerns the nature and scope of the powers delegated to courts. The Member States, as parties contracting into a market-building project, built judicial discretion into the Treaty of Rome. The Treaty established the Court as the authoritative interpreter of EC law, and charged it with enforcing that law even (or especially) against the contracting parties

---

[11] Inexplicably, Alter attacks all extant approaches for failing to notice intra-judicial conflict or to address the questions she has posed. However, the literature cited in this section focused squarely on supremacy conflicts (including Slaughter, Stone Sweet, and Weiler (eds.) 1998, to which Alter contributed).

themselves. The Treaty also fixed further details of the Court's jurisdiction. The ECJ, for example, may resolve disputes brought to it by one Member State against another (Art. 227); between the Commission and a Member State charged with failing to comply with its obligations under EC law (Art. 226); and between the various supranational organs whose form and mandates have also been constituted by the Treaty, such as the Commission, the Parliament, and the Council of Ministers (Art. 230). As discussed, the Treaty also made it possible for national judges to refer preliminary questions to the Court (Art. 234), as a means of ensuring the uniform application of EC law throughout the Union. Jurisdiction and rules governing who has standing before the Court condition caseload, and without a caseload, the topic of the Court's authority is a moot one.

In addition to these direct grants of authority to the ECJ, the Member States also delegated in a "tacit," or "implicit," manner (Bengoetxea 2003), and they continue to do so on an ongoing basis. Legal norms are always at least partly indeterminate, and some types of constitutional norms are arguably the least determinant, or open-ended, of normative structures. Read as a constitutional text, the Rome Treaty leaves much vague, which constitutes a wide grant of discretion to the Court, given demand for normative clarity. The Member States did not lay down a clear blueprint for how the national and supranational legal orders were to fit together, for example, and they did not provide for the supremacy of EC law. The Court generated its own blueprint, in its interactions with private litigants and national judges, under Art. 234. Today, the judicial architecture of the EC is founded on the primacy of EC law vis-à-vis national law. The Member States did not mean the Treaty to confer judicially enforceable rights on private individuals, businesses, and other legal persons. But the Court inferred rights from certain crucial provisions, such as those obligating states to remove hindrances to trade, or to guarantee equal pay for men and women. Legal integration is therefore largely a record of how the ECJ has made creative use of its discretionary powers to remake the Treaty, and how private actors, national judges, and political elites have responded to these moves.

Like any constitution (Stone Sweet 2000: ch. 2), the Treaty of Rome can be analyzed as an incomplete contract. The idea of the incomplete contract is basic to a wide range of approaches to delegation and to courts. Generally, contracts are said to be "incomplete" to the extent that there exists meaningful uncertainty as to the precise nature of the commitments made. Due to the insurmountable difficulties associated with negotiating rules for all possible contingencies, and given that, as time passes, conditions will change and the interests of the parties to the agreement will evolve, all contracts are incomplete in some significant way.[12] Most agreements of any complexity are generated by what Milgrom and Roberts (1992: 127-33) call "relational contracting." The parties to an agreement seek to "frame" their relationship broadly. They agree on a set of basic "goals and objectives," fixing outer limits on acceptable behavior and establishing procedures for "completing" the contract over time.

The Treaty of Rome, read as an enforceable constitution meant to last indefinitely, is a paradigmatic example of a relational contract. Much is left general, even vague. Of course, any state of normative uncertainty constitutes a delegation of discretion to judges. From the point of view of the Member States, generalities and vagueness may have facilitated agreement. But vagueness, by definition, is normative uncertainty, which threatens to undermine rationales for contracting in the first place. For those who are governed by EC law, indeterminacy itself may generate conflict and thereby spur litigation; and litigation provides judges with opportunities to make law real and effective for these same actors. The establishment of the ECJ therefore can be understood as an institutional response to the incomplete contract, that is, as a solution to a set of general commitment problems. Each contracting party to it has an interest in seeing that the other parties honor their obligations, and will be punished for failure to do so. One job of the Court, then, is to clarify, over time, the meaning of the contract, and to monitor and punish noncompliance.

The second factor is the mix of control mechanisms available to the contracting parties, vis-à-vis the Court. We can sort control mechanisms into two broad categories: direct and indirect. Direct controls are formal (they are established by explicit rules) and negative (they annul or authoritatively revise the court's decisions, or curb the court's powers). The following point can hardly be overemphasized: the decision rule that governs reversal of the Court's interpretations of the treaty—unanimity of the Member States plus ratification—constitute a weak system of control, thereby favoring the ongoing dominance of the ECJ over the constitutional evolution of the system. Put differently, the ECJ operates in an unusually permissive environment when it interprets the Treaty. When it interprets secondary

---

[12] A "complete' contract" would specify precisely what each party is to do in every possible circumstance and arrange the distribution of realized costs and benefits in each contingency so that each party individually finds it optimal to abide by the contract's terms (Milgrom and Roberts 1992: 127).

legislation, permissiveness shrinks in those domains governed by majority or qualified majority voting, other things equal.[13]

Indirect controls are effective only insofar as the judges internalize the interests of the contracting parties, or take cues from the revealed preferences of the latter, and act accordingly. The extent to which any court does so is usually taken to be commensurate to the credibility of the threat that direct controls will be activated. Indirect controls operate according to the logic of deterrence (an anticipatory reaction): the more credible the threat of punishment, the more the court will constrain itself. In the EU, since the system of direct controls operated by the Member States is relatively weak, we have no good reason to think that the ECJ, when it interprets the Treaty, will be systematically constrained, in its use of its discretionary powers, for fear of being punished.

Member States can also be said to exercise indirect influence over the ECJ through their powers of appointment. Each Member State could choose only to appoint members to the Court whom they believed share their policy preferences on key issues, for example. During the course of a judge's tenure, governments could make it clear that they will not reappoint a judge who disregards their interest in some important or systematic way. Social scientists have shown, conclusively in my view, that appointment makes a difference to outcomes: the personal policy preferences of judges help to produce judicial outcomes. On the other hand, it has not been shown that appointing authorities control outcomes through their power to choose judges, at least not in any uniform (across time and policy sector) way. In any case, it is virtually impossible to undertake proper research on the relationship between appointments and outcomes in Europe. The Court presents its decisions as unanimous judgments: no votes are published and dissenting opinions are not permitted. In consequence, wherever possible, this book evaluates the extent of indirect control, or influence, by juxtaposing (a) the revealed preferences of the Member States and national governments; and (b) the outcomes produced by the Court.

These first two determinants—delegated powers and the mix of control mechanisms—constitute a strategic "zone of discretion." As defined above, this zone is constituted by the powers possessed by the Court minus the sum of control instruments available for use by the Member States to constrain or void outcomes that emerge as the result of the Court's performance

---

[13] Other things, however, are not equal, since in legislative processes the Court's principal is a complex and hybrid one, including the Commission, the Council of Ministers, and the Parliament.

of its tasks. When it interprets the Treaty, the Court's discretionary authority is close to unlimited.

Conceptualizing discretion in this way cannot tell us what the ECJ will actually do with its powers. The question—what values are judges maximizing when they exercise discretion?—is crucial, if we are to make sense of European legal integration and the impact of the construction of the legal system on nonjudicial actors. I proceed on the assumption, one implicitly shared by nearly all legal scholars who have helped social scientists understand legal integration, that the Court seeks to enhance the effectiveness of EC law in national legal orders, to expand the scope of supranational governance, and to achieve the general purposes of the Treaty broadly conceived. The Court cares about compliance with its decisions because compliance serves these overlapping values, not because it fears being punished by the Member States. There is no compelling, a priori institutional justification for modeling the Court (or the European judiciary) as servants of national governments (Garrett 1992, 1995; Garrett, Keleman, and Schultz 1998, to the contrary). Where governments work to promote the same values, they work in tandem with judges in the service of integration; when they do not, they risk judicial censure

The third determinant of the Court's discretion is endogenous to its own decisionmaking: relative levels of discretion will vary partly as a function of the Court's case law, but only if some minimally robust idea of precedent governs the Court's decisionmaking. The capacity of the Court to organize integration prospectively depends on its success in generating a relatively coherent jurisprudence on the Treaty. I will return to doctrine and precedent shortly. For now, it is enough to note that the zone of discretion will, in part, be determined by the Court's evolving jurisprudence, unless practices associated with precedent do not operate at all. In elaborating constraints that bind all governmental authority in the EU, the Court also constrains itself.

AGENCY AND TRUSTEESHIP

To this point, the discussion in this section may appear to fit comfortably with the so-called positive theory of delegation (Kiewet and McCubbins 1991; Epstein and O'Halloran 1999; Bergman, Müller, and Strøm (eds.) 2000). The analyst typically begins with an exposition of the underlying functional logics for delegation, in order to "explain" why "principals" (political rulers) would delegate to "agents" (new organizations). The standard line is that delegation is functional for principals insofar as delegation reduces the costs associated with governing: of bargaining and commitment; of monitoring and enforcing agreements; and of developing rational policies in the face of technical complexity, incomplete information, and powerful incentives for rent-seeking. The analyst then turns to how the P–A relationship is constructed, focusing on the mix of *ex ante* and *ex post* incentives and control mechanisms that principals use (*a*) to preprogram the agent's performance with respect to their policy preferences, and (*b*) to monitor and punish the agent for nonperformance.

There are good reasons to be dissatisfied with this approach to delegated governance (see Moe 1987; Pierson 1998; Thatcher and Stone Sweet (eds.) 2002). First, the P–A framework loses much of its relevance in situations in which the agent's task is to govern the principals, and when the agent's rulemaking is effectively insulated from *ex post* controls. Following Majone (2001), when one analyzes situations in which relational contracting and commitment problems have induced political rulers to delegate broad "fiduciary" powers to a particular kind of agent—a *trustee*—and then to guarantee the latter's independence, the *agency* metaphor is less appropriate than one of *trusteeship*. The ECJ, like other European constitutional courts, is just such a trustee (Stone Sweet 2002), given that the relevant "political property rights" (Moe 1990) have been transferred to the Court. The Commission constitutes a trustee in the anti-trust field, but an agent of the EC legislator, of which it is a part, when it produces delegated legislation under an EC statute. Strong intergovernmentalism rested on the untheorized assumption that the EU's organizations operate as relatively perfect agents, under the control of the Member States. But, given the Court's expansive zone of discretion, we should not be surprised to see the Treaty develop in ways that were neither intended nor anticipated by the contracting parties at these constitutional-design moments.

A second problem relates to testing. The "positive theory of delegation," as with Moravcsik's weak intergovernmentalism, offers a set of appropriate, if pre-packaged, concepts and logics that can be applied to virtually any delegated governance situation. As causal theory, it remains woefully inadequate. Analysts typically assert a logic for delegation and institutional design derived from alleged needs and preferences of the principals; they then model the resulting situation. These models rarely specify variables or causal mechanisms that would make the formulation of testable hypotheses or comparative research on governance-through-delegation possible (Huber and Shipan 2000). Propositions that have been derived have not found support in subsequent empirical research designed to test them (Moe 1987; Balla 1998). It turns out that such models, largely because they fetishize the *ex ante* functional needs of principals, are not well equipped to deal with the evolutionary dynamics of agency, let alone trusteeship.

Any theory of European integration must attend to the motivations of the Member States in choosing to establish or enhance the powers of supranational organizations. Functional logics can help us to do so. They can also help to generate some very general expectations about how the system of governance constituted by delegation is likely to evolve. A trustee, for example, will likely exert more independent impact on the evolution of EU institutions than will an agent. The Court operates in an expansive zone of discretion, and its activities—such as its interactions with national judges and private parties—cannot be directly controlled by the Member States. Ultimately, trusteeship constitutes a necessary condition for feedback and spillover to emerge and become entrenched, a point stressed throughout the book.

More generally, I, or an intergovernmentalist, or a neofunctionalist can always account for some of the scope of supranational governance by paying attention to previous acts of delegation. The Member States chose to constitute the Court and the Commission as trustees on a host of matters, for rational purposes. They did so, obviously enough, because a trustee would be more likely to succeed in building the common market than an agent would be, or the Member States on their own would have been. But questions of how supranational governance actually proceeds—through what processes, generating what kinds of outcomes, with what dynamic effects?—cannot be answered in this way, except in the most mundane, *post hoc*, and circular way.

The implications of trusteeship make weak intergovernmentalism quite vulnerable, in so far as it means to be taken seriously as a theory of integration.[14] By definition, the greater the Court's or the Commission's zone of discretion, the less able the analyst is to predict the outcomes of supranational governance from the preferences of the Member States at *any* selected moment in time. Moravcsik's strategy is to stipulate some underlying functional need of the Member States for supranational governance, and then to

---

[14] I view weak intergovernmentalism as a theory of how governments interact with one another at specific moments in the process of integration, not as a theory of integration. Moravcsik (1995, 1998) proposes certain testable propositions about national preferences and intergovernmental bargaining, and he finds support for these propositions in the bargaining episodes he analyzes.

interpret outcomes produced by the EU's organizations in light of a prior act of delegation, thereby "explaining" them. As far as can be known, *all* outcomes of interest will *always* fall within the parameters fixed by state purposes. The move, however, does nothing to help us understand how the EU's organizations actually operate, or what kinds of outcomes they will produce. Instead, the empirical domain is eviscerated: integration proceeds; supranational governance spreads and deepens; but the intergovernmentalist's model of the EU, and of state control of the system, never changes. Indeed, Moravcsik asserts that the system has never produced important "unintended consequences."

A similar problem afflicts the so-called "unified model" of EU politics proclaimed by Tsebelis and Garrett (2001; discussed further in Chapters 4 and 5): a series of game theoretic insights about how EU organs can be expected to interact within legislative rules established by the Treaty. Moravcsik and Garrett and Tsebelis proceed on the basis of a crucial, but unstated, assumption: that the "rules of the game," within which the EU's various legislative bodies play, never evolve through the activities of the EU's trustees. The assumption is indefensible. EU institutions not only evolve in this way, but have done so routinely over the past three decades (also Sandholtz and Stone Sweet (eds.) 1998; Héritier 1999, 2001; Farrell and Héritier 2003). Tsebelis and Garrett, too, claim that "unintended consequences" never occur,[15] although they neither define the phrase, "unintended consequences," nor discuss the evidence or arguments to the contrary. These issues are addressed in each chapter of the book.

IV   Precedent and the Path Dependence of Legal Institutions

To this point, I have argued that judicial power is heavily conditioned by two variables: the size of a court's zone of discretion, and the extent to which people activate it, through litigation. Higher levels of judicialization are most likely in systems governed by a trustee court that confronts a steady or growing caseload. I have also claimed that a third variable—the robustness of practices associated with precedent—is basic to judicial power and to the dynamics of judicialization. In this section, I sketch the theory of

---

[15] Presumably Moravcsik and Tsebelis and Garrett mean outcomes to be compared against the intentions of the Member States.

precedent that guides this book. Although the discussion is abbreviated here (see Shapiro and Stone Sweet 2002: 112–35), I focus on why legal institutions tend to develop in path dependent ways, not least because judicialization is a form of path dependence.

The more a legal system is path dependent, the more *historical process* rather than initial conditions or purely functional logics determine outcomes. That is, the analyst will only be able to explain the state of the law, at any given moment in time, in relation to a particular sequence of intermediate events that take place "between initial conditions and the endpoint" (Goldstone 1998: 834). In more technical language, the more any intermediate choice determines the sequence and content of subsequent choices, the more the observed process will exhibit *non-ergodic* properties.[16] In so far as legal actors (those who are being regulated, their lawyers, judges, legal scholars) adapt their behavior to the law, as it develops, the cost of transition away from any existing set of rules or doctrines will rise. The law will continuously develop, through interpretation and application, but it will do so along "pathways" traced by case law (history).

Brian Arthur (1994) and Paul David (1992, 1993, 1994) have shown that path dependent systems possess a common dynamic structure. At a beginning point, a range of choices, formats, or templates—read "law" or "doctrine" —for a particular form of behavior are available; at one or several "critical junctures,"[17] one of these choices gains an advantage, however slight, and this advantage is continuously reinforced through social adaptation effects, called "positive feedback." Ultimately, the choice becomes dominant, or "locked-in," when it becomes a relatively taken-for-granted state of affairs. As shown in Chapter 2 of this book, the Court's decisions on direct effect and supremacy were an obvious critical juncture in European legal integration: they organized what happened next in the grand narrative of constitutionalization. Similarly, *Dassonville* (ECJ 1974) and *Defrenne II* (ECJ 1976) are critical junctures for the development of the law in the areas of free movement of goods and sex equality, discussed in Chapters 3 and 4 respectively.

I begin by conceptualizing precedent. I then present an argument as to how, and under what conditions, legal systems will develop in path dependent ways. I conclude by discussing the book's methods for analyzing precedent in Europe.

---

[16] In David's (1993) terms, "A path dependent process is 'non-ergodic': systems possessing this property cannot shake off the effects of past events, and do not have a limiting, invariable probability distribution that is continuous over the entire state space."

[17] Critical junctures are not necessarily events that actors understood as "big" or "important" when they took place. Their importance may only become clear further downstream.

PRECEDENT AND ANALOGICAL REASONING

Three basic claims about the nature of law and judging underlie my conception of precedent. The first has already been discussed: the law, as developed through judicial decisionmaking, is fundamentally indeterminate. The generic source of the law's indeterminacy lies in the essential tension between the abstract nature of social norms, on the one hand, and the concrete nature of human experience, on the other. Any particular social situation is in some meaningful sense unique, whereas norms are specified in light of an existing or evolving typology of fact contexts, an abstraction that deprives situations of their richness. Second, judging is just one, highly formalized, manifestation of a deeply rooted human penchant for using analogic reasoning to make sense of, and to manage, the complexity of the social environment. Third, judges curate precedent in the form of *argumentation frameworks*. The social function of precedent is to organize legal arguments.

For cognitive psychologists, analogical reasoning is the process through which people "reason and learn about a new situation (the target analog) by relating it to a more familiar situation (the source analog) that can be viewed as structurally parallel" (Holyoak and Thagard 1997: 35–44). The ability to construct analogies is widely considered to be an innate part of thinking (Vosniadou and Ortony 1989; Holyoak and Thagard 1995). Unfamiliar situations, those that individuals cannot understand through their generalized knowledge, stimulate the formation of analogies, which are used to conceptualize *and* to find solutions to problems (Keane 1988: 103). The set of potential source analogs is defined jointly by (*a*) the specific, immediate problem to be resolved (or situation to be conceptualized), and (*b*) the past experiences of the individuals constructing the analogy. Legal argumentation constitutes a species of analogical reasoning: actors reason through past decisions of the court (source analogs) to characterize the interplay of new fact contexts and legal interests raised by a dispute (the target analog), and to find an appropriate solution to it.

Psychologists have also engaged the question of what constitutes an appropriate or effective analogy. Research has shown that the most successful analogies (those that best enable people to conceptualize situations and solve problems) maximize certain structural values (Spellman and Holyoak 1992). The greater the conceptual similarity between source and target, the more the internal relationships between their core elements are structurally parallel, and the better able to offer solutions to the problems posed, the more effective is the analogy. Holyoak and Thagard (1997) have shown that problem solvers generally do seek to maximize these values, which enhances the overall coherence of such reasoning. Moreover, even when the choice of source analog is guided by the conscious, goal-oriented purposes of the individual, the constraints guiding analogy formation nonetheless impose a degree of consistency on the sorts of mappings that will be considered effective and legitimate.

Analogic reasoning is also a functional instrument of decisionmaking, which judges use to structure their environments. Litigation raises questions concerning how legal norms are to be applied to concrete situations, and with what social consequences. Judges will answer these questions in light of how they have answered questions raised with respect to prior, analogous situations, rather than willy-nilly, because skilled analogic reasoning is not only basic to skilled action per se, but to the judges' own social legitimacy. By formalizing the results of analogic reasoning into precedents, say through abduction, judges give the legal system a measure of "relative determinacy." In providing analogs to other actors, they enhance the coherence of the litigation environment, thus reducing randomness and filtering "noise." By grounding judicial rulemaking in discourses present in existing case law, the judges mitigate the crisis of legitimacy discussed earlier. None of these points is incompatible with the view that those who litigate and those who judge are goal-oriented (or even ideologues). Indeed, the argument is that legal actors will sharpen their analogic reasoning skills through training and use, precisely because they are purposive, strategic actors operating within an organizational code that requires such skills of them.

It is an obvious, but not a trivial, thing to note that analogy formation is a perfectly path dependent process, in that each transfer or adaptation of a source to a target analog is only possible by virtue of a prior outcome of analogic reasoning which, in turn, depends upon the sequence of situations and problems that individuals have *already* confronted and resolved. Research has shown that, at any given moment in time, people have some discretion, or exercise some degree of conscious choice, over which analogs get mapped onto unfamiliar situations and how; but the set of available analogs is finite, having been determined by prior events and choices. In adjudication, analogic reasoning has been institutionalized as a set of relatively stable practices. Lawyers and judges use it self-consciously, and the results of their deliberations are, I repeat, heavily documented, which facilitates the identification and mapping of appropriate analogies. Of course, in crafting their arguments and decisions, litigators and judges also work to achieve logical or systemic coherence through other methods, such as deduction and abduction.

Argumentation frameworks

I now turn to how judges govern through precedent, that is, through the propagation of formal *argumentation frameworks*. Prior legal decisions constitute the materials that enable the construction of such frameworks. Legal systems are webs or clusters of relatively autonomous argumentation frameworks.

Argumentation frameworks are discursive, doctrinal structures that organize (*a*) how parties to a legal dispute ask questions of judges and engage one another's respective arguments, and (b) how courts frame their decisions.[18] Following Sartor (1994), these can be analyzed as a series of inference steps, represented by a statement justified by reasons (or inference rules) that lead to a conclusion. Such frameworks embody inconsistency, to the extent that they offer, for each inference step, both a defensible argument and counter-argument, from which contradictory—but defensible—conclusions can be reached. In resolving disputes within these structures, judges typically choose from a menu of those conclusions.

In practice, legal argumentation, unlike purer forms of logical deduction, tends to be "non-monotonic." In monotonic reasoning, "no logical consequence gets lost by extending the premises from which it has been deducted" (Sartor 1994: 191). The primary source of non-monotonicity in legal discourse is the dialectic relationship between new facts or information about the context of the dispute, and the existing premises that underlie normative conclusions. Particularly susceptible to this dialectic are those argumentation frameworks that contain normative statements that (*a*) announce general rules and then justified exceptions to those rules and (*b*) govern how conflicting legal interests ought to be balanced, or how the conflict between two otherwise applicable norms is to be resolved (e.g. when two rights provisions conflict). In balancing situations, which are ubiquitous in constitutional and administrative law, "only the particular circumstances of a case allow a choice to be made," while any new situation "may render new arguments possible, which may defeat previously valid ones" (Sartor 1994: 191, 197).

I have returned to the point made earlier: judicial outcomes, and therefore legal institutions, are indeterminate. Nonetheless, argumentation frameworks provide a measure of (at least short-term) systemic stability, to

---

[18] Only the main features of such frameworks are discussed here.

the extent that they condition how litigants and judges pursue their self-interest, social justice, or other values through adjudication. To be effective actors, legal actors have to be able to identify the type of dispute in which they are involved, reason through the range of legal norms that are potentially applicable, and assess available remedies and their consequences. Such frameworks, being formalized analogs, help actors do all of these things, and more. They require actors not only to engage in analogic reasoning, but in argumentation.

Considered in more sociological terms, doctrinal structures are highly developed, meso-level structures that connect institutions (the law) to the domain of individual agency (decisionmaking, strategic behavior), by sustaining deliberation about the nature, scope, and application of norms. In culturalist terms, they enable specially positioned social actors to adjust existing "guides to action" to "the relentless particularity of experience" (Eckstein 1988: 795–6) on a continuous basis. Precedent is basic to judicial governance, allowing it to proceed incrementally, from preexisting institutional materials.

COURTS AS ORGANIZATIONS

Certain common features of adjudication favor the path dependence of these institutions, *if some minimally robust conception of precedent exists.* I do not claim that these features are essential characteristics of all legal systems, or that they exert the same effect everywhere. Indeed, where these features are not present, or where the effects of the factors discussed are mitigated by other unspecified factors, we expect the path dependence of legal institutions to be commensurably weaker. One purpose of this book is to show that the European legal system has steadily developed these qualities.

First, courts typically do not control the temporal order of cases that come before them. In any legal domain, judicial rulings on cases that come first will exert influence on subsequent litigation and judicial decisionmaking. This will be so to the extent that courts frame their decisions in light of past decisions, and litigants adapt their claims to the courts' rulemaking. Where a judicial decision itself provokes a stream of cases—such as when a ruling expands the opportunities, or enhances the benefits, of litigating for some class of individuals—path dependent properties are most obvious. In negative terms, the claim is that if one could run a sequence of cases differently, one would find that judicial outcomes too would be different, and they would trace a different path.

Second, adjudication constitutes a dichotomous discursive field, in which specific legal questions are typically asked in a "yes–no" format (Kornhauser 1992: 171). Each party seeks different answers from the judge, and each makes counter-arguments in light of the other's claims, behavior that is structured by argumentation frameworks. Judges not only answer at least some of the questions posed to them, but they give reasons for why they have chosen one result over another. (In some polities, some courts are legally required to provide written legal justifications for rulings made.) Dispositive answers given to yes–no questions possess the inherent capacity to block one path of development while encouraging another. Further, when judges justify their rulings with reasons, they (at least implicitly) announce prospective rules, which subsequent litigants will understand and use as templates for future argumentation in cases that are similar in some salient way. If this is so, the *path independence* of legal institutions will be unlikely or exceptional.

Third, adaptation and network effects, to be registered on the behavior of judges, lawyers, and professors, are facilitated by the fact that records of judicial activity are heavily documented. Published decisions typically include a description of the relevant or settled fact context of the case, a survey of the main arguments and counter-arguments, the dispositive decision, and the justification. The lawyers' briefs and other summaries of the parties' arguments are also usually available. Lawyers, who through training and practice learn to take their cues from these materials, are commonly organized into relatively autonomous groups that roughly map onto relatively autonomous domains of the law. If domains of law develop along separate path dependent lines, than the processes that serve to construct various networks of legal professionals will also be path dependent.

Fourth, judicial rulemaking is typically embedded in dense matrices of legal rules, some of the properties of which will favor, again, increasing returns logics. At any given point in time, the existing law relevant to any specific dispute may itself be relatively inflexible and path dependent, in the sense of *being more or less immune to change except through adjudication*. Modern legal systems typically organize legal acts hierarchically, and this fact has consequences for system inflexibility, that is, for the capacity of other political actors to alter or reverse judicial outcomes.

We have already discussed this last point with reference to the zone of discretion enjoyed by the European Court. But more generally, wherever constitutional judicial review operates in a routine and minimally effective manner, the path dependence of constitutional law, because of its normative supremacy vis-á-vis other legal norms, will be assured. Given network effects, the relative inflexibility of any body of law will be largely determined by two factors: (*a*) the density of judicial rulemaking in that area and (*b*) the relative ease or difficulty of overturning the lawmaking effects of judicial decisions through nonjudicial means.

In summary, how courts typically operate and how legal actors typically behave are likely to provoke and then sustain the path dependent development of litigation and judicial rulemaking. Given some underlying notion of precedent, these processes can be expected (*a*) to exhibit some significant degree of non-ergodicity (through the vagaries of sequencing, and the survival of rules announced in past rulings), and (*b*) to provoke feedback effects (more litigation and the construction of litigation networks), and to move the law along paths that are relatively inflexible (increasingly costly to reverse).

RATIONALITY AND ADAPTATION

In this book, I assume that all legal actors are instrumentally rational, in the sense of generally pursuing their own individual or corporate interests, however defined. Judges, I expect, will seek to maximize, in addition to their own private interests, at least two corporate values. First, they will seek to enhance their legitimacy, vis-à-vis all potential disputants, by portraying their own rulemaking as meaningfully constrained by, and reflecting the current state of, the law. Second, they will work to strengthen the salience of judicial modes of reasoning vis-à-vis disputes that may arise in the future. Propagating argumentation frameworks allows them to pursue both interests simultaneously. To the extent that these assumptions and expectations hold some purchase on reality, then judges will behave in ways that reinforce the path dependence of the legal system. Of course, frameworks produced can never entirely reduce normative indeterminacy, at least not from the point of view of the litigator operating in a rapidly changing environment.

I assume that litigators are seeking to shape the law in ways that will most benefit their clients, at the moment and in the future. Given the costs of litigation, private actors will pursue their interests through adjudication only to the extent that expected returns exceed those costs. In litigating EC law, this calculation will be partly conditioned by perceptions of the relative cost and likelihood of achieving the same policy change through other means (such as lobbying for legislation in national or supranational arenas).

They will do so in full knowledge that there will be others who will work to block legal change. In any given domain of law, rationality means deploying those litigation strategies best adapted to achieving desired legal outcomes, given the current state of the law, as that law is constituted by argumentation frameworks. Those who litigate more frequently in any given domain will invest more heavily in mastering the intricacies of relevant frameworks, and in charting their evolution over time. This is another way of saying that the more the law is path dependent the more we can expect it to branch, and the more incentives legal elites will have to specialize, not least in order to participate in the development of the law. In the EU today, specialization is now, for all practical purposes, obligatory.

THE INDETERMINATE NORM AND JUDICIAL DISCRETION

Figure 1.1 helps to simplify and summarize the argument made thus far, namely, that adjudication functions to reduce the indeterminacy of legal norms through (*a*) use, that is, argumentation, interpretation, application, and (*b*) the propagation of argumentation frameworks. The line between point ID (absolute indeterminacy) and point AD (absolute determinacy) defines the extent to which any given rule can vary along one dimension, that of determinacy. Point ID represents a theoretical pole at which there exist no stable, collective understandings of the meaning and scope of application of the rule. Point AD represents the opposite theoretical pole, at which the collective understandings of the meaning and scope of application of the norm are perfect. (Neither ID nor AD is realistic.) For any given

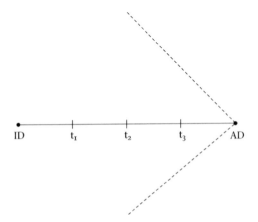

Figure 1.1. The Indeterminate Norm and Judicial Discretion

norm, indeterminacy is a relative condition: it will vary, in context and over time. If the law is path dependent, for the reasons given, the position of the norm on this continuum will move, from left to right, over time, as the rule is adjudicated. The broken lines spreading from point AD define the range of defensible arguments available for how a rule must be applied to resolve disputes arising within that rule's purview. The space constitutes the judge's *zone of discretion*, within which the judge chooses among available options and justifications. If the law is path dependent, this zone will narrow, over time, as the rule is adjudicated. That is, argumentation frameworks that appear will move from left to right: choice narrows and frameworks become more articulated. As this space narrows, so does the discretion of the judge.

The argument made here bears directly on certain debates within contemporary legal theory. Insofar as legal institutions are in fact path dependent, certain strains of positive legal theory must be considered at least presumptively right, or supportive of the theory presented here, and other strains of legal theory must be presumptively wrong. In the former category, we find the positivist legal theory of H. L. A. Hart and his heirs. Hart (1994: especially 124–41), understood judicial discretion to be inversely proportional to normative indeterminacy, so long as judges did their jobs in an "adequate," or "reasonably defensible," rather than in an "arbitrary" or "irrational," manner. Judicial lawmaking (the use of discretion) is defensible, rather than arbitrary, to the extent that it proceeds through analogic reasoning, in light of precedent, and to the extent that it "renders" legal rules "more determinate." The underlying criteria governing a justified extension of the law into new areas is the "relevance and closeness" of the new situation to a pre-existing, norm-governed, situation.

For Neil MacCormick (1978), a close student of Hart's, the primary objective of legal theory is the development of standards for evaluating judicial decisions as "good or bad," "acceptable or not acceptable," "rational or arbitrary." Bad decisions are those that cannot (ultimately) be packaged as a deduction, that is, where the justification given does not proceed logically from explicated norms and principles. Bad decisions also fail to adhere to the "principle of formal justice," defined as *like cases shall be decided in like fashion*. For MacCormick (1978: 67, 68), judges can only produce good decisions through a combination of *good* analogical reasoning and *good* justification—precisely the mix of ingredients that generates argumentation frameworks and makes them path dependent. Further, good decisions definitively structure lawyers' strategies (positive feedback): good strategies will reinforce existing frameworks and will plead for incremental adjustments to the law from judges. Last, even where consequentialist (policy) arguments trump purely legal ones, judges are likely to choose from a menu comprised of defensible rulings, not all rulings that are imaginable. These points, because they link the production of doctrine to the dynamics of prospective judicial lawmaking, are generally consistent with arguments made in this chapter and elsewhere in this book.

But they also contrast with what the law and economics movement typically asserts. Law and economics imagines a market for legal institutions. Stable institutions that do emerge are assumed to be Pareto efficient, since if they were not they would be abandoned and replaced. In the world imagined, institutions are plastic (both malleable and disposable), and new ones can be generated with little or no cost. In such a world, the analyst needs to know a great deal about the needs of the economy and about how to calculate transaction costs and efficiencies, but little or nothing about how the law has developed through use. I agree that there is a market for legal rules that litigation and adjudication helps to construct. But I see no reason to assume, a priori, that the world constructed is an optimally efficient one.

This view is not, however, necessarily hostile to the views of critical legal studies or so-called deconstructionists. In the critical tradition, scholars commonly seek to show that doctrinal structures develop in ways that privilege certain "dominant principles," and "suppress" or "subordinate" others; they then may analyze the fact that a "marginalized" narrative or principle actually means marginalization in the world, as the law works its effect on constructing human relations (Balkin 1987, 1990). I do not see how it could be otherwise. Argumentation frameworks develop in ways that foreclose certain kinds of arguments, deforming certain narratives or situations into types recognizable by judges. Relatively foreclosed, "marginalized interests" can be expressed, but often only as exceptions, or as second- or third-best legal representations.

PRECEDENT IN EUROPEAN LAW

I have discussed precedent at some length because the ideas presented here are taken for granted in subsequent chapters. One purpose of book is to chart the development of precedent-based practices in the EC and to assess their impact on the course of integration. The basic unit of observation is the argumentation framework. In principle, the analyst should be able to chart the development of frameworks that should, in principle, chart the evolution of the legal system more broadly. We have good reasons to think that the development of legal institutions will provoke the development of networks of legal actors specializing in that area of the law. For these actors, existing argumentation frameworks establish the basic parameters for action. Further, if a legal system exhibits path dependent qualities, then the following expectations will be met *and* will be causally related to one another.

First, argumentation frameworks will link, through feedback loops, the activities of litigators and judges over time. Litigation will provide opportunities for judges to construct such frameworks, and subsequent litigants will take their cues from judicial rulemaking. If such frameworks are path dependent, the sequence—litigation > judicial rulemaking > subsequent litigation > subsequent rulemaking—will tend to reproduce itself as a self-reinforcing process sustained by a mix of analogic reasoning and the self-interest of legal actors, that is, potential litigants and judges.

Second, legal outcomes will be both indeterminate and incremental. By indeterminate, I mean that the further downstream we are from any given, prior point in the process of selecting or refining legal institutions through adjudication, the more unpredictable will be the content of the rule selected. By incremental, I mean that the substantive law and argumentation frameworks produced through this process will be predicated on outcomes and frameworks that had emerged upstream. Stated differently, how cases are sequenced and decided will have an effect on how the future is organized.

Third, legal institutions will produce network effects that embed them in wider social practices and interests. Substantive legal outcomes and argumentation frameworks will become parameters for (focal points of) social action. They will be referenced and used by an increasing number of individuals and groups, including those not otherwise directly associated with adjudication.

Fourth, legal institutions will be relatively resistant to rollback or deinstitutionalization. This outcome will be governed partly by the zone of discretion, and partly by the relative embeddedness, through positive feedback, of outcomes over time.

V Case Selection and Data

This book extends research that blended econometric and other statistical methods with detailed cased studies in order to test a theory of European integration. Although we have chosen not to replicate the quantitative analyses published previously,[19] our findings are summarized in Chapter 2. Instead, my collaborators and I assess the impact of adjudication on the institutional evolution of the EC. In Chapters 3–5, we move away from the broad, macro perspective on integration adopted in Chapter 2, to a detailed examination of the impact of the legal system on the evolution of three policy domains: free movement of goods, gender equality, and environmental protection. The data collected allow us to do so systematically, at least in the three areas of EC law that we have chosen to research intensively. The choice of these three sectors, and not others, requires a defense.

Generally, case selection is defended in terms of representativeness and variance. While I can hardly claim a representative sample (it is a purposive sample of three domains), I do argue that the cases selected provide for meaningful variation along a number of dimensions. One of our policy areas is concerned with negative integration (free movement of goods), and the other two concerns positive integration (social policy, environment). Compared with free movement of goods, the efficiency logic of positive integration is not always straightforward. At the same time, the development of common EC policies can raise distributional issues, set constituencies off against one another, and threaten the institutional interests of the national administrations. The sectors are more or less developed, due to their longevity as an important EC policy area, or to the density of EC legislation in the area. Further, the data analyzed in subsequent chapters reveal large variance in practices associated with litigation. In avoiding similar cases, one reduces the probability that patterns found are due to specific factors not likely to be replicated in other settings. While one cannot generalize results to all issue areas or sectors, steps have been taken to assure that the results are not completely idiosyncratic.

A second justification for selection of cases has to do with robustness, defined as the persistence of uniformities in the face of theoretically extraneous variables. In specifying the theory in a certain way, I consciously open the door to other variables. Precisely because of these confounding influences, the design is stronger. Again, to the extent that patterns found are similar or invariant across different conditions, the theory is better supported.

The third justification relates to process tracing in general. Micro-sectoral accounts of the operation of the legal system can be used to corroborate or crosscheck results produced by analysis of more highly aggregated data.

---

[19] See Stone Sweet and Brunell (1998a); Stone Sweet and Caporaso (1998a, b); and Fligstein and Stone Sweet (2002).

This rationale does not imply the selection of specific cases. By focusing on three sectors, I hope to understand better the mechanisms at work in the legal integration process. Detailed process tracing, for example, should allow one to "see" the aggregate patterns in different and hopefully complementary ways. Just as important, my arguments about the path dependent development of legal systems imply a privileged place for process tracing—a concern for history and sequencing—as a means of evaluating the various propositions put forward in the last section. Last, research on judicialization requires assessment of the cumulative impact of adjudication on the decisions of nonjudicial lawmakers. Thus, each chapter examines the extent to which the relevant institutions governing a specific domain do or do not evolve as a function of judicial lawmaking.

Seven databases, compiled specifically for this project, are used in this book. The first contains basic information on the nearly 4,000 preliminary references sent to the ECJ from national judges from the first (1961) through mid-1998 (Stone Sweet and Brunell 2001). It was also used as the master key for the second and third data-sets. The second contains information on the relationship between (a) amicus briefs, what are called observations in the EU, filed by the Member States and the Commission in ECJ decisions rendered pursuant to an Art. 234 reference; and (b) the decision of the Court, in that case, with reference to each observation, and to the claims of the private party or group pleading EU law. Thus, we are in a position to know who "wins" or "loses" each case decided, in each of the three domains. We use these data as one means of evaluating the impact of "revealed preferences" of Member State governments and the Commission on the decisionmaking of the Court. The third database allows us to track the development of precedent: it contains comprehensive information on self-citation by the ECJ in all cases decided pursuant to a preliminary reference from a national court. The fourth contains basic information on all infringement proceedings brought by the Commission against Member States under Art. 226, through 1998. Finally, in Chapter 2, we present aggregate data compiled on trading, lobbying, and legislating in the EC.

VI The Judicial Construction of Europe

The book proceeds as follows. Chapter 2 presents a dynamic theory of integration, surveys the ECJ's major activities, and examines how national judges have responded to the Court's move to constitutionalize the Treaty.

Chapters 3–5 trace outcomes produced by the legal system in three areas of EU law. Among other things, this part of the research is designed to evaluate the impact of Member States' governments on the evolution of the Court's case law, and the impact of the Court's case law on the activities of legislators and judges. I conclude by addressing certain major features of the overall course of European integration in light of the book's priorities and findings.

Constructing a Supranational Constitution

With Thomas Brunell

This chapter charts the evolution of the European Community (EC). To do so, we combine three different perspectives. First, we examine the major features of the integration process since 1959. We argue that the European market and polity developed symbiotically, as the activities of economic actors, organized interests, litigators and judges, and the EC's legislative and regulatory organs became linked, creating a self-sustaining, dynamic system. Second, we examine the "constitutionalization" of the treaty system, and survey the activities of the European Court. Among other things, constitutionalization secured property rights for transnational market actors, expanded the discretionary powers of national judges, and reduced the EC's intergovernmental character. Third, we consider the relationship between the European Court of Justice (ECJ) and the national courts, focusing on how intra-judicial conflict and cooperation have shaped the production of specific constitutional doctrines. Through these "constitutional dialogues," the supremacy of EC law was gradually achieved, rendering it judicially enforceable.

I The Community System

With the Treaty of Rome, Belgium, France, Germany, Italy, Luxembourg, and the Netherlands sought a long-term solution[1] to a pressing problem: how to channel political and economic reconstruction, and particularly

---

[1] The EEC Treaty (1958) was adopted for an "unlimited period" (ex-article 240).

that of Germany, to collective and peaceful ends. European integration would provide that solution, helping to make war unthinkable within Western Europe. In providing governance for a common market, the EC also organized the steady growth of economic interdependence between the Member States, and of a new, transnational society invested in sustaining the project. Anxious to share in the benefits of integration (Mattli 1999), the original six Member States were joined by Denmark, the United Kingdom, and Ireland in 1973; by Greece in 1981; by Spain and Portugal in 1986; and Austria, Sweden, and Finland in 1995. With eastward enlargement, the European Union's (EU's) membership has just grown to twenty-five members.

The Rome Treaty laid down a blueprint for the building of a single market. As defined by the Treaty, the Common Market is comprised of: (*a*) a zone of free movement, wherein restrictions on the movement of labor, goods, services, and capital within the area have been abolished; (*b*) a common external customs policy, whereby goods imported from outside the area are subject to uniform treatment; and (*c*) an EC-wide system of market rules and regulation, produced and enforced by the EC's governing bodies. As market integration has proceeded, the scope of supranational governance has expanded (Pollack 1994; Fligstein and McNichol 1998). Establishing and maintaining free movement animated the Community's governing bodies in the first decades. As this project moved forward, new issues— including fiscal and monetary policy, social policy and health care, consumer and environmental protection, and human rights—steadily moved onto the agenda. In the Single European Act (SEA) (1986), the Treaty on European Union (1993), and the Treaty of Amsterdam (1999), the Member States formally incorporated some of these and other policy domains into the Rome Treaty, and expanded the EC's competences to govern to domains outside of the EC framework.

The Rome Treaty constituted the EC. Like all modern constitutions, the Treaty distributed governing authority among functionally differentiated institutions and established procedures to produce legal rules (Stone 1994). The Community, however, has never easily fit traditional typologies of political systems, blending, in complex and fluid ways, elements of governance found in international law and organizations with elements akin to national constitutional law and federalism (Caporaso 1996). Some observers prefer to characterize it as an intergovernmental organization, an interstate "regime," constituted by a voluntary "pooling of sovereignty" (Keohane and Hoffmann 1991; Moravcsik 1991). Others see it as having evolved into a quasi-federal state system (Sbragia 1993), or into a "multilevel" polity (Marks, Hooghe, and Blank 1996). Wessels (1997) describes the EC/EU as "fusionist", whereby the national governments have combined some of their functions. Still others see it as a complex blend of supranational and intergovernmental modes of governance, a mixture that varies across time and policy arenas (Sandholtz and Stone Sweet (eds.) 1998).

For present purposes, the larger debate about the nature of the Community is less important. In this chapter, we are mainly interested in the development of the EC's capacity to make and enforce the legal rules that it produces. The EC is principally governed by four organizations:

The Commission, which combines legislative and executive powers, is the supranational nerve center of the Community system. The Commission possesses the exclusive authority to draft and propose legislation. New measures are usually not submitted to the EC's legislative organs until extensive negotiations with relevant lobby groups have taken place. The Commission is divided into Directorates, each in charge of one or more of the policy areas delineated by the Treaty of Rome. There are always a great number of proposals, large and small, floating around the Commission, and much political activity among people who work for the Directorates and lobbying groups. This complicated structure requires the various kinds of actors working in the organization to build coalitions in support of divergent agendas. The Commission also monitors Member State compliance with EC law, and has the power to initiate enforcement actions against Member State governments, including before the ECJ. There are currently twenty Commissioners, named by Member State governments and responsible to the European Parliament, who collectively manage a sprawling bureaucracy based in Brussels, Belgium.

The Council of Ministers (Council), composed of sitting ministers of Member State governments, is the intergovernmental center of gravity in the EC. Until the mid-1980s, the Council could be characterized as the Community's legislature, since it usually took the final decision on important EC legislation, and could block unwanted legislative proposals. Each member of the Council possesses a weighted vote, roughly determined by its relative size. The Council has developed its own Brussels-based bureaucracy, organized along national lines, to monitor the Commission's activities and to help its members defend their national and the Council's collective interests. Heads of national governments, joined by some heads of state, also meet regularly in intergovernmental fora, such as the European

Council and the Intergovernmental Conference, to consider more ambitious initiatives and to discuss the overall direction of the EC and the EU.

The European Parliament (EP) is the only Community institution whose members are directly elected (since 1979). The subject-matter of proposed legislation—more precisely, the provisions of the Treaty under which any bill has been proposed—determines the extent of the EP's powers, relative to the other legislative organs, in the lawmaking process. For most initiatives, the EP's powers range from the right of amendment, which may be overridden by the Council, to veto power. The Parliament, now composed of 626 members, meets in Strasbourg, France, and Brussels. Members serve five-year terms.

The ECJ is a constitutional court based roughly on the European model of constitutional review (Stone Sweet 2000: ch. 2). The Court resolves legal disputes that arise between the various EC organs, between EC institutions and the Member States, and between the Member States themselves. It also provides authoritative interpretations of European law to national judges, by way of the preliminary reference procedure. The ECJ's fifteen members, who are appointed by, and drawn from each of, the Member States, serve six-year, renewable terms. The Court sits in Luxembourg.

The evolution of supranational governance must be considered against the backdrop of permutations in the Community's decisionmaking processes. Simplifying, the original understanding of these processes distinguished between (*a*) treaty amendments—including the accession to the Treaties of new Member States, an alteration in the weighted votes of Council members or in legislative procedures, and the transfer of new powers from the Member States to the EC—and (*b*) "secondary legislation"—statutes produced pursuant to the Treaty. The Treaty's provisions could be amended, as in traditional international law, by the unanimous vote of the Member States followed by successful ratification at the national level. Secondary legislation, including most legislation concerned with the construction of the common market, would be proposed by the Commission, and then amended and adopted by a supermajority (about two-thirds) of the weighted votes of the Council, what is called "qualified majority voting" (QMV). Unanimity is an intergovernmental mode of governance, wherein each Member State possesses a veto; QMV tends toward supranationality, since a Member State can be bound by a policy it has not voted for.

The Treaty of Rome fixed a timetable for the completion of the common market, which was to be realized through two processes. The first is called "negative integration": the obligation of all Member States to remove barriers to free movement within EC territory. It is negative because governments renounce their authority to regulate a range of economic transactions within their borders. States were obliged by the Treaty to progressively reduce and ultimately eliminate, by the end of 1969, all import tariffs and quotas, for example. The second type is called "positive integration": the creation of new European policies to regulate problems common to all Member States. The two processes were meant to go hand in hand. The most prominent example was the proposed Common Market. Successful negative integration was to erase whole classes of national laws and regulations, leaving important "holes," which positive integration would then fill with EC laws. The kaleidoscope of disparate national laws that functioned to hinder trade in 1960—taxes, duties, and rules governing health, licensing, and environmental protection standards—would be replaced by uniform, or "harmonized," European law by the end of the 1960s. Most harmonization, according to the Treaty, would proceed, beginning in January 1966, by QMV.

This is not what occurred. Just as the deadline approached, France's President, Charles De Gaulle, provoked a constitutional crisis. De Gaulle distrusted the supranational elements of the Community, including the Commission and QMV. The crisis was resolved by the "Luxembourg Compromise" of January 1966, an intergovernmental understanding among the Member States. The compromise permitted a Member State, after asserting that "very important interests [were] at stake," to demand that legislation be adopted by unanimity voting rather than QMV. In other words, each Member State, on the grounds of a declared national interest, could veto the Commission's proposals. The veto radically strengthened the intergovernmental element of the Community—the Council and the Member States—and positive integration often stalled.

Since the mid-1970s, the EC has developed a powerful momentum of its own evidenced by, among other things, a succession of institutional reforms. The Single Act reinstated QMV as the dominant legislative process for achieving the common market by the Single Act, and the Treaty on European Union (TEU) extended majority voting to other areas. Beginning with the Single Act, the powers of the Parliament have also been steadily enhanced, and the Member States ratified the ECJ's development of juridical notions of European citizenship and rights. Under the guise of the "European Union," the project now also includes explicit treaty-basis for security and foreign policy (Smith 1998, 2001), for new modes of cooperation in policing and border control (Turnbull and Sandholtz 2001), and the move to a European central bank and a common currency (Sandholtz 1993; Cameron 1998; McNamara 2001).[2]

II European Integration and Supranational Governance

The theory of European integration that underlies this book was built from materials developed in North (1990), recent economic sociology (Fligstein 2001), and a general theory of judicialized governance (Shapiro and Stone Sweet 2002). Stripped to bare essentials, the theory focuses on specific causal relationships between three factors, or variables: (a) dyadic contracting, or social exchange; (b) triadic dispute resolution, or "governance"—defined as the capacity of political organizations to regulate such exchange; and (c) normative structure, including law. Under certain conditions, these three factors will tend to evolve interdependently and, in so doing, constitute and reconstitute a polity (Stone Sweet 1999). In the context of the EC, these variables are operationalized in ways that highlight their supranational character. Thus, the variable, "social exchange," includes both economic activity across borders and the growth of transnational civil society. The "governance" variable includes the evolution of the capacities of the EC's legislative and judicial bodies to authoritatively manage what is, in effect, supranational "space" (Stone Sweet, Sandholtz, and Fligstein 2001). And the variable, "normative structure," includes the increased density and articulation in the rule system produced by the EC lawmaking organs and the Court.

There exists a huge body of sophisticated research on European integration that relates to the various themes of this chapter. It is important, therefore, to be clear about the nature of our argument and methods, and the scope of our findings. First, compared with virtually any other contemporary approach to integration, the theory is pitched at a higher level of abstraction, and the data analyzed are more comprehensive and more highly aggregated. Our approach is both macro and dynamic, directing attention to how large processes interact, across multiple dimensions, over

---

[2] The EC is now called the "first pillar" of the European Union, foreign and security policy being the second pillar, and justice and home affairs being the third. The pillar system was introduced by the Maastricht Treaty on European Union (1993). This book's focus is on the first pillar, the Treaty of Rome.

time. Our goal is to be able to "see," and make sense of, the main features and patterns exhibited by the integration process, as it proceeds. The theory is relevant to, but cannot on itself explain, many discrete economic, legislative, or judicial events or decisions, at least without being supplemented by detailed case studies. For this reason, Parts III–V of this chapter examine the doctrinal underpinnings of constitutionalization in more detail; and Chapters 3–5 of the book trace the development of the EC's institutions in three different areas of the law, and assess this evolution in light of the materials presented here and in Chapter 1. These points accepted, we do not ignore relevant scholarship, but rather incorporate the main streams of research on European integration within our more macro theory.

Second, this book takes on one of the more intractable puzzles of the social sciences: how to account for institutional change in political systems. Even within an increasingly generic "institutionalist" social science (see Hall and Taylor 1996), there are important disagreements about whether one should focus primarily on actors (the micro-level), organizations (the meso-level), or on rule systems (institutions and culture, the macro-level). In our view, privileging one level of analysis over another can be justified by the nature of the inquiry, for example, with respect to a specific mechanism of change being explicated or assessed. However, any satisfactory explanation of institutional change must pay close attention to all three levels, as they interact with one another over time.

Third, because at this point we are primarily interested in the relationship between market and political integration in Europe, the issue of how to evaluate the efficiency of rules and governance structures in promoting social exchange is necessarily raised. Organizational economists (e.g. Fama and Jensen 1983; Williamson 1985) and most rational-choice political scientists (e.g. Bates et al. 1998) assume that viable, relatively stable institutions are presumptively (usually Pareto) efficient, although efficiency is rarely demonstrated empirically. Economic sociology and students of political culture (e.g. Eckstein 1988) tend to be agnostic on this same question, or seek to evaluate the functionality of institutions in other than economistic ways, such as with respect to how, and to what extent, they enable human communities to reproduce themselves over time, given changing circumstances. We do not rely on an assumption that EC institutions are optimal, in the sense of being at least as economically "efficient" as all other possible institutional arrangements. Supranational governance has organized the steady expansion of intra-EC trade and the development of transnational society, primarily by making, interpreting, and enforcing Community law.

In the absence of such governance, or in situations in which rule-innovation in the EC has been stalled, transnational exchange would have been stifled, or would have expanded more slowly. For our purposes, it is enough that new EC institutions are functional for market actors in that they are at least relatively efficient compared to preexisting arrangements.

Fourth, our main finding is that, over time, the activities of the EC's organizations mixed with the activities of traders and other transnational actors to produce a self-reinforcing system whereby evolving rule structures and market integration became linked. Our results provide broad support for some of the core claims of "neofunctionalist" theory, first developed by Ernst Haas (1958, 1961). Haas, not unlike North (1990), tried to show that market expansion and political development could be connected to one another through positive feedback loops that would push steadily for more of both. We formalized these insights as hypotheses, gathered data on the processes commonly associated with European integration, and tested out hypotheses in diverse ways. The evidence supports Haas' basic intuitions.

The next section—based on Fligstein and Stone Sweet (2002) and Stone Sweet and Brunell (1998a)—summarizes our theory and empirical findings. We have chosen not to reproduce the complete statistical analyses here.

EUROPEAN INTEGRATION

In our view, integration has been driven by the ways in which specific, otherwise relatively autonomous, fields of action gradually came to be connected to one another. We emphasize three such fields: between firms engaged in cross border trade (seeking to open and expand markets); between litigants (seeking to vindicate or develop rights under EC law), national judges (seeking to resolve disputes to which EC law is material), and the European Court; and between lobbying groups (seeking to exercise influence on EC regulation that affects them) and the EC's legislative bodies (seeking to maximize their control over policy outcomes). We assume that the Commission and the Court primarily work to extend the scope of supranational governance over market activities, and to enhance the effectiveness of EC law within national legal systems. We assume that national governments pursue their own interests, which are at least partly determined by their calculations on how best to win the next election and remain in power; but we also expect the activities of governments, as they relate to the EC, to be conditioned by the constraints of growing economic interdependence, and by EC rules and procedures as they evolve over time.

We begin by taking up four different, but well-known, stories that scholars have told about market and polity building under the Treaty of Rome.

The first focuses attention on the consequences of rising economic transactions across borders. The flow of goods, services, investment, and labor across national boundaries not only generated economic growth that states came to rely upon, but created or accentuated a host of transnational governance problems (the *negative externalities* of economic interdependence). Those who transacted across borders actively pressured governments and the EC's organizations to remove national barriers to further economic exchange (negative integration), and to regulate, in the form of European legislation (positive integration), the emerging Common Market (Moravscik 1993, 1998; Scharpf 1996; Stone Sweet and Brunell 1998*a*; Mattli 1999). Certain groups, like large export-oriented firms, have benefited more from market integration than have smaller nonexporting firms (Fligstein and Brantley 1995); and some believe that integration has contributed to the erosion of national systems of social welfare and interest representation (e.g. Schmitter and Streek 1991).

The second narrative traces the causes and effects of the "constitutionalization" of the Treaty of Rome (Stein 1981; Weiler 1990, 1999*a*, *b*; Shapiro 1992; Burley and Mattli 1993): the mutation of the EC from an international regime to a quasi-federal polity through the consolidation of the doctrines of direct effect and supremacy. Among other things, the doctrine of direct effect enables private actors to plead rights found in EC law against public authorities in national courts, and the doctrine of supremacy requires national judges to resolve conflicts between EC and national law with reference—and deference—to the former. Two basic dynamics were quickly established (Stone Sweet and Caporaso 1998*a, b*). First, transnational economic actors litigated to remove national hindrances to their activities; and, second, individuals and groups not directly engaged in cross-border exchange—such as those who seek to enhance women's rights—sought to use the EC legal system to destabilize or reform national rules and practices. In many legal domains, including those governing the free movement of goods and of workers, social policy, and environmental protection, the operation of the legal system has pushed the integration project a great deal further than the Member State governments, operating under existing decision rules, would have been prepared to go on their own (Chapters 3–5).

These outcomes were in no sense preordained. The Member States did not design the legal system that ultimately emerged. Legal elites (lawyers activated by their clients, and judges activated by lawyers) had to figure out how to use European law, to make it work in their interests. A modicum of consistency in the Court's constitutional case law helped, but it also forced national judges to confront complicated problems concerning the nature and enforceability of EC law, standing requirements, and remedies (Ward 2000*a*, *b*). Hardly passive, national judiciaries negotiated their relationship to the European Court of Justice within a set of multidimensional, intra-judicial, "constitutional dialogues" (Slaughter, Stone Sweet, and Weiler (eds.) 1998). The system, built by judicial lawmaking, evolved through use, not by institutional design.

Our third integration narrative traces the myriad effects of the growth and institutionalization of interest group representation at the supranational level. Given its many responsibilities, the Commission is a relatively small organization. Even today, only about 16,000 people work for it, and probably fewer than 2,000 are directly involved in policymaking (Fligstein and McNichol 1998). Given the potentially huge scope of its jurisdiction and responsibilities, the organization possesses relatively little capacity to generate serious study of complex issues in order to facilitate agreements, and even less capacity to enforce and administer European rules once they are adopted. The Treaty did not design a system of accommodating lobbying organizations in Brussels, nor did it outline procedures for incorporating them into the policy process.

Early on, the Commission worked hard to co-opt technical experts and directly affected parties into the policy process, to help draft new and assess existing market rules, and to help legitimize new proposals proposed. Producer groups, who had the biggest, immediate stake in market integration, dominated lobby activity. As the scope and density of EC rules increased, more and more groups, including those representing "diffuse," public interests, discovered that it paid to set up shop in Brussels (Mazey and Richardson (eds.) 1993; Pollack 1997). In the 1980s, Brussels became "a lobbyist's town" (Harlow 1992), as complex symbiotic relationships developed between lobby groups and the Commission. Today, a wide range of policy outcomes can only be understood by taking into account the influence of these groups (Anderson and Eliasson 1991; Greenwood and Aspinwall (eds.) 1998), within increasingly institutionalized procedures for consultation and participation (Dogan 1997; Joerges and Neyer 1997; Mazey and Richardson 2001).

A fourth stream of scholarship seeks to explain the sources and consequences of permutations in the EC's legislative procedures (Moravcsik 1998; Tsebelis and Garrett 2001; Jupille 2004). As noted, the most important changes have been the move away from unanimity voting and the enhancement of the role of the European Parliament, beginning in the mid-1980s. Perhaps controversially, we see intergovernmental bargaining and the evolution of procedures that structure it as being embedded in the overall process of integration (Stone Sweet and Sandholtz 1997, 1999, 2002).

We had good a priori reasons to think that the activities of market actors, lobbyists, legislators, litigators, and judges were in fact connected to one another, both directly and through feedback loops. For the sake of brevity, we will provide stylized examples of such linkages, without fully developing the theoretical foundations for these expectations (see Fligstein and Stone Sweet 2002). Thus, given certain necessary causal conditions—the most important of which is the acceptance of supremacy and direct effect by national judges, and the entry into force of free trading rules in 1970— rising intra-EC trade could be expected to generate litigation, as importers found their activities hampered by national hindrances to trade. A more stringent hypothesis: relatively more trade would produce relatively more litigation, and thus relatively more references to the Court. These hypotheses are testable, both cross-nationally and across time. Further, to the extent that the legal system actually did remove trade obstacles, more cross-national exchange would be stimulated. A feedback loop would thereby be constituted, one that connects intra-EC trade to the litigation of EC law. There were also good reasons to expect that as EC secondary legislation was produced, in more and more domains, an increasing number of lobby groups would choose to set up shop in Brussels; and we expected—the feedback loop again—that lobbyists would help produce more legislation in the arenas in which they operated. A third example: we expected that legislating and litigating could also become connected, since new regulations and directives (if directly effective) give private actors new grounds on which to plead rights under EC law, before national courts. These latter two logics could be formalized as testable hypotheses, not only across time, but across policy domains: new legislation in specific domains of EC law (e.g. agriculture, consumer protection, sex equality, etc.) would stimulate more lobbying and more litigating, which might then generate the attendant feedback effects.

DATA AND ANALYSIS

We collected data on indicators of our variables, measures of the "outputs" of the system. For legislating, lobbying, and litigating in the EC, we compiled comprehensive information on activity across the sixteen main policy domains designated by the Commission to be under the EC's jurisdiction, for the 1959–98 period. These data allowed us to compare, and to analyze statistically, the extent to which any given policy domain has been the site of each form of activity, relative to other domains, across time. For the indicator of economic interdependence within Europe, we used different measures of intra-European trade; unfortunately, comprehensive data on other kinds of economic transactions, such as capital and labor flows since 1959, do not exist. However imperfect, the choice of trading as an indicator of transnational economic activity is defensible given the fact that creating a free trade zone within Europe was the original core objective of the Rome Treaty.

Figures 2.1–2.6 report, as time series, the outputs of each of our four processes. Taken together, these figures depict what any theory of integration must seek to explain. In our analysis of the data, we found that European integration has been sequenced in three main periods. In the first period, roughly 1958–69, actors were engaged in the process of building the EC's main organizations and figuring out how to make the Treaty of Rome work; and they succeeded in establishing the common agricultural policy and important competition rules. The pivotal institutional innovation during this period was the constitutionalization of the Treaty through the diffusion of the Court's doctrines of supremacy and direct effect. During the second period, roughly 1970–86, the EC's organizations worked to dismantle barriers to intra-EC trade and other kinds of transnational exchange (negative integration). At the same time, the Commission and the Council sought to replace the disparate regulatory regimes in place at the national level with harmonized, EC regulatory frameworks (positive integration). Although the data show that positive integration proceeded more steadily than is often appreciated, many important harmonization projects stalled, not least because more ambitious initiatives required the unanimous vote of national ministers. The unanimity rule, a product of the Luxembourg compromise, made it very difficult to forge such agreements, at a time when an increasing number of social and economic actors were pressing for wider and deeper integration. This period ended with the passage of the SEA 1986, which altered the voting rules for adopting most legislation pertaining to the Single Market Program from unanimity to QMV. Our final period, post-SEA, has been the most active from the perspective of positive integration.

This periodization of the EC's activities can help make sense of the broad patterns of growth in trade, legislation, litigation, and lobbying across the

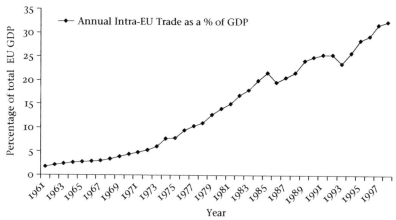

Figure 2.1. Annual Levels of Intra-EC Trade, Per Capita

Note: Data have been calculated by dividing total amount of intra-EU trade per year by total population of all EU Member States.

Source of the trade data: Pitarkis and Tridmas (2003).

life of the EC. Figure 2.1 presents the growth in intra-EC trade per capita for the period 1961–98. One observes a slow increase, but relatively low levels of trade during the 1960s. In 1970 as EC rules start to bite, exports rise more steeply. Following 1985 with the announcement of the Single European Act, growth in trade accelerates.Changes in patterns of intra-European trade coincide with important events within the EC. The rules governing free movement of goods, such as the prohibition of maintaining national quotas and other measures of equivalent effect, entered into force on January 1, 1970, and thereby became directly effective for traders. In 1986, the EC agreed to the completion of the Single Market and to important changes in the voting rules just discussed.

Changes in trade are mirrored in changes in litigating and legislating. Figure 2.2 tracks annual levels of preliminary references and preliminary rulings by the European Court, since the first such reference in 1961. This measure is the best indicator now available of the degree to which EC law is litigated in national courts. It bears emphasis, however, that these numbers represent only the tip of the iceberg,[3] since today most cases resolved by national judges involving European law do not lead to a referral. The figure

---

[3] A far better measure of the "EC litigation" variable would be information concerning cases brought before national judges (over time, and across policy domains and jurisdictions) in which at least one of the parties based pleadings on EC legal norms. These data have never been collected.

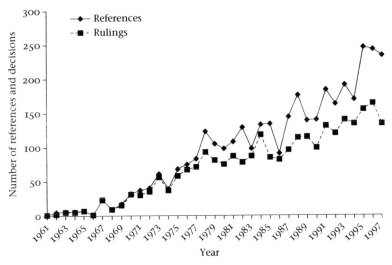

Figure 2.2. Annual Levels of Preliminary References and Rulings

Note: 'Rulings' in the caption includes references ended by a judgment or an order of the Court.

Source: Alec Stone Sweet and Thomas L. Brunell Data Set on Preliminary References in EC Law, 1956–98, Robert Schuman Centre for Advanced Studies, European University Institute (San Domenico di Fiesole, Italy: 1999). See Stone Sweet and Brunell (2000).

shows that levels of references were very low during the 1960s, and began to pick up after 1970, when common market rules entered into effect, and as the doctrines of supremacy and direct effect gradually diffused throughout the system. References doubled by 1980, leveled off in the mid-1980s, and climbed dramatically after the Single Act.

The adoption of EC statutes is a reasonable indicator of positive integration, since much of this activity is oriented towards producing "harmonized" market rules to replace national regulation. Unfortunately, obtaining reliable data on the EC's lawmaking activities is fraught with difficulty, given inconsistencies in the methods used by reporting services (see Page and Dimitrakopoulos 1997; Maurer and Wessels 2003). Figure 2.3 tracks the annual production of secondary legislation—Directives and Regulations—produced by the EC legislator through the complete legislative process. Figure 2.4 depicts the number of EC legislative acts in force, measured at annual intervals for the 1983–98 period. Legislative activity during the 1960s was relatively low, if rising. It picks up during the 1970s, and peaks in 1978. Between 1978 and 1985, the production of statute stabilizes, and then takes off after the passage of the Single Act. The data we collected show that legislative activity actually begins to decline in the 1990s (as do

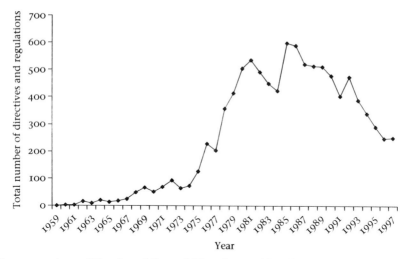

Figure 2.3. Annual Number of Council Directives and Regulations Adopted
Source: Compiled by Christine Mahoney and Alec Stone Sweet from *EU Directory of Legislation in Force* (2003).

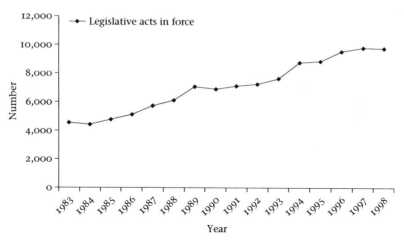

Figure 2.4. Annual Number of EC Legislative Acts in Force
Source: Maurer and Wessels (2003).

the data compiled by Maurer and Wessels 2003). What Figure 2.4 does not show is the huge growth in delegated legislation (including the so-called legislative decisions) that takes place in the 1990s.

Figure 2.5 presents information on the formation of lobbying groups in Brussels, over time. We were able to compile information on almost 600 significant lobbying groups; our database understates the number of groups

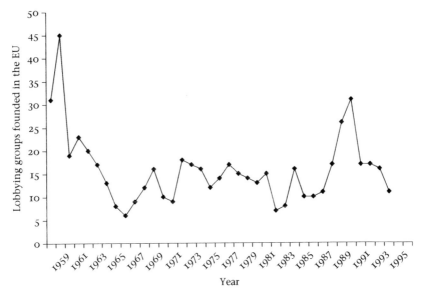

Figure 2.5. Annual Number of EC Lobby Groups Founded
Source: Fligstein and Stone Sweet (2002).

at any point in time, and reflects the activities of bigger and more stable groups. The beginning of the EC witnessed a flurry of foundings, which decreased during the mid-1960s, and then bounced around during the 1970s and early 1980s. Following the passage of the Single Act, the establishment of new lobbying groups shot upward.

Figure 2.6 presents data on the cumulative number of lobbying groups in Brussels, over time. Clearly, the SEA convinced groups that being in Brussels mattered, and that new legislative initiatives further stimulated the formation of new lobbying groups.

We used these data, and our cross-domain data on legislating, lobbying, and litigating in the EC, to test a series of hypotheses about how integration has proceeded, using econometrics and other statistical methods. Our most important findings can be briefly stated.

First, trading, litigating, legislating, and lobbying—key indicators of European integration and supranational governance—grew over time, along roughly similar paths. Indeed, we found that two large "parameter shifts"— whereby important qualitative events generated quantitatively significant transformations in how our variables interact—have occurred in the development of the EC: the first around 1970; the second after 1985. The claim is not that in 1970, and again in 1986, everything that matters suddenly changed.

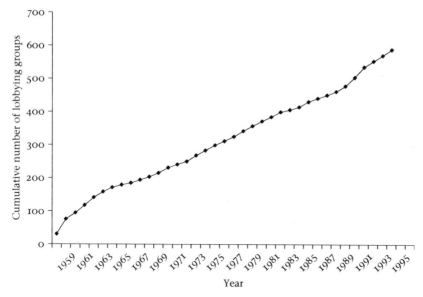

Figure 2.6. Cumulative Number of Lobby Groups in the EC, Per Year
Source: Fligstein and Stone Sweet (2002).

On the contrary, each period generated, and passed forward to the next, institutional materials that structured what took place thereafter. To take one pertinent example, the doctrines of supremacy and direct effect, established in the first period, constituted necessary conditions for the expansion of litigation and the subsequent development of the Court's famous doctrine of mutual recognition[4] during the second period. During the second period, the Commission, in alliance with transnational business coalitions, built on the Court's work, successfully converting Member State governments to the idea that mutual recognition could ground a general strategy for moving market integration forward (see Chapter 3).[5]

Second, market integration and the construction of the legal system have been mutually reinforcing processes. Intra-EC trade has been the

[4] A good produced and marketed lawfully under the rules of any one Member State must be allowed to circulate freely within the market of every other Member State.

[5] If it makes sense to analyze some of the broad dynamics in terms of three periods that comprise a single overall process, we also recognize that this process has always been messy and complex. Much of importance will not be captured by schema that aggregate complex phenomena across time and policy space. Nevertheless, the claim is that how our three meta-variables interact—that is, the various relationships between (*a*) transnational activity like cross-border trade and the activities of supranational interest groups; (*b*) the litigation of EC law; and (*c*) the rulemaking capacities and activities of EC organizations—alter meaningfully from one period to the next.

fundamental determinant of litigating EC law in the national courts. The underlying logic of this relationship should be obvious. In the beginning, those who had the most to gain from economic transactions across borders were the most likely benefactors and users of the EC Treaty, and were the most likely to use litigation in the service of negative integration. As important, they possessed the resources to use litigation as a means of evolving EC rules in their favor, and in pro-integrative directions. At the same time, we found that legal integration stimulated intra-EC trade. Blending a modified neofunctionalism with a concern for the transaction costs of trade, we had proposed that to the extent that the legal system actually removed barriers to transnational exchange, more intra-EC trade would be generated (Stone Sweet and Brunell 1998a). Both the aggregate quantitative analysis and the qualitative assessment (Chapter 3) of the adjudication and evolution of the EC's trading institutions show the causal connections between trading and litigating to be extraordinarily robust.

Following from this analysis, Jean-Yves Pitarkis and George Tridimas, recently subjected the latter hypothesis—the operation of the EC's legal system stimulates intra-EC trade—to a more sophisticated set of statistical tests, using updated measures. They concluded (Pitarkis and Tridimas 2003: 365) that "the establishment of an EU-wide legal order and a system of dispute resolution with the ECJ at the top, leads to deeper economic integration expressed as a larger share of intra-EC trade in economic activity." Their findings provide solid support for our theory, and for the modified neo-functionalist view.[6]

Third, we found that EC legislative activity and the litigation of EC law were connected in various ways. Most important for present purposes, the impact of trade on litigating is declining over time, while the impact of the EC rule structure is rising. Put differently, the relative importance of negative integration and positive integration has been reweighted in favor of the latter. We will discuss the relationship between legislating and litigating in the EC further in part III of this chapter.

---

[6] Curiously, Pitarkis and Tridimas (2003) state that their analysis does not provide support for neofunctionalist integration theory. Yet we derived their central hypothesis from our theory, explored the same relationship, and predicted their findings (Stone Sweet and Brunell 1998a). Haas (1961) explicitly states that his theory is principally concerned with how new EC institutions feed back on transnational society to stimulate more cross-border exchange, thereby raising the costs of intergovernmental stalemate. In any case, the theoretical underpinnings of the even more generic proposition—that complex social exchange depends heavily on rules, property rights, and contract enforcement—is central to the approach of this book, as well as to that of North (1990); Stone Sweet (1999); and Stone Sweet and Fligstein (2002), among others.

Fourth, we found, at the domain level, that the growth in EC legislative activity attracted interest groups to Brussels. Further, it was the higher density of lobbying groups in any given policy domain that helped to produce more legislation, while encouraging new groups to set up shop in Brussels. This is a relatively pure measure of the political success of the EC. As some groups achieved influence over legislation, others perceived the necessity of joining them in Brussels, or suffering being left out of processes that would impact them. The positive integration project was pushed, in part, by this 'bandwagon' effect. There is also evidence that the impact of big export or trading concerns has declined, as more diffuse, public interests have become better organized in Brussels.

Last, trading and legislating in the EC are strongly correlated. Rising economic interdependence has led the EC's legislative organs to produce an extensive, highly differentiated regulatory structure. At the same time, positive integration further reduced the transaction costs of transnational economic activity, through opening markets and harmonizing standards and other market rules.

We found no significant causal connections between lobbying and trading, or between lobbying and litigating.

SUMMARY

When we observe the overall sweep of European integration, we see that transnational economic activity, litigating, legislating, and lobbying did not take place in isolation from, but in fact became connected to, one another. The Treaty of Rome created vast potential for export-oriented European firms to derive benefits associated with larger and more open markets. It created two sets of organizations, one legislative and one judicial, to help governments achieve their goals. Market actors began to take decisions in light of this new institutional structure, and to orient themselves to emerging European spaces; the EC legislative organs began to operate, opening up new sites for political activity; and the EC's legal system was (re)constituted on the basis of the Court's constitutional doctrines, creating an avenue of direct action for private parties. As an ever-widening range of national regulation and administrative practices were placed in the shadow of EC law, and as actors advantaged by EC institutions pushed for more integration through lobbying and litigation, EC legislators found that the search for supranational solutions to the problems posed by the expansion of transnational society and economic interdependence were the only feasible response. And, as the EC's rule structure became more dense and differentiated, so did the grounds for legal action, and actors moved to push the EC to establish or interpret new rules in their favor.

III Constitutionalization and its Effects

We have argued that the broad expansion of supranational governance in Europe since 1960 is embedded in two other large processes: rising economic interdependence and the growth of transnational society. Despite the difficulties of achieving agreement among the Member States on many key issues, market and political integration proceeded, propelled forward by the expansive dynamics of the causal system just described. Still, that system could not have been forged without a measure of individual property rights, a system of effective adjudication, and a lawgiver. For well-known reasons (Waltz 1979), these conditions have been notoriously difficult to create and sustain in the interstate system.

In Europe, the six states that signed the Treaty of Rome were able to overcome some of these difficulties, but only in part. The Treaty contained important restrictions on state sovereignty, such as the prohibition, within the territory constituted by the EC, of tariffs, quantitative restrictions, and national measures "having equivalent effect" on trade after December 31, 1969. It enabled the "pooling of state sovereignty," creating legislative institutions and a process for elaborating common European policies. And it established "supranational" institutions, including the Commission and the ECJ, to help the Council of Ministers—and later the EP—to legislate and resolve disputes about the meaning of EC law. Nonetheless, despite these and other important innovations, the Member States founded an international organization, not a constitutional, or federal, polity. Some Treaty provisions announced principles that, if implemented, would directly impact individuals—including the free movement of workers, and equal pay for equal work between men and women—but the Member States did not mean for the Treaty to confer judicially-enforceable rights on individuals. Further, even within a free trade zone, the transaction costs facing traders would be higher than transaction costs within a single national market, to the extent that traders could not rely on a secure legal framework comparable in its efficacy to that furnished by national legal systems. In contrast to the American constitution, the Rome Treaty neither contains a supremacy clause nor provides for a hierarchically arranged judicial system (i.e. with a supreme court at its apex).

In this section, we consider the impact of the ECJ's moves to reconstruct the legal system on the basis of supremacy, direct effect, and related constitutional doctrines. We begin with a summary of the Court's "constitutional" case law. These judgments reconfigured the normative foundations of the Community, thereby upgrading the capacity of the legal system to respond to the demands of transnational society. It bears repeating that this case law constitutes a necessary condition for European integration to have proceeded in the ways that it has. Our argument is not a purely functional one—that the growth of intra-EC trade inexorably led to the construction of the legal system—or that functional demands for new institutions somehow magically produced them. Instead, we claim that legal integration has been powerfully conditioned by the causal linkages that developed between transnational economic activity and the litigation of EC law in the courts of the Member States; and we insist that these linkages depended critically on the Court's success in having its constitutional vision of the EC accepted by the national courts. Thus, in our account, supremacy and direct effect—which are basic to the emergence of secure property rights for European market actors—come first, causally. We then examine more closely how the legal system has operated, and provide an overview of the ECJ's main activities.

THE CONSTITUTIONALIZATION OF THE TREATY OF ROME

The *constitutionalization of the EC* refers to the process by which the Rome Treaty evolved from a set of legal arrangements binding upon sovereign states into a vertically integrated legal regime conferring judicially enforceable rights and obligations on legal persons and entities, public and private, within EC territory. The phrase thus captures the transformation of an intergovernmental organization governed by international law into a multi-tiered system of governance founded on higher-law constitutionalism. Today, legal scholars and judges conceptualize the EC as a constitutional polity (Lenaerts 1990; Mancini 1991; Weiler 1991; Shapiro 1992; Timmermans 2002).[7] This is an orthodox (but by no means unanimous[8]) position,

---

[7] Scholars in the international relations field have been more reticent to do so (e.g. Hoffmann and Keohane 1991), probably for reasons internal to the development of international relations theory (Stone 1994).

[8] There remain good arguments for conceptualizing European law as treaty law (e.g. Schilling 1996; Hartley 2001).

although it also accommodates strong anxiety about the constitution's aesthetic imperfections (de Witte 1998), its piecemeal, judicial construction (Curtin 1993; Mortelmans 1996), and its weak "political" legitimacy (Habermas 1995; Weiler 1999a; Weatherill 2003: 697–714). The ECJ has implicitly treated the Treaty as a constitutional text from the start; and, in 1986 (*Parti Écologiste "Les Vert"* v. *European Parliament*, ECJ 294/83, 1986), the Court began to refer to the treaties as a "constitutional charter," or as "the constitution of the Community" (Fernandez Esteban 1994).

It cannot be stressed enough that the Court initiated and sustained this process in the absence of express authorization of the Treaty, and despite the declared opposition of Member State governments (Stein 1981: 25–7). National governments could have blocked or reversed the process, but only by revising the Treaty of Rome. Treaty amendment requires the unanimous vote of the Member States, acting as a constituent assembly, followed by ratification in each member state, according to diverse procedures, including referenda. The Court's trustee status (see Chapter 1) served to shield the process from direct interference on the part of the Member States. At the same time, *constitutionalization* strengthened the Court's position as trustee, expanding the zone of discretion of both the Court and national judges.

Moravcsik (1998) and Tsebelis and Garrett (2001), if for different reasons, have pointedly argued that the activities of the EC's supranational organizations have *never* produced "unintended consequences" from the point of view of the Member States. We submit that the constitutionalization of the Treaty of Rome is an "unintended consequence" of monumental proportions.

The Member States neither provided for the supremacy of the Rome Treaty in national legal orders, nor for the direct effect of Treaty provisions and EC directives. Instead, they designed an enforcement system that we would characterize as "international law plus," the "plus" being (*a*) the compulsory nature of the Court's jurisdiction, and (*b*) the participation of a supranational authority—the Commission—in various proceedings. Under Art. 227,[9] a Member State may bring a complaint against another Member State; if the

---

[9] Article 227 EC:

   A Member State which considers that another Member State has failed to fulfill an obligation under this Treaty may bring the matter before the Court of Justice. Before a Member State brings an action against another Member State for an alleged infringement of an obligation under this Treaty, it shall bring the matter before the Commission. The Commission shall deliver a reasoned opinion after each of the States concerned has been given the opportunity to submit its own case and its observations on the other party's case both orally and in writing. If the Commission has not delivered an opinion within three months of the date on which the matter was brought before it, the absence of such opinion shall not prevent the matter from being brought before the Court of Justice.

Commission determines that the complaint is founded, and if the defendant state refuses to settle, the case could go to the Court. Art. 227 is a virtual dead letter, having been used on only a handful of occasions, producing not one important ruling on the part of the ECJ.

Under Art. 226,[10] the Commission may initiate "infringement proceedings"—also called "enforcement actions"—against a Member State for noncompliance with EC law; rounds of negotiation with the government then ensue; if these fail, the Commission may refer the matter to the Court for decision. The Commission is under no obligation to bring proceedings; its discretion under Art. 226 is absolute. The Commission was reticent to use Art. 226 aggressively until the late 1970s, a posture it gradually abandoned as legal integration through Art. 234, and EC rulemaking (harmonization), proceeded. The Treaty of European Union added a new provision (to Art. 228) enabling the ECJ to fine Member States for failure to comply with an enforcement ruling.[11]

Article 234,[12] the linchpin of legal integration, was not intended to be an enforcement mechanism at all, although that is exactly what it became. Art. 234 established a procedure connecting the ECJ to the national courts. National judges make references to the European Court in order to obtain a formal interpretation of EC law—either of the Treaty or of secondary legislation—when EC law is material to the resolution of a case at bar. The ECJ's interpretation, called a "preliminary ruling," is then applied by the judge of reference to resolve the case. The provision was designed to help national judiciaries avoid conflicts of interpretation, thereby promoting the

---

[10] Article 226 EC:

> If the Commission considers that a Member State has failed to fulfill an obligation under this Treaty, it shall deliver a reasoned opinion on the matter after giving the State concerned the opportunity to submit its observations. If the State concerned does not comply with the opinion within the period laid down by the Commission, the latter may bring the matter before the Court of Justice.

[11] The relevant provision states: "If the Court of Justice finds that the Member State concerned has not complied with its judgement, it may impose a lump sum or penalty payment on it." The first Member State to be fined under this provision was Greece (*Commission* v. *Greece*, ECJ C-387/97, 2000).

[12] Article 234 EC:

> The Court of Justice shall have jurisdiction to give preliminary rulings concerning . . . the interpretation of this Treaty [and] the validity and interpretation of acts of the institutions of the Community . . . Where such a question is raised before any court or tribunal of a Member State, that court or tribunal may, if it considers that a decision on the question is necessary to enable it to give judgment, request the Court of Justice to give a ruling thereon. Where any such question is raised in a case pending before a court or tribunal of a Member State, against whose decisions there is no judicial remedy under national law, that court or tribunal shall bring the matter before the Court of Justice.

consistent application of EC law within national legal orders. The Member States did not mean to give citizens a means of suing their own governments, or of defending themselves against prosecution. Nor did they mean to confer on national judges the power of judicial review of national legislation with respect to "higher" EC law. These outcomes, it turned out, inhered in the ECJ's vision of an integrated Community legal order.

The constitutionalization process has been driven primarily by the relationship between private litigants, national judges, and the ECJ, interacting within the framework provided by Art. 234. In the 1962–79 period, the Court secured the core, foundational principles of supremacy and direct effect. The doctrine of supremacy, first announced in *Costa* (ECJ 6/64, 1964), lays down the rule that, in *any* conflict between an EC legal rule and a rule of national law, the former must be given primacy. Indeed, according to the Court, every EC norm, from the moment of entry into force, "renders automatically inapplicable any conflicting provision of . . . national law" (*Simmenthal*, ECJ 106/77, 1978), including national constitutional rules. Where the doctrine of direct effect holds, EC norms confer—directly upon individuals—legal rights that public authorities must respect, and which can be pleaded in the national courts. During this period, the ECJ found that provisions of the Rome Treaty (*Van Gend en Loos*, ECJ 26/62, 1963) and a class of secondary legislation, called "directives" (*Van Duyn*, ECJ 41/74, 1974), were, under certain conditions,[13] directly effective. This latter move provoked a great deal of controversy, including heavy criticism from Member State governments (Craig and De Burca 2003: 204), since the wording of the Treaty (Art. 249) strongly implies that EC directives only acquire their legal force in national law once they have been fleshed out and transposed by national executive or legislative authorities.[14] The "regulation," the other major form of secondary legislation, is the only EC legal norm that the Member States meant to be directly applicable within national legal orders (Art. 249 EC). The supremacy of EC law was further reinforced by the doctrine of preemption (e.g. *Kramer*, ECJ 3/76, 1976), which holds

---

[13] The conditions are that the rights and duties created by the directive must be "precise" and "unconditional," and not depend upon further action by the Member States or EC legislative bodies.

[14] Article 249 EC:

In order to carry out their task and in accordance with the provisions of this Treaty, the European Parliament acting jointly with the Council, the Council and the Commission shall make regulations and issue directives . . . A regulation shall have general application. It shall be binding in its entirety and directly applicable in all Member States. A directive shall be binding, as to the result to be achieved, upon each Member State to which it is addressed, but shall leave to the national authorities the choice of form and methods.

that where the EC's competence to act is exclusive, the taking of measures by the Community deprives national authorities of their powers to act independently.

These doctrines—in so far as national judges were to accept them—would integrate national and supranational legal systems, and establish a decentralized enforcement mechanism for EC law. The mechanism relies on the initiative of private actors, enabled by the doctrine of direct effect. Direct effect is actually shorthand for a complex set of rules and principles of construction. As a point of law, the Court distinguishes between "vertical" and "horizontal" direct effect. *Vertical direct effect* refers to the capacity of Community law to create rights that individuals may invoke against national governments—and virtually all other public authorities—in disputes before a national judge. The Treaty, EC regulations, and EC directives can produce such effects. *Horizontal direct effect* refers to the capacity of Community law to create rights and obligations between any two private individuals or companies. Provisions of the Treaty and of EC regulations produce such effects, which allow, for example, a firm to sue another firm on the basis of such provisions, or an employee to sue an employer. After skirting the issue for a decade, the ECJ decided, in *Marshall I* (ECJ 152/84, 1986), that EC directives were not directly effective horizontally, that is, between two private parties. The Court's posture has been heavily debated (Tridimas 1994; Prechal 1995: ch. 8; Ellis 1998: 30; Lenz 2000; Ward 2000: 197–200), and may appear as an anomaly, however justifiable,[15] in its otherwise consistent record of pushing hard to enhance the effectiveness of EC law within national legal orders. The Court subsequently resisted opportunities to reverse itself (e.g. *Dori*, ECJ C-91/92, 1994), choosing instead to develop other instruments to pressure governments to properly implement directives in a timely fashion. Direct effect, of course, depends on supremacy for its efficacy. The doctrine of supremacy prohibits public authorities from relying on national law to justify breaches of EC law, and it requires national judges to resolve conflicts between national and EC law in favor of the latter.

In a second wave of constitutionalization, the Court supplied national courts with enhanced means of guaranteeing the effectiveness of EC law.

---

[15] The decision is typically defended with reference to principles of fairness (legal certainty). If directives had been held to be horizontally directly effective, firms or individuals could have been made responsible for failure to comply with, say, an improperly implemented directive, even though compliance with the directive would have meant contravening national law on the books. Further, until the TEU entered into effect, the EC was not required to publish directives, which would have placed a serious burden on private actors to monitor continuously the activities of the EC legislator.

In *Von Colson* (ECJ 14/83, 1984), the doctrine of indirect effect was established, according to which national judges must interpret national law in conformity with EC law. In *Marleasing* (ECJ C-106/89, 1990), the Court clarified the meaning of indirect effect, holding that when a Member State has not transposed a directive, or has transposed it late or incorrectly, national judges are obliged to interpret the entire relevant corpus of national law as if it were in conformity with the directive. The doctrine thus requires national judges to interpret national statutes in ways that render EC law applicable, and thereby effective for individuals, even in the absence of implementing measures. Once national law has been so (re)constructed, EC law, in the guise of a de facto national rule, can be applied in legal disputes between private legal persons. The doctrine of indirect effect partly mitigates the problem that EC directives are not horizontally effective. In *Francovich* (ECJ C-6 and 9/90, 1991), the Court went even further, announcing the doctrine of state liability. According to this rule, a national court can, among other things, hold a member state financially responsible for damages caused to individuals due to transposition or implementation failures. The national court may then require member states to compensate such individuals for their financial losses. As subsequently clarified in *Brasserie du Pecheur* (ECJ C-46 and C-48/93, 1996), individuals are entitled to reparation where Community law is "intended to confer rights upon them, the breach is sufficiently serious, and there is a direct causal link between the breach and the damage sustained by the individuals." Where state liability is found, it is up to the national court to assess damages (normally determined by the domestic law of remedies).

The ECJ has thus imagined a particular type of relationship between the European and national courts, a working partnership in the construction of a rule-of-law Community. In that partnership, national judges become agents of the Community order—they become Community judges—whenever they resolve disputes governed by EC law (Maher 1994). The Court obliges national judges to uphold the supremacy of EC law (even against conflicting statutes, and even where parliamentary sovereignty otherwise holds sway); encourages them to make references concerning the proper interpretation of EC law to the Court; and empowers them, even without a referral, to interpret national rules so that these rules will conform to EC law and to set aside national law that does not.

The effectiveness of the system, therefore, depends critically on the willingness of national judges to refer disputes about EC law to the ECJ, and to settle those disputes in conformity with the Court's case law. Although national judges embraced the various logics of supremacy with differing degrees of enthusiasm (part IV below), by the end of the 1980s every supreme court in the EC had formally accepted the doctrine (Slaughter, Stone Sweet, and Weiler (eds.) 1998). Although judicial adaptation to constitutionalization has neither been simple nor painless, the ease with which judges at the Member State level were able to accommodate supremacy deserves to be assessed against the slower—and more conflictual—consolidation of federal supremacy in the United States system (Goldstein 2001).

Preliminary references

Figure 2.7 plots the annual rate of Art. 234 references and rulings, beginning with the first in 1961. Without the doctrines of supremacy and direct effect, the level of preliminary references would doubtlessly have remained stable and low. In proclaiming supremacy and direct effect, the Court broadcast the message that EC law could be used, by individuals, businesses, and interest groups, to pursue their private interests. With use, firms and groups learned that Art. 234 could also be used to obtain policy outcomes that would otherwise have been impossible or more costly to obtain from executives and legislators. A victim of its own success, the system is today in deep crisis (Chapter 6). Overloaded, the average delay between reference and ECJ ruling is now more than three years.

Table 2.1 provides domain-level data on preliminary references. We coded information on the domain being litigated using a reference system

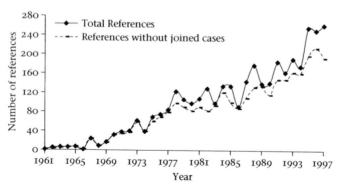

Figure 2.7. Annual Number of Preliminary References and Joined Cases

Note: The line plots the annual number of Article 177 references to the ECJ. The broken line plots the annual number of references minus those that have been joined to another case. The ECJ typically joins together references that are filed by the same judge, on the same day, involving the same legal dispute (although each involves a separate litigating party). The ECJ also joins pending cases, referred by different judges, when they involve the same legal dispute.

Source: Alec Stone Sweet and Thomas L. Brunell Data Set on Preliminary References in EC Law, 1958–98, Robert Schuman Centre for Advanced Studies, European University Institute (San Domenico di Fiesole, Italy: 1999). See Stone Sweet and Brunell (2000).

Table 2.1. Distribution of Preliminary References by Legal Domain and Period (Art. 234)

Subject matter	%(n)							
	1958–98[a]	1958–69	1970–4	1975–9	1980–4	1985–9	1990–4	1995–8[a]
Agriculture	1,008	13.4 / 13	41.5 / 129	35.8 / 232	26.9 / 202	21.4 / 170	15.3 / 163	9.5 / 99
Free movement of goods	832	17.5 / 17	18.7 / 58	19.4 / 126	21.6 / 162	21.3 / 169	16.2 / 172	12.3 / 128
Social security	444	26.8 / 26	10.3 / 32	12.2 / 79	7.9 / 59	8.9 / 71	10.2 / 109	6.5 / 68
Taxation	344	14.4 / 14	3.2 / 10	4.2 / 27	6.1 / 46	7.4 / 59	8.1 / 86	9.8 / 102
Competition	318	12.4 / 12	7.1 / 22	4.3 / 28	4.9 / 37	5.5 / 44	10.5 / 112	6.1 / 63
Approximation of laws	217	1.0 / 1	1.0 / 3	1.5 / 10	4.9 / 37	4.2 / 33	3.9 / 41	8.9 / 92
Transportation	77	0 / 0	1.6 / 5	1.5 / 10	1.2 / 9	1.1 / 9	2.6 / 28	1.5 / 16
Establishment	289	1.0 / 1	1.9 / 6	3.7 / 24	2.1 / 16	6.4 / 51	8.4 / 89	9.8 / 102

Social provisions	236	**0** / 0	**0.3** / 1	**1.2** / 8	**2.8** / 21	**3.9** / 31	**8.5** / 90	**8.2** / 85
External	109	**1.0** / 1	**2.6** / 8	**2.3** / 15	**3.1** / 23	**1.8** / 14	**1.6** / 17	**3.0** / 31
Free movement of workers and persons	202	**1.0** / 1	**2.9** / 9	**2.9** / 19	**2.9** / 22	**5.2** / 41	**3.7** / 39	**6.8** / 71
Environment	75	**0** / 0	**0** / 0	**0.2** / 1	**1.7** / 13	**1.0** / 8	**1.0** / 10	**4.1** / 43
Commercial policy	72	**0** / 0	**1.3** / 4	**1.2** / 8	**1.3** / 10	**1.4** / 11	**2.4** / 25	**1.4** / 14
Other domains	483	**11.3** / 11	**7.7** / 24	**9.6** / 62	**12.5** / 94	**10.5** / 83	**7.9** / 84	**12.3** / 125
Total claims	4,706	97	311	649	751	794	1,065	1,039
% of total claims by period	100[b]	2.1	6.6	13.8	16.0	16.9	22.6	22.1

[a] The table contains information from the complete data-set. The data for 1998 are incomplete, ending, for most countries, in May or June 1998.

[b] 'Joined references' (see fig. 2.1) are excluded from these calculations. Due to rounding, percentages of total claims by period add to 100.1%.

Source: Alec Stone Sweet and Thomas L. Brunell Data Set on Preliminary References in EC Law, 1958–98, Robert Schuman Centre for Advanced Studies, European University Institute (San Domenico di Fiesole, Italy: 1999). See Stone Sweet and Brunell (2003).

developed by the European Court. The Court classifies each reference in terms of the substantive issues raised by the referring judge, as issues are delineated by the Treaty. We sorted the references into the largest thirteen "meta-categories" which, taken together, contain roughly 90 percent of the total number of domains invoked. Our data-set contains slightly more than 3,700 specific references, raising more than 4,700 separate substantive issues; judges often ask questions concerning more than one area of EC law in the same reference (no reference concerns more than five domains).

Table 2.1 vividly records how Art. 234 activity has expanded in scope and intensity, across an increasing number of policy domains. During the 1970–4 period, over 60 percent of the questions raised in references fell in just two domains, agriculture and the free movement of goods; these areas today generate less than 20 percent of total activity. In the meantime, we see an important diffusion of reference activity to other domains, such as environmental protection, taxation, commercial policy and competition, and the free movement of workers. Strikingly, in the 1990s nearly one-in-twelve references concerned sex discrimination law (which the Court codes as "social provisions"). It is clear that as the scope of EU rules expanded, the legal system became not simply a vehicle for farmers, producers, and traders, but also for more diffuse, "public" interests.

These data are relevant to one of the central claims of this book: negative and positive integration are linked to one another, notably through feed-back loops that connect adjudicating and legislating. By definition, negative integration entails the removal of obstacles to transnational economic activity. To the extent that litigating trading rights under EC law serves to remove the most obvious hindrances to transnational exchange (border inspections, fees and duties, and so on), new obstacles to cross-border exchange will be revealed (laws and administrative practices designed to protect consumers, the environment, public safety, etc.). Traders can be expected to target these newly exposed strata of national regulatory systems in subsequent rounds of litigation. In this way, layers of the regulatory state can—potentially at least—be peeled away, like layers from an onion. We think of this dynamic as a kind of legal "spillover," in that it has the potential to develop an expansive logic of its own. In fact (see Chapter 3), by the late 1970s governments had discovered that adjudication in the area of free movement of goods had exposed to challenge virtually any national rule that might affect intra-EC trade. Governments experienced mounting pressure to replace national regulatory regimes, even those designed to pursue otherwise legitimate public policy purposes, with supranational ones. Negative integration shaped how positive integration proceeded in these and other ways. At the same time, as the corpus of EC law grew more dense and articulated, so did the grounds for pleading rights under EC law in national courts. Other kinds of private actors litigated, including those not engaged in cross-border economic exchange or in market integration, per se. Some use Art. 234 overtly, for general policy purposes: to subvert local regimes, to replace national rules with more advantageous European ones, to enhance the role of the judiciary as an arena for policy innovation, and to reduce that of the national government and parliament. Legislating and litigating are thus connected in yet another way.

Chapters 3–5 focus intensively on the relationship between (*a*) negative and positive integration, and (*b*) legislating and litigating, as this relationship is organized by the preliminary reference procedure.

Enforcement actions

Figure 2.8 tracks the number of Art. 226 infringement proceedings and rulings, by period, since the Commission's first enforcement action (1961). The gap between the line plotting the number of proceedings and the line plotting the number of rulings represents the number of cases withdrawn from the Court's docket. In the vast majority of such instances, the Member State agrees to resolve the matter to avoid adjudication. The behavior makes good sense, since the European Court finds a breach of EC law by Member States in about 90 percent of its Art. 226 rulings, a success rate for the Commission that hardly varies across domains. Tables 2.2 and 2.3 provide

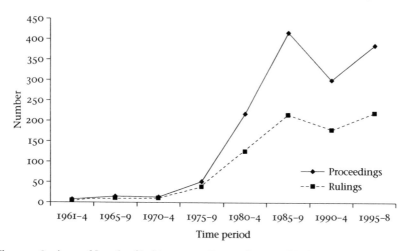

Figure 2.8. Annual Levels of Infringement Proceedings and Rulings

Source: Data compiled by Markus Gehring and Alec Stone Sweet from the *European Court Reports*, the *Official Journal of the EC*, and the *Official Journal of the EU*.

Table 2.2. Distribution of Infringement Proceedings by Legal Domain and Period (Art. 226)

Subject matter[a]	%(n)							
	1958-98	1958-69	1970-4	1975-9	1980-4	1985-9	1990-4	1995-8[b]
Agriculture	14.8 296	16.0 4	28.6 4	24.7 19	13.6 43	13.8 83	16.4 70	13.6 73
Free movement of goods	11.2 223	36.0 9	28.6 4	18.2 14	22.5 71	13.3 80	8.9 38	1.3 7
Social security	1.3 25	0.0 0	0.0 0	2.6 2	0.3 1	1.7 10	1.2 5	1.3 7
Taxation	6.5 129	28.0 7	0.0 0	13.0 10	6.6 21	7.3 44	5.4 23	4.5 24
Competition	2.8 56	8.0 2	7.1 1	5.2 4	3.8 12	3.0 18	2.3 10	1.7 9
Approximation of laws	28.5 569	0.0 0	14.3 2	18.2 14	24.4 77	27.5 165	31.9 136	32.7 175
Transportation	3.3 66	0.0 0	0.0 0	2.6 2	2.8 9	3.3 20	3.0 13	4.1 22
Establishment	8.2 163	4.0 1	0.0 0	1.3 1	9.8 31	7.2 43	8.7 37	9.3 50
Social provisions	2.6 52	0.0 0	0.0 0	0 0	4.4 14	1.5 9	2.1 9	3.7 20

Domain								
External	0.7 / 14	4.0 / 1	0.0 / 0	0 / 0	0.3 / 1	0.7 / 4	0.7 / 3	0.9 / 5
Free movement of workers and persons	2.7 / 54	0.0 / 0	7.1 / 1	1.3 / 1	0.6 / 2	2.5 / 15	5.2 / 22	2.4 / 13
Environment	10.6 / 212	0.0 / 0	0.0 / 0	6.5 / 5	4.7 / 15	9.7 / 58	8.9 / 38	17.9 / 96
Commercial Policy	0.2 / 4	0.0 / 0	0.0 / 0	0.0 / 0	0.0 / 0	0.2 / 1	0.7 / 3	0.0 / 0
Other domains	6.6 / 131	4.0 / 1	14.3 / 2	6.5 / 5	6.0 / 19	8.3 / 50	4.7 / 20	6.4 / 34
Total proceedings by domain	1,994	25	14	77	316	600	427	535
% of total proceedings by domain	100[c]	1.3	0.7	3.9	15.8	30.1	21.4	26.8

[a] Based on filing dates (not date of decision).

[b] Infringement proceedings can be filed in more than one issue area for the same case. The table counts domains not rulings. There are 1,406 Art. 226 proceedings in our data-set.

[c] Percentages are rounded.

Source: Data compiled by Markus Gehring and Alec Stone Sweet from the *European Court Reports*, the *Official Journal of the EC*, and the *Official Journal of the EU*.

Table 2.3. Distribution of Art. 226 Rulings by Legal Domain and Period

Subject matter[a]	%(n)							
	1958–98	1958–69	1970–4	1975–9	1980–4	1985–9	1990–4	1995–8[b]
Agriculture	15.0 180	22.2 4	27.3 3	25.8 16	18.2 39	18.0 59	13.3 33	8.1 26
Free movement of goods	11.5 139	33.3 6	36.4 4	14.5 9	18.7 40	14.1 46	11.2 28	1.9 6
Social security	1.3 16	0.0 0	0.0 0	1.6 1	0.5 1	0.6 2	2.0 5	2.2 7
Taxation	8.4 101	33.3 6	0.0 0	14.5 9	6.1 13	10.4 34	7.6 19	6.2 20
Competition	3.6 43	5.6 1	9.1 1	4.8 3	4.7 10	3.7 12	3.2 8	2.5 8
Approximation of laws	22.2 267	0.0 0	0.0 0	16.1 10	22.4 48	16.2 53	26.4 66	28.0 90
Transportation	4.0 48	0.0 0	0.0 0	3.2 2	3.3 7	4.3 14	2.8 7	5.6 18
Establishment	9.6 115	0.0 0	0.0 0	1.6 1	8.4 18	8.9 29	11.6 29	11.8 38
Social provisions	2.8 34	0.0 0	0.0 0	0.0 0	4.7 10	1.8 6	2.4 6	3.7 12

								Total rulings by domain
External	0.3 1	0.8 2	1.2 4	0.5 1	0.0 0	0.0 0	5.6 1	0.7 9
Free movement of workers and persons	3.4 11	7.2 18	3.4 11	0.9 2	1.6 1	9.1 1	0.0 0	3.7 44
Environment	19.9 64	9.6 24	10.7 35	4.7 10	8.1 5	0.0 0	0.0 0	11.5 138
Commercial policy	0.0 0	0.8 2	0.3 1	0.0 0	0.0 0	0.0 0	0.0 0	0.2 3
Other domains	6.5 21	1.2 3	6.4 21	7.0 15	8.1 5	18.2 2	0.0 0	5.6 67
Total rulings by domain	322	250	327	214	62	11	18	1,204
% of total rulings by domain	26.6	20.8	27.2	17.8	5.1	0.9	1.5	100[c]

[a] Based on filing dates (not date of decision).

[b] Infringement proceedings can be filed in more than one issue area for the same case. The table counts domains not rulings. There are 801 ECJ enforcement rulings in our data-set.

[c] Due to rounding, percentages of total claims by period add to 99.9%.

Source: Data compiled by Markus Gehring and Alec Stone Sweet from the *European Court Reports*, the *Official Journal of the EC*, and the *Official Journal of the EU*.

domain-level information on infringement proceedings and rulings pursuant to Art. 226. For purposes of comparison, we have sorted enforcement actions into the same meta-categories as those used for preliminary references. Our database includes information on 1,406 individual proceedings, resulting in 801 rulings; each proceeding and ruling has been coded into a minimum of one, and a maximum of three, domains.

In practice, as Snyder (1996) notes, "the Commission can use litigation as an element in developing longer-term strategies. Instead of simply winning cases, it is able to concentrate on establishing basic principles or playing for rules" (see also Börzel 2003). As discussed in Chapter 3, the Commission also uses its prosecutorial powers in the service of its legislative agenda. Prior to the signing of the Single Act, for example, it initiated a wave of proceedings based on the Court's expansive reading of Art. 28 (free movement of goods) to challenge national regulatory autonomy, and to give agency to its emerging mutual recognition strategy. At the same time, it began to prosecute Member States more aggressively for failures to properly implement EC directives governing the Common Market (approximation of laws). After 1986, this latter activity became the dominant source of enforcement actions, and free movement of goods proceedings dropped off sharply. As the EC legislator pushed to "complete" the internal market by 1992, it withdrew whole classes of potential disputes from the Court's free movement of goods docket, while making the politics of harmonization and implementation more salient.

Comparing Table 2.1 with Table 2.2 reveals some striking differences. Litigation in the sex equality (social provisions) domain has been driven by private parties using national courts under Art. 234, not by the Commission using Art. 226. That said, the Commission does not hesitate to prosecute Member States in the area, not least in order to force them to update their national law to conform to the Court's interpretations (Chapter 4). In doing so, victims of sex discrimination are better positioned to use the national courts to vindicate their rights under EC law. In contrast, litigation in the environment domain is dominated by enforcement actions, accounting for between 10 and 20 percent of all Art. 226 activity since the 1985–9 period. Although preliminary references in the environmental protection field have grown steadily since 1980, to about 5 percent of all references today, restrictive standing rules, among other factors, has limited public interest litigation in the national courts (Chapter 5).

We now turn to a more fine-grained analysis of the doctrinal politics of supremacy and constitutionalization, focusing on interactions between the European Court and the national courts.

IV The Constitutional Politics of Supremacy

The Court's supremacy doctrine was *constitutional* in that it sought to organize the juridical relationship between otherwise distinct legal orders: the national and the supranational. The reception of supremacy, by national judges, was *political*, in that it entailed choices that would necessarily impinge upon the activities of executives, legislators, administrators, and private actors. Though legal integration proceeded steadily, national judges have not been passive actors in the process (Slaughter, Stone Sweet, and Weiler (eds.) 1998).

Most strikingly, constitutional courts refused to accept supremacy without exacting important concessions from the ECJ. Constitutional judges do not typically adjudicate conflicts about EC law, except insofar as questions referred to them directly raise a controversy framed by their own constitution. Compared with judges who routinely deal with commercial disputes, for example, constitutional judges do not "need" EC law to perform their tasks effectively. As repositories of constitutional review powers, they could not benefit from the "judicial empowerment" logics that scholars suggest appealed to judges on the "ordinary" courts (see Chapter 1). For these and other reasons, one would not have expected them to welcome the development of a new "constitutional" order that could subsume the order that it would remain their task to defend, while diffusing judicial review powers, in areas governed by EC law, to the whole of the judiciary.

In this section, we examine the impact of constitutional and supreme courts on the evolution of the supremacy doctrine. As we will see, the resolution of intra-judicial conflict about the nature and scope of the doctrine has been a primary mechanism of legal integration. These "constitutional dialogues" (*a*) organized the evolution of a wide-reaching supremacy doctrine; (*b*) induced the construction of an enforceable charter of rights for the EC; and (*c*) provoked a still unsettled controversy about the underlying democratic legitimacy of the EC polity. The politics of supremacy are also connected to the Court's other constitutional doctrines, the most important of which concern direct effect and remedies.

SUPREMACY AND THE PROBLEM OF JUDICIAL REVIEW

National constitutional law governs the relationship between international law and national law, with rules that are commonly classified as either more or less *monist*, or more or less *dualist*. Simplifying, in monist systems, international and national law is considered to comprise a single legal order, wherein international law usually takes juridical precedence in any conflict of norms. Although there are exceptions (the Dutch tradition), European legal systems have traditionally tended toward dualism: international law and national law are taken to be separate systems of norms. In dualist systems, treaty law normally enters into the national legal order after having been *transposed*—or ratified—by parliament. Once transposition has been achieved, statute and treaty law, having been produced by formally equivalent acts of the legislature, occupy the same rung on the hierarchy of norms (both are binding, as parliamentary acts, on ordinary judges, and both are inferior to constitutional norms). In dualist systems, the juridical relationship between statute and treaty-based law typically is organized by the doctrine of *lex posteriori*: when an irresoluble conflict between the two arises during the course of litigation, the most recently produced rule prevails. Thus, when international rules conflict with a subsequent legislative act, the latter prevails in court, on the theory that the Parliament's last word on the matter is controlling.

What was innovative—what was "constitutional"—about the ECJ's supremacy doctrine was that it required national judges to treat EC law as if it were (*a*) a source of law superior to, and autonomous from, national statutes, and (*b*) capable of being applied, directly, within the national legal order, by a national judge. The European Court sought to constitute the Community legal order on the basis of a sophisticated monism, mandating, among other things, that the orthodoxies of constitutional dualism, like *lex posteriori*, be abandoned. The doctrine of *lex posteriori*, however, is a corollary of the prohibition of judicial review, which itself is deeply embedded in the doctrine of parliamentary sovereignty. With supremacy, the Court was, in effect, requiring national judges to engage in judicial review, even of legislative acts, in order to make EC law effective for individuals within national legal orders.[16] In France, Germany, and Italy, the constitution conferred on constitutional courts the exclusive exercise of constitution review of statutes. It is therefore unsurprising that, once announced, the Court's success in securing supremacy, on the ground, would largely be determined by the response of constitutional judges.

Tension between the ECJ and the Italian Constitutional Court (ICC) produced the supremacy doctrine in the first place. The story begins in

---

[16] The ECJ does not require a national court to void as invalid a national rule held to be contrary to EC law but, rather, requires that the national court apply the EC rule and to disapply the national one (*IN.CO.GE'90*, ECJ C-10-22/97, 1998).

1962, when Mr Costa went on trial for refusing to pay the equivalent of a three-dollar electrical bill in protest at the nationalization of electrical companies. Costa, a shareholder in one of the companies expropriated, alleged that the nationalization violated Art. 31 EC (nationalized monopolies are not to be managed in a discriminatory manner). Taking the initiative, the trial judge referred the matter to both the ECJ and the ICC.

The Italian Court, which disposed of the case first, was faced with determining the relative primacy of two sets of constitutional provisions. The first governs the relationship between international and national law: Art. 10 provides that "the Italian legal order shall conform to the general principle of international law"; and Art. 11 authorizes the state to "limit" its sovereignty in order to "promote and encourage international organizations," such as the EC. The second, Art. 80, states that treaty law enters into force only upon an act of the Italian Parliament. In its decision (ICC 1964/14), the ICC declared that because treaty law occupies the same rung on the hierarchy of legal norms as legislation, the latter rule prevails, and Costa lost his case.

Five months later, the European Court (*Costa*, ECJ 6/64, 1964) rejected Costa's claim as unfounded, while announcing its views on supremacy. The ECJ emphasized that the Treaty of Rome had "created its own legal system which, on the entry into force of the Treaty, became an integral part of the legal systems of the Member-States . . . which their courts are bound to apply." The Court continued:

[T]he law stemming from the Treaty, an independent source of law, [can]not, because of its special and original nature, be overridden by domestic legal provisions, however framed, without being deprived of its character as Community law and with the legal basis of the Community itself being called into question.

The decision thus repudiated *lex posteriori* doctrines, to the extent that they would inhibit the effective application of EC law in national legal orders.

Ignoring the European Court's ruling, the ICC let stand its position on *lex posteriori* for more than a decade. In a series of rulings from 1975–7 (ICC 1975/232; ICC 1976/206; ICC 1977/163), the ICC gradually shifted control from Art. 80 of the Constitution to Arts. 10 and 11. At this point, however, the traditional approach to the problem of judicial review proved awkward. The Court held that the constitutional rule prohibiting the courts from reviewing of the legal validity of a parliamentary act also denied ordinary judges the authority to enforce EC law against subsequent, conflicting legislation. EC law could be applied in such cases, but only after the ICC authorized courts to do so, on a case-by-case basis, pursuant to a preliminary reference. Thus, in cases where the supremacy doctrine would come into play, the applicability of EC law would be subject to the infamous delays attending Italian constitutional review processes. The enforcement of directly applicable, legal rights under EC law would be held hostage to an idiosyncratic, national procedure.

Some Italian judges, apparently hoping to gain a measure of autonomy from the Italian Constitutional Court, worked to undermine the ICC's case law. The crucial case involved the importation of French beef into Italy by the Simmenthal company. In 1973, Italian customs authorities billed Simmenthal nearly 600,000 lire to pay for mandatory health inspections of its meat as it crossed the border. The border inspections, required by Italian legislation passed in 1970, conflicted with the EEC Treaty, and with two EC regulations adopted in the 1960s. Simmenthal challenged the border inspections before an Italian judge, who referred the matter to the ECJ. The European Court (*Simmenthal*, ECJ 35/76, 1976) ruled that the border inspections violated free movement of goods provisions and various EC regulations, and authorized the Italian judge to order the Italian government to return Simmenthal's payment. The Italian government appealed the judge's order, on the grounds that only the ICC could authorize an Italian judge to set aside national legislation. At that point, the trial judge stayed the proceeding, and requested the ECJ to declare the ICC's jurisprudence incompatible with the ECJ's supremacy doctrine!

The European Court (*Simmenthal*, ECJ 106/77, 1978) agreed, declaring that EC norms, from their entry into force, become immediately enforceable in every courtroom throughout the Community. Consequently, "any provision of a national legal system and any legislative, administrative, or judicial practice which might impair the effectiveness of Community law"—such as a mandatory concrete review process—"are incompatible with . . . *the very essence* of Community law." Despite the clarity of the European Court's statement, the ICC waited more than fifteen years to decide that EC law could be directly applicable by ordinary judges, without a preliminary reference to the ICC.[17] In that case (*Granital*, ICC 1984/170), the Italian Court took pains to stress that (*a*) the Italian constitution, not the ECJ, governed the relationship between Community law and national legislation, and (*b*) contrary to the European Court's vision of the world,

---

[17] The ICC finessed the constitutional review issue, ordering judges simply to ignore national law conflicting with antecedent EC law. Upon discovering a conflict between national and EC norms, the ordinary judge must choose not to recognize the existence of the former; the ICC no longer considers such a choice to be judicial review of statute.

the European and national legal orders were "independent and separate" of one other. In later cases (e.g. *Fragd*, ICC 1989/168), it also reserved for itself the power to examine potential conflicts between EC law and fundamental rights guaranteed by the Italian constitution.

In this saga, the ECJ and the ICC have remained stubbornly attached to their own "inalienable conceptual orders" (Barav 1985: 314). Nevertheless, the ICC has been forced to adapt to the case law of the European Court, rather than the other way around. The ECJ, for its part, has refused to back down, using its interactions with the Italian Court to clarify and extend its message. In comparing the reception of this message crossnationally, we notice that it was in those states where constitutional review by specialized constitutional jurisdictions exist—France, Germany, and Italy—that the reception of supremacy proved to be the most problematic.

In France, the story has been, until recently, one of fragmentation. The constitution of 1958 is strongly monist: Art. 55 clearly states that treaty law is both part of French law and superior to statute. Each of France's three high courts, however, had to determine if it could enforce EC law. In 1975, in a decision having no relationship to the Community, the Constitutional Council (1975) ruled (contrary to the ICC's position) that constitutional review of statute and the review of the conformity of national legislation with treaty law were inherently different juridical exercises, and that its powers were limited exclusively to the former. Although this decision is now commonly read as constitutional authorization to the judiciary to accept supremacy (Favoreu and Philip 1994), the fact is that the civil courts had proceeded to do so beforehand.

In 1971, a Paris trial court had set aside customs rules, adopted in a law of 1966, that taxed certain imports from other EC countries more than the same products produced in France. The French administration had argued that the civil courts could only do so by "making themselves judges of the constitutionality of laws," which would be impermissible under separation of powers doctrines. The trial court disagreed, basing its decision on Art. 55 of the French constitution, and on the "autonomous nature of EC law" emphasized by the ECJ. The Paris Court of Appeal and the Supreme Court (the *Cour de Cassation*) upheld the decision, ruling that the primacy of Community law over conflicting statute inhered in both the nature of EC law and in Art. 55 (*Jacques Vabre*, Cour de Cassation 1975).

France's high administrative court, however, waited until 1989 to accept supremacy. Until that point, the Council of State's position was that, notwithstanding Art. 55 of the constitution, the administrative courts could not enforce international law, because (*a*) judicial review was prohibited and (*b*) the authority to set aside legislation conflicting with a constitutional provision rested exclusively with the Constitutional Council. In *Nicolo* (*Conseil d'État* 1989), the Council of State simply overruled itself, without mentioning the ECJ, the status of Community law, *Cassation*'s case law, or the Constitutional Council's jurisprudence on Art. 55. The arguments of the *Commissaire du Gouvernement*, presented to the Council of State as part of the proceedings in *Nicolo*, probably held sway among a large number of judges:

Art. 55 in itself necessarily enables the courts, by implication, to review the compatibility of statutes with treaties. Indeed, we must attribute to the authors of the Constitution an intention to provide for actual implementation of the supremacy of treaties . . .

On this basis, therefore, I propose that you should agree to give treaties precedence over later statutes.

I am aware that the ECJ . . . has not hesitated . . . to affirm the obligation to refuse to apply in any situation laws which are contrary to Community measures.

I do not think you can follow the ECJ in this judge-made law which, in truth, seems to me at least open to objection. Were you to do so, you would tie yourself to a supranational way of thinking which is quite difficult to justify, to which the Rome Treaty does not subscribe expressly, and which would quite certainly render the Treaty unconstitutional . . .

The sometimes tortuous accommodation of supremacy by the French, Italian, and—as we will shall soon see—the German legal systems contrast sharply with how smoothly the doctrine was received by judiciaries of the other three original members of the EC. In the Netherlands, the constitutional prohibition against judicial review was simply overridden by a strongly expressed monism. Arts. 93 and 94 of the Dutch constitution, which date from the 1950s, provide for the direct applicability of international law as well as their primacy in any conflict with national legal norms. Even more extraordinary, the consensus of legal scholars is that this supremacy clause bestows on international agreements primacy over even the constitution itself (see Claes and de Witte 1998). Belgium and Luxembourg, dualist constitutional orders, provided tougher tests. Nevertheless, the high courts in both countries quickly and easily swept aside entrenched *lex posteriori* doctrines, without explicit constitutional or political authorization.

One might have expected supremacy to have met its chilliest reception in the courts of the United Kingdom, a relative latecomer to the EC, joining in 1973. A central organizing precept of UK constitutional law is the doctrine of Parliamentary Sovereignty: the only legal limitation to legislative power is that a Parliament of today cannot, with legislative instruments, bind a parliament of tomorrow. The doctrine further prohibits judicial review of legislation, and mandates a *lex posteriori* solution to conflicts between treaty law and statute. In many respects, the United Kingdom constitutes the archetype of a dualist regime.[18] Nevertheless, that Member State's highest court, the House of Lords, formally accepted supremacy of EC law—but not the supremacy of any other species of international law—in 1991. Prior to 1991, British judges either (*a*) applied the UK norm, under the guise of an "implied repeal" of the antecedent EC norm, a solution in open conflict with the ECJ's supremacy doctrine, or (*b*) engaged in "principled construction of the UK statute," reading it—as far as possible—as if it were adopted in light of requirements of EC law (see Craig 1998). The change caps a long process through which British judging has been "Europeanized" (Levitsky 1994), to the detriment of traditional conceptions of legislative sovereignty (Craig 1991).

SUPREMACY AND THE PROBLEM OF HUMAN RIGHTS

One hugely important, but wholly unintended, consequence of the ECJ's elaboration of the supremacy doctrine has been the progressive construction of a charter of rights for the Community. The Treaty of Rome originally contained no mention of rights, although some provisions could be read as rights provisions. Ex-Art. 7 EC (the principle of nondiscrimination based on nationality) and Art. 141 EC (the principles of equal pay for equal work among men and women), to take the most prominent examples, were designed to counter potential sources of distortion within an emerging common market, not to create individual rights. In 1959, the ECJ declared itself to be without power to review European Coal and Steel Community acts with reference to fundamental rights (*Stork*, ECJ 1/58, 1959); in 1969, the Court recognized that fundamental rights were part of the general principles of EC law that it was obliged to protect (*Stauder*, ECJ 29/69, 1969); and, in 1989, the Court secured the power to review the acts of the Member States for rights violations (*Wachauf*, ECJ 5/88, 1989). The Court has thus radically revised the treaties, "wisely and courageously" in Weiler's terms (1986: 1105–6).

---

[18] That is, any international legal norm that modifies the legal rights and obligations of UK citizens must be transposed to have effect within the United Kingdom. This law is then subject to implied repeal (*lex posteriori*).

The move, however, was not voluntary.[19] An incipient rebellion against supremacy, led by national constitutional courts, drove the process. Just after the doctrine of supremacy was announced, Italian and German judges noticed that supremacy could work to insulate EC law from national rights protection. They began challenging—in references to the ECJ and to their own constitutional courts—the legality of a range of EC legislative acts, on the theory that these acts violated national constitutional rights. The *Internationale Handelsgesellschaft* litigation provided the most important early example. The case involved a financial penalty (the forfeiture of an export deposit) permitted by EC regulations adopted in 1967, and administered against a German exporter by the German government. In its referral to the ECJ, the administrative court of Frankfurt complained that the regulations appeared to violate German constitutional rights. In its response, the European Court (ECJ 11/70, 1970) declared that EC law could not be overridden by national rights provisions "without the legal basis of the Community itself"—that is, supremacy—"being called into question." But recognizing the seriousness of the challenge, the Court declared that "respect for fundamental rights"—which is "inspired by the constitutional traditions of the member states"—"forms an integral part of the general principles of law protected by the Court of Justice." Although the German government argued that the Court had no power to do so, the ECJ then reviewed the regulations for their conformity with these fundamental rights, but found no violation.

The case did not end there. Disappointed with the ECJ's ruling, the Frankfurt court asked the Constitutional Court to declare the EC rules unconstitutional, not least since they could lead to a "constitutional and legal vacuum." Although the GFCC (1974) refused to do so, it declared (by a 5–3 vote) that "*so long as* the integration process has not progressed so far that Community law also possesses a catalogue of rights . . . of settled validity, which is adequate in comparison with a catalogue of fundamental rights contained in the [German] constitution," the German Court would permit German constitutional review of EC acts. The decision is today known as the *Solange I* (the first "so long as") decision.

In response to cases like these, the ECJ became increasingly explicit about the fundamental rights it had promised to protect. Thus, in *Nold* (ECJ 4/73, 1974), the Court declared that it would annul "[Community] measures

---

[19] Mancini and Keeling (1994) argue that the ECJ was not "bulldozed," but only "forced," by national courts into recognizing fundamental rights.

which are incompatible with fundamental rights recognized and protected by the constitutions of the Member States." In the same case, the Court also announced that international human rights treaties signed by the member states, including the European Convention on Human Rights, would "supply guidelines" to the Court. The Court has thereafter referred to the Convention as if it were a basic source of Community rights, and has invoked it in review of member state acts (e.g. *Rutili*, ECJ 36/75, 1975). Although some uncertainty remains, national courts have generally been persuaded by these moves. In 1986, the GFCC set aside *Solange I*. In *Solange II*, it declared that "a measure of protection of fundamental rights has been established . . . which, in its conception, substance and manner of implementation, is essentially compatible with the standards established by the German constitution." The GFCC then prohibited concrete review references "*so long as* the EC, and in particular the ECJ, generally ensures an effective protection of fundamental rights" (GFCC 1987).

The European Court's jurisprudence of supremacy and fundamental rights are tightly bound to a particular vision of the Community. Without supremacy, the ECJ had decided, the common market was doomed. And without a judicially enforceable charter of rights, the German courts had decided, the supremacy doctrine was doomed. The ECJ could have maintained its original position that held, in effect, fundamental rights to be part of national—but not EC—law; the courts of the Member States might have begun to annul EC acts judged to be unconstitutional. If either had occurred, legal integration would have been fatally undermined. (The courts of several Member States[20] still assert the power to review EC acts, but none has actually found one to be unconstitutional.)

Instead an expansive constitutional politics of rights emerged at the Community level. A 1989 decision, *Wachauf* (ECJ 5/88, 1989), illustrates the main features of these new politics. The case involved a German farmer who, along with his parents before him, had built a thriving dairy business on leased land over a period of twenty-five years. After having been denied a renewal of his lease by the landowner, Mr. Wachauf decided to take advantage of a 1984 EC Regulation providing for monetary compensation to dairy farmers who agreed to downsize or abandon their milk production.[21] The

---

[20] In the United Kingdom, a 2002 opinion of a division of the High Court noted that an important matter of law might be raised "[i]n the event, which no doubt would never happen in the real world, that a European measure was seen to be repugnant to a fundamental or constitutional right guaranteed by the law of England" (reported in Craig and de Burca 2003: 312).

[21] The regulation was adopted as part of a general scheme to reduce chronic surpluses in the EC agricultural sector.

federal government, charged with implementing the regulation, refused to grant this compensation, about DM150,000, on the grounds that the EC rule required, in cases where land leases were involved, the consent of the landowner. The landowner, in an attempt to profit from Wachauf's labors, had denied his consent. The case was brought to the Frankfurt administrative court. In its reference to the ECJ, the German judge offered "a suggested interpretation" to the effect that the implementation of the EC rule had "deprived [Wachauf] of the fruits of his labor," and "amounted to an unconstitutional expropriation without compensation." The ECJ agreed with this interpretation, but declined to annul the regulation. It instead declared that the measure could be construed to include compensation in cases like Wachauf's, despite the language of the regulation to the contrary, in order to render the act compatible with "fundamental rights in the Community legal order." The ECJ left it to the national court to determine if Wachauf's rights had indeed been violated, and the Frankfurt court subsequently awarded the farmer compensation and trial costs.

The decision has far-reaching implications, three of which deserve emphasis. First, the ECJ announced that it was now in the business of balancing rights claims against the interests of government, using proportionality tests. The Court stated:

The fundamental rights recognized by the Court are not absolute . . . but must be considered in relation to their social function. Consequently, restrictions may be imposed on the exercise of these rights . . . provided that these restrictions in fact correspond to objectives of general interest pursued by the Community and do not constitute, with regard to the aim pursued, a disproportionate and intolerable interference, impairing the very substance of those rights.

Second, Member State governments, when they administer EC law within their territory, are considered by the Court to be *agents of the Community*, and thereby bound by Community rights provisions. Third, national courts are enlisted to monitor respect for Community rights, and the ECJ is present to authorize national judges to annul member state acts that violate these rights. Taken together, *Wachauf* has strengthened the capacity of the ECJ, in partnership with the national courts, to control policy outcomes.

Despite being conflictual in origin, the dialogue on fundamental rights has served to deepen legal integration, to widen the scope of EC constitutional politics, and to strengthen the supranational aspects of the Community.[22] Playing catch-up, the Member States did not block, but

---

[22] For a more complete survey, see Weiler and Lockhart (1995*a*, *b*).

ratified, these developments. In 1977, the EP, the Commission, and the Council adopted a joint resolution approving the Court's move. In the TEU, the Member States revised the Rome Treaty, echoing the Court: "the Union shall respect fundamental rights as guaranteed by the European Convention on Human Rights . . . and as they result from the constitutional traditions common to the member states as general principles of Community law." The statement is not merely a symbolic one. In case after case over the past decade (e.g. *Commission* v. *Netherlands*, ECJ C-353/89, 1991) Member States have been induced to defend themselves, in cases involving rights guaranteed by the Community, in the Court's preferred language of proportionality balancing. In doing so, the Member States legitimize the centrality of the Court's position as constitutional balancer of rights against the general interest, in partnership with national judges. In December 2000, the Member States produced a codified Charter of Rights (De Burca 2001), the precise legal status of which is scheduled to be determined by an Inter-Governmental Conference in 2004. In Craig and de Burca's (2003: 359) words, the Charter is "a creative distillation of the rights contained in the various European and international agreements and national constitutions on which the ECJ had for some years already been drawing."

SUPREMACY AND THE CONSTITUTIONAL LIMITS TO POLITICAL INTEGRATION

Interactions between the European and national constitutional courts ultimately led to a stable accommodation on rights and the obligation of ordinary courts to enforce EC law. But they have not resolved another fundamental problem posed by supremacy: which jurisdiction has the *ultimate* authority to determine the constitutionality of EC acts? The problem may in fact be irresoluble. On the one hand, the logic of supremacy suggests that the ECJ alone should have such authority, as guardian of the constitutional order of the EC, and the Court has declared as much in *Foto Frost* (ECJ 314/85, 1987). On the other hand, national constitutional courts, guardians of their own constitutional orders, cling to the view that Community law is a species of international law which enters into national legal orders through, and must conform with the provisions of, their own constitution. These courts, even at their most integration-friendly moments, have always been careful to reserve for themselves the final authority to determine the legality of EC acts.

The most far-reaching ruling in this regard is the German constitutional court's decision on the TEU, signed at Maastricht in January 1992. The ruling sent shock waves through the Community that are still felt.[23] Because of its far-reaching scope, the TEU required an accommodation between the European and national constitutions. In addition to committing the Member States to enhanced cooperation in foreign policy, security, and social policy, the TEU established European citizenship for all EC nationals and a step-by-step process to European Monetary Union (EMU). These latter provisions required the amendment of most Member States' constitutions: the granting of a right to vote in local elections to all EC citizens, wherever they lived within the Community, conflicted with provisions restricting voting rights to nationals; and the transfers of sovereignty involved in the EMU, the core of which is a single European currency managed by an independent European Central Bank, also required constitutional authorization. In December 1992, four articles of the German Constitution were amended to enable ratification, and the German Bundestag (the lower house of the legislature, by a 543–25 vote) and the Bundesrat (the upper house, unanimously) ratified the Treaty. In amending the constitution, the government and the legislature were careful to pay tribute to the GFCC's jurisprudence on the issue of supremacy. Art. 23, for example, now states that Germany:

shall cooperate in the development of the European Union in order to realize a united Europe which is bound to observe democratic . . . principles . . . and which guarantees the protection of basic rights in a way which is substantially comparable to that provided by this constitution.

Further, rules (Art. 23) governing transfers of governmental authority from Germany to the EC were tightened: such transfers, which previously could be effected by a simple majority, now were to be approved by two-thirds of the Bundestag and the Bundesrat.

The law ratifying the Treaty was suspended[24] after four members of the German Green Party, joined by a former German EC Commissioner, attacked its constitutionality in separate constitutional complaints. Although a dozen often contradictory arguments were invoked, complainants focused on the alleged "democratic deficit" afflicting the EC: that the expansion in the EC's policymaking powers had so far outpaced democratization in the

---

[23] The Danish Supreme Court issued a similar ruling in 1998. Reported in Craig and de Burca (2003: 312); see Høegh (1999).

[24] The German President refused to sign the bill pending the GFCC's decision.

Community that in many areas Germans do not effectively participate in their own governance.

In a long and complex ruling, the German Court (GFCC 1993) dismissed the complaint as unfounded, thus clearing the way for German ratification of the Treaty. Given the care in which the Constitution had been revised, the outcome was hardly surprising. The Court, however, used the opportunity to introduce a new basis in which to challenge EC norms: the *ultra vires* nature of EC acts. (*Ultra vires* acts are governmental acts that are not legally valid to the extent that the governmental entity taking them has exceeding its prescribed authority.) The ruling thus conflicts with the ECJ's holding in *Foto Frost.*

The decision rests on two interpretive pillars. First, the Court subjugated Art. 23 to Art. 38, the latter of which establishes that the Bundestag is to be elected by "general, direct, free, equal, and secret" elections. The GFCC read Art. 38 to mean not only that Germans possessed a right to participate in such elections, but that "the weakening, within the scope of Art. 23, of the legitimation of state power gained through an election" was prohibited. Thus, a vote of the Bundestag, issuing from legislative elections, constitutes the sole means of conferring legitimacy to acts of public authority within Germany, *including acts of the EC.* Second, the German Court announced that it would view the expansion of supranational governance as compatible with the constitution only to the extent that Member State governments "retain their sovereignty," and "thereby control integration." Willfully ignoring reality, it then declared the EC to be a strictly "intergovernmental Community," in which each national government is its own "master" of the treaties, possessing the power to veto Community acts and the right to withdraw from the EC.

The operative part of its ruling is derived from these two interpretive moves. Most important, the Court declared that integration must, in order to conform to constitutional dictates, proceed "predictably," that is, intergovernmentally. At the Community level, the German government negotiates and authorizes, by treaty law, whatever there is of EC governance; at the national level, the Bundestag legitimizes and transposes these authorizations in national law. The Court then asserted its jurisdiction over EC acts:

If . . . European institutions or governmental entities were to implement or develop the Maastricht Treaty in a manner no longer covered by the Treaty in the form of it upon which the German [ratification act] is based, any legal instrument arising from such activity would not be binding within German territory. German state institutions would be prevented, by reasons of constitutional law, from applying such legal instruments in Germany. Accordingly, the GFCC must examine the question of whether or not [these] legal instruments . . . may be considered to remain within the bounds . . . accorded to them, or whether they may be considered to exceed these bounds.

Thus, the German Court possesses the authority to void any EC act having the effect of depriving German legislative organs of their substantive control over integration. In terms of constitutional review processes, litigants now possess the right to plead the *ultra vires* nature of Community acts before all German judges, who would then be obliged to initiate concrete review processes before the GFCC.

Not surprisingly, the German Court's decision has been the target of sharp criticism, particularly by Community lawyers who see a repudiation of the underlying bases of European legal order. Weiler (1995), for example, sees a "sad and pathetic decision" that employs "a surface language of democracy," but ultimately rests on a "deep structure" of ethno-centric nationalism. A glaring irony runs through the decision. Supranational aspects of the Treaty of European Union, such as the enhancement of certain powers of the EP and the establishment of a general right to vote in local elections, sought to close, however slightly, the Community's democratic deficit. The revision of the German constitution, necessary for ratification of the Treaty, also strengthened democratic controls over integration. Nevertheless, in privileging a traditional "international law and organization" approach to the EC, the German Court legitimates as democratic what for many is the very source of the alleged deficit: the Community's intergovernmental elements. The irony can be drawn out further. The process by which the treaties were constitutionalized, widely viewed as both strengthening the supranational and the democratic character of the Community/Union, escaped the control of national governments. Had the rules the German Court laid down there been enforceable since the beginning, the construction of an EC charter of rights—which the GFCC itself required in the name of democracy, but which were not a product of an intergovernmental bargain—would clearly have been unconstitutional.

REMEDIES

Supremacy and direct effect imply that national courts are appropriate sites for remedial action where an individual is damaged by a breach of EC law. One of the more subtle—and ongoing—dialogues between the ECJ and the national courts concerns the extent to which EC law pertains to the provision of remedies in national courts (Caranta 1995; Hoskins 1996;

Dougan 2004). The Treaty of Rome makes no mention of remedial requirements, which is unsurprising since the Member States did not consider establishing the direct effect of EC law or of individual rights. Once private parties could plead rights before national judges, however, the question of remedies could not but follow. In its early decisions on the problem (*Rewe-Zentralfinanz*, ECJ 33/76, 1976; *Comet*, ECJ 45/76, 1976), the ECJ recognized the broad autonomy of national courts to tailor remedies according to their own established rules and practices, so long as the remedies provided for breaches of EC law were both (*a*) available in practice and (*b*) broadly equivalent to remedies available for similar breaches of domestic law. The Court subsequently made it clear that, subject to these two conditions, EC law did not require the Member States to develop new remedies (see *Rewe-Handelsgesellschaft Nord*, ECJ 158/80, 1981).

During this same period, the Court steadily pushed to strengthen the effectiveness of EC law, notably through the expansion of individual rights. The strategy rapidly undermined the minimalism of its jurisprudence on remedies (Craig and de Burca 2003: 237–53). At the end of the 1980s, the ECJ began to curtail the principle of national remedial autonomy. Most importantly, it asserted that national legal systems must provide remedies whose purpose is to enable individuals to secure fully their rights under EC law. In 1993, for example, the Court (*Marshall II*, ECJ C-271/91, 1993; see Chapter 4) held that national rules establishing a ceiling on damages for sex discrimination claims were contrary to EC law, to the extent that a victim of discrimination might be less than fully compensated for his or her injury under national law. It further held that full compensation must include interest payments, whereas the pertinent UK statute expressly prohibited such awards. In this and other cases, the ECJ found that EC law required remedies that were not otherwise available under national law. Inevitably, the Court developed a proportionality-based, balancing test according to which the importance of the EC right at bar is weighed against the underlying purposes of the remedy, wherein the restrictions on the remedy available must not place an undue burden on those who seek to have their rights under EC law vindicated in national courts. Throughout this saga, the EC's legislative organs have not moved to harmonize remedies, partly due to the inherent complexity of doing so (Kilpatrick et al. 2001).

The most spectacular development in this field came with the Court's development of the principle of state liability, initiated in 1991 (*Francovich*, ECJ C-6 and 9/90, 1991). As noted in part III, in *Brasserie du Pecheur* (ECJ 46/93, 1996) the Court refined the rules governing a right to be compensated for losses due to a Member State's breach of EC law. During the proceedings, Germany, as defendant party to the case, argued that ordinary national remedies sufficed, implying that the Court had erred in its *Francovich* judgment. The Court dismissed the argument, declaring that "the right to reparation is the necessary corollary of the direct effect of the Community provision whose breach caused the damage."[25] Echoing *Marshall II*, the Court then announced that "the reparation for loss or damage to individuals as a result of breaches of Community law must be commensurate with the loss or damage sustained." Thus, the principles of state liability and the right to full compensation inhere in EC law, and supremacy requires national legal systems to accommodate them. In *Brasserie du Pecheur* and subsequent cases, the Court did not simply codify a pre-existing minimum common denominator position of the Member States; these decisions, in the words of Steiner and Woods (2003: 149), "[broke] new constitutional ground in most if not all of the Member States" (see also Craig 1997; Anagnostaras 2001).

SUMMARY

The constitutionalization of the treaty system generated a dynamic and inherently expansive set of dialogues between the ECJ and national judges on the nature of the relationship between the national and the Community legal orders. We have focused on the relatively formal aspects of these dialogues in this section, but formalism should not disguise what has been at stake politically. Most important, the evolution of the supremacy doctrine steadily upgraded the capacity of both the ECJ and the national courts to intervene in policy processes, to dictate political outcomes, and to shape various processes associated with judicialization. It has helped to undermine the dogmas of legislative sovereignty, freeing national judges from the dictatorship of statute (and legislative intent), while enhancing the ECJ's position as the locus for the elaboration of European constitutionalism. Finally, supremacy, when coupled with the doctrine of direct effect and the Court's jurisprudence on remedies, opened up the EC legal system to individual litigants, making national judges major players in the overall process of European integration.

[25] The German government had also claimed that establishing such a right was a matter for the EC legislative organs, implying that the ECJ had exceeded its authority. In response, the Court stated that the issue of state liability fell within the purview of the Treaty, which it was bound to interpret and apply.

V Adjudicating EC Law in the National Courts

In this section, we examine data on precedent and preliminary reference activity. The success of European legal integration, as a political project, depended on the institutionalization of practices associated with precedent. The EC is a decentralized polity, comprised of multiple legal systems, each operating according to local rules and traditions; for its part, the ECJ does not possess mechanisms to coerce and directly control national judges. For legal integration to proceed, various coordination problems had to be faced and resolved. Private parties had to learn how to conceive of EC law instrumentally, and how to press their claims before national judges. National judges had to be persuaded that the system worked, overall, to their benefit; and the ECJ had to be capable of tailoring its message to the specifics of concrete cases, while maintaining a minimum of overall consistency. The emergence of a precedent-based, discursive politics provided a means of doing these things and more.

Through use, the preliminary reference procedure has evolved to become the central nervous system of the EC polity. With the diffusion of the Court's doctrines of supremacy and direct effect, the national judges gradually assumed a new function: agents of the Community legal order, and thus judges and enforcers of EC law in their own right. Precedent-based decision-making helped them perform these new tasks. At the same time, the constitutionalization of the Treaty expanded the discretionary powers of national judges. They decide (*a*) if a reference is necessary or should be sent; (*b*) how preliminary questions should be worded and framed; and (*c*) if and how a preliminary ruling will be implemented. National judges have always exercised these discretionary powers to great effect (Arnull 1989; Rasmussen 2000). Today, the overload and attendant delays now afflicting the system put even more pressure on judges to act as European judges. When judges decide not to send a reference, in order to save on costs to the parties, for example, then they will be required to interpret and apply EC law on their own, albeit aided by the Court's move to a heavily precedent-based case law.

PRECEDENT

The EC was founded as an international legal order by Member States sharing civil law traditions. Although neither international nor civil law formally recognize the doctrine of *stare decisis*, the Court not only used its discretion to reconstruct the treaty system, but worked assiduously to develop what is now a robust and taken-for-granted set of practices associated with precedent.

McCown and Stone Sweet compiled a comprehensive data-set of ECJ citation practices for all preliminary rulings, 1958–98. Excluding references withdrawn or joined to another case by the Court,[26] our database contains information on a total of 2,674 rulings citing 2,057 different cases (1961–98) The analysis does not conflate the practice of citation with the concept of precedent, or with argumentation frameworks (see Chapter 1); rather, we take citation to be a highly reliable indicator of the presence of such phenomena. Chapters 3 through 5 of this book involve detailed, case-by-case analysis of specific domains of EC law, which focus, in part, on the Court's construction of doctrine. In these chapters, we are primarily interested in the extent to which these doctrinal structures influence the decision-making of legislators, judges, and the Member States. Here we present only some of the aggregate data analysis on citation practices, and some of the inferences taken from this analysis.

We conceptualize precedent as a set of practices organized by argumentation frameworks, also called "doctrine" (Chapter 1). The more any argumentation framework constrains litigation and adjudication of EC law—through delimiting the set of defensible arguments available to litigants and judges—the more robust the precedent. The process of building argumentation frameworks has been institutionalized as an inherently expansionary process. The number of decisions using precedent arguments increase, over time, as do the number of precedent-rules used to construct each argument. As Figures 2.9 and 2.10 show, the frequency with which decisions cite past rulings, and the density of citation, have both increased.

These findings provide some initial support for claims, made by Bengoetxea (2003) and others using traditional doctrinal analysis, that under the tutelage of the ECJ, EC law has steadily developed an internal coherence organized, in a self-referential manner, by precedent. Chapters 3 and 4 analyze the structure and impact of precedent more fully.

REFERENCE ACTIVITY

Until the beginning of the 1980s, the ECJ went out of its way to encourage national courts to send preliminary references. The Court relied upon

---

[26] Although including the primary case of each set of joined cases as is consistent with ECJ practice.

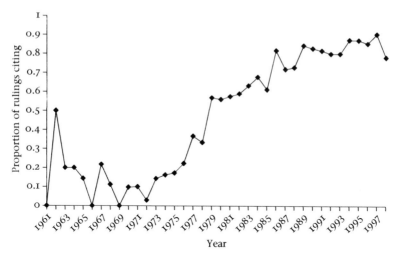

Figure 2.9. Proportion of ECJ Rulings, Per Year, Containing Citations to Prior Judgments

Note: We count only those rulings made pursuant to a preliminary reference.

Source: Data compiled by Margaret McCown and Alec Stone Sweet (see Stone Sweet and McCown 2003).

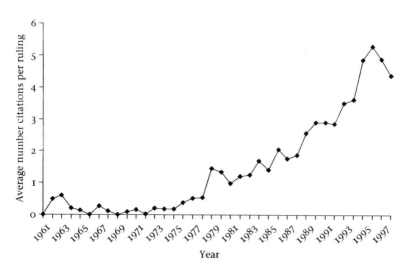

Figure 2.10. Average Number of Citations Per ECJ Ruling, Per Year

Note: We count only those rulings made pursuant to a preliminary reference.

Source: Data compiled by Margaret McCown and Alec Stone Sweet (see Stone Sweet and McCown 2003).

references to develop its doctrines and to socialize litigants and judges into the ways of EC law. By the end of the 1980s, the Court began making it clear that litigants and national judges should rely as much as possible on precedent, whereas references should be used primarily for problem cases or ones that raise new questions of law. Massive overload, perhaps the best measure of the Court's success in its bid to enhance effectiveness through supremacy and direct effect, has largely dictated the change. Today, reform of the Art. 234 procedure is on the agenda (see this book's conclusion).

Not enough attention has been paid to compliance (judicial and political) with the Court's rulings, or with the impact of the Court's interactions with national judges on national politics. Two recent studies, however, deserve mention. In the first, Stacy Nyikos (2002) analyzed preliminary questions raised pursuant to an Art. 234 reference in three legal domains— free movement of goods, free movement of workers, and sex discrimination—and traced their various effects on latter stages of the process. In their questions, national judges often (38 percent of all references; $n = 574$) signal to the Court the answer they hope to obtain; such signaling has risen over time, and is far higher among judges who use the Art. 234 procedure repeatedly. The ECJ sometimes (in about 33 percent of cases) redefines the issue, through restating the referring judge's question. In a majority of instances in which national judges signal the desired response, the ECJ provides it. Nyikos also examined if and how national judges comply with the ECJ's preliminary rulings. She found overall compliance to be well above 90 percent. In less than 3 percent of cases did the national court (*a*) seek to evade a preliminary ruling through resending the reference (and indicating that it did not agree with the ECJ's preliminary ruling), or (*b*) refuse to apply it (in only two cases). Although Member State governments were parties in 86 percent ($n = 575$) of the cases that generated preliminary references, their *amicus* briefs to the Court were largely ineffectual in influencing the decisionmaking of either national judges or the ECJ.

Second, Lisa Conant (2002) argues rightly that a focus on the ECJ's output—its formal decisionmaking—tells us next to nothing about the Court's actual influence on national law and politics. EC law and litigation must find agency in national environments that are full of obstacles and complexities. The effectiveness of EC law varies widely, across jurisdictional boundaries and policy domains, conditioned by myriad factors operating with different effects, at different places and times. When observed in this way, the scope and effectiveness of EC law will always look "patchwork" and "fragmented," not least because quasi-federal governance is constantly being, in Conant's terms, "negotiated" by organized groups and officials, operating different levels of government, and possessed of different amounts and kinds of resources to shape outcomes. Of course, these same points apply to other federal polities, such as Canada and the United States.

Cross-national data on the subject matter of preliminary references reveal just how complicated the situation is at the Member State level. Each cell of Table 2.4 provides three pieces of information. First (labeled "actual number"), we give the number of references, generated by each Member State, for each of the major legal domains. Second (labeled "proportional share"), we assign to each Member State the number of references for each legal domain that would have been generated had there been no difference between percentages of rates of litigation overall and rates of litigation in specific legal areas. If a Member State accounted for 12 percent of total references, we assigned, as the proportional share, a number corresponding to 12 percent of the total number references in each legal domain to that member state. Thus, "proportional share" is a calculated expected frequency. Third, we highlight in bold a number expressed as a percentage, a percentage calculated as follows. We subtracted, for each domain and for each Member State, the proportional number from the actual number referenced. The percentage difference highlighted in bold is the difference between the actual and predicted level of references for each country standardized, by percentage, in terms of the total number of cases in each column.

The process may seem complex, but these calculations make comparing Art. 234 across Member States and across legal domains simple and instantaneous. Cell entries in bold consist of positive and negative percentages: a high positive value indicates that national judges are filing more references in a particular legal domain relative to other countries and other domains; a negative value indicates that national judges are filing fewer referrals than we would expect based on overall rates of reference activity, relative to judges in other Member States and relative to all other policy areas. Among other things, Table 2.4 shows clearly that it makes little sense to characterize judges, and their relative proclivities to participate in the construction of EC law through Art. 234 procedures, in strictly national terms, as many now do. All national judges send relatively more referrals in some areas than most other national judges, and relatively fewer references in other areas. It would be impossible to explain these patterns with reference to a factor that is specified nationally—such as German or French "legal culture"—unless one is somehow able to specify the attributes of a national legal culture

Table 2.4. Art. 234 References: Number, Proportional Share, and Percentage Difference, by Legal Domain

	A	B	C	D	E	F
Austria	−0.02%	−1.07%	−0.84%	−0.55%	−1.47%	−0.20%
Actual Number	12	4	2	1	0	3
Proportional Share	12.2	14.8	4.7	1.6	6.5	3.5
Belgium	−3.84%	−5.66%	1.94%	−1.15%	18.73%	−0.16%
Actual Number	54	47	39	10	129	24
Proportional Share	85.9	104.1	32.8	11.3	45.9	24.4
Denmark	−0.63%	−0.79%	0.15%	−1.76%	−2.23%	5.80%
Actual Number	17	19	9	1	2	20
Proportional Share	22.3	27.0	8.5	2.9	11.9	6.3
Finland	0.52%	−0.12%	−0.32%	−0.32%	−0.32%	−0.32%
Actual Number	7	2	0	0	0	0
Proportional Share	2.7	3.2	1.0	0.3	1.4	0.8
France	1.80%	−0.51%	13.02%	2.81%	−1.09%	−10.32%
Actual Number	129	133	85	18	56	8
Proportional Share	114.0	138.2	43.6	14.9	60.9	32.3
Germany	5.78%	11.62%	−13.98%	9.73%	−6.32%	−2.68%
Actual Number	303	426	53	44	108	66
Proportional Share	254.9	308.9	97.4	33.4	136.0	72.3
Greece	−0.53%	0.06%	−0.50%	−1.13%	−0.68%	−0.70%
Actual Number	5	12	2	0	2	1
Proportional Share	9.4	11.4	3.6	1.2	5.0	2.7
Ireland	−0.35%	1.09%	0.38%	0.64%	−0.74%	0.93%
Actual Number	7	23	5	2	2	5
Proportional Share	9.9	12.0	3.8	1.3	5.3	2.8
Italy	−0.36%	1.57%	5.20%	−4.21%	−12.50%	−9.22%
Actual Number	116	160	62	11	8	12
Proportional Share	119.0	144.2	45.5	15.6	63.5	33.8
Luxembourg	−0.02%	−0.48%	−0.66%	−0.98%	−0.30%	−0.55%
Actual Number	8	5	1	0	3	1
Proportional Share	8.1	9.9	3.1	1.1	4.3	2.3
Netherlands	−0.77%	−1.12%	−0.80%	0.41%	6.26%	0.28%
Actual Number	97	114	37	14	83	30
Proportional Share	103.4	125.3	39.5	13.5	55.2	29.3
Portugal	0.64%	−1.04%	0.85%	0.79%	−0.82%	−0.62%
Actual Number	14	0	6	2	1	1
Proportional Share	8.7	10.5	3.3	1.1	4.6	2.5
Spain	−0.47%	−1.71%	1.23%	−1.91%	1.02%	−0.22%
Actual Number	12	2	10	0	13	4
Proportional Share	15.9	19.3	6.1	2.1	8.5	4.5
Sweden	0.30%	−0.36%	−0.66%	−0.66%	−0.43%	0.61%
Actual Number	8	3	0	0	1	3
Proportional Share	5.5	6.6	2.1	0.7	2.9	1.6
UK	−2.06%	−1.47%	−5.02%	−1.72%	0.88%	17.35%
Actual Number	43	58	7	6	36	58
Proportional Share	60.1	72.8	23.0	7.9	32.1	17.1

G	H	I	J	K	L	M	N
−1.47%	**1.99%**	**2.49%**	**−0.30%**	**−1.47%**	**−1.47%**	**3.60%**	**1.43%**
0	10	8	4	0	0	11	14
1.1	4.2	3.0	5.0	1.1	1.1	3.2	7.1
−4.99%	**5.59%**	**7.49%**	**−2.77%**	**9.15%**	**−8.94%**	**−0.65%**	**−3.29%**
4	46	36	26	15	1	21	34
7.7	29.8	20.9	35.5	8.0	7.4	22.4	49.9
−0.01%	**−1.29%**	**−2.68%**	**2.85%**	**6.41%**	**0.10%**	**1.47%**	**0.43%**
2	4	0	19	7	2	9	15
2.0	7.7	5.4	9.2	2.1	1.9	5.8	12.9
−0.32%	**0.72%**	**−0.32%**	**0.26%**	**0.98%**	**−0.32%**	**−0.32%**	**−0.32%**
0	3	0	2	1	0	0	0
0.2	0.9	0.6	1.1	0.2	0.2	0.7	1.5
−0.37%	**−0.21%**	**−5.29%**	**0.54%**	**−3.32%**	**−2.59%**	**−1.72%**	**−1.49%**
10	39	17	49	8	8	26	59
10.3	39.6	27.7	47.1	10.6	9.9	29.7	66.2
−25.31%	**−14.38%**	**7.48%**	**−3.03%**	**−3.37%**	**13.80%**	**−11.29%**	**−4.97%**
4	47	77	95	21	32	42	124
23.0	88.6	61.9	105.4	23.6	22.1	66.5	148.0
−1.13%	**4.06%**	**0.36%**	**0.04%**	**−1.13%**	**−1.13%**	**−1.13%**	**0.74%**
0	15	3	4	0	0	0	9
0.8	3.3	2.3	3.9	0.9	0.8	2.4	5.4
−1.19%	**−0.50%**	**−0.69%**	**−1.19%**	**−1.19%**	**1.59%**	**−0.73%**	**0.05%**
0	2	1	0	0	2	1	6
0.9	3.4	2.4	4.1	0.9	0.9	2.6	5.7
33.70%	**4.38%**	**−6.88%**	**0.23%**	**−7.81%**	**3.75%**	**7.36%**	**3.09%**
36	54	15	50	5	13	47	84
10.7	41.3	28.9	49.2	11.0	10.3	31.0	69.1
−0.98%	**1.44%**	**1.00%**	**−0.69%**	**0.32%**	**−0.98%**	**−0.06%**	**1.71%**
0	7	4	1	1	0	2	13
0.7	2.8	2.0	3.4	0.8	0.7	2.1	4.7
6.24%	**−3.43%**	**−3.52%**	**0.94%**	**−2.04%**	**−2.71%**	**2.32%**	**−0.22%**
14	26	18	46	8	7	32	59
9.3	35.9	25.1	42.8	9.6	9.0	27.0	60.0
−1.04%	**0.34%**	**−1.04%**	**0.99%**	**0.26%**	**3.13%**	**−0.12%**	**0.62%**
0	4	0	7	1	3	2	8
0.8	3.0	2.1	3.6	0.8	0.7	2.3	5.0
−1.91%	**3.28%**	**−0.92%**	**0.70%**	**−1.91%**	**−1.91%**	**2.24%**	**0.99%**
0	15	2	9	0	0	9	14
1.4	5.5	3.9	6.6	1.5	1.4	4.2	9.2
0.67%	**1.42%**	**−0.66%**	**−0.08%**	**0.64%**	**−0.66%**	**−0.20%**	**0.38%**
1	6	0	2	1	0	1	5
0.5	1.9	1.3	2.3	0.5	0.5	1.4	3.2
−1.89%	**−3.42%**	**3.17%**	**1.50%**	**4.46%**	**−1.67%**	**−0.77%**	**0.85%**
4	11	21	30	9	4	14	39
5.4	20.9	14.6	24.9	5.6	5.2	15.7	34.9

Note: A: Free movement of goods; B: Agriculture; C: Competition and dumping; D: External policy; E: Social security; F: Social provisions; G: Environment; H: Establishment; I: Free movement of workers; J: Taxes; K: Transportation; L: Common policy; M: Approximation of laws; N: Other. *Actual Number* indicates the number of Art. 177 references in that legal domain for each Member State. *Proportional share* entries are the number of cases that each Member State *would have registered* in each legal domain if there were no difference between (a) overall litigation rates for each Member State; and (b) rates of litigation for each Member State in each policy area. The *Proportional Share* is the "table of no association" (the basis of the chi-squared test). $P < 0.0001$. Bold entries, or *Percentage Differences*, are calculated as follows: (Actual number—Proportional share)/number of references in the legal domain. Bold entries indicate the positive or negative extent to which national judges are filing preliminary references in a particular legal domain, relative to other Member States and other areas.

Source: Alec Stone Sweet and Thomas L. Brunell Data Set on Preliminary References in EC Law, 1958–98, Robert Schuman Centre for Advanced Studies, European University Institute (San Domenico di Fiesole, Italy: 1999).

in multiple ways, as a function of the legal domain in which judges are operating.

Table 2.4 raises a crucial question: what factors account for, or explain, the cross-national variation in references in any given area of EC law? Proposed answers to this question, once formed as a set of hypotheses, would generate a research agenda of great importance.[27] We conclude by suggesting ways of thinking about how the variation depicted in Table 2.4 might be explained, not least in order to demonstrate some of the fierce difficulties that would be involved. Although we have chosen to mention a range of potential approaches, we do so for the sake of illustration rather than to offer firm candidate hypotheses.

Let us begin by paying attention to the variation contained in the entire table. It may be that some significant percentage of cross-national difference in the intensity of Art. 234 activity, as measured by all of the cells in the table, may be accounted for by one (or a small number of) factors. To take just one example, one might reasonably argue that variation is a function of the relative extent to which EC rulemaking, as it evolves through case law or legislation, generates tensions or disjunctures between EC and national legal regimes. One logic of legal integration developed in this project (Sandholtz and Stone Sweet (eds.) 1998; Stone Sweet and Caporaso 1998*b*) posits that the perceived costs and benefits of using national courts to effect policy change will be more attractive to some individuals and groups than to others, and such differences will be registered as crossnational variation in references. A related set of propositions begins with the assumption that EC rulemaking—including judicial lawmaking—will always affect national legal regimes differentially. Thus, a secondary hypothesis might be that the more any national legal system is required to change in order to meet the new demands of EC law, the more references will be produced in that system, since we might expect change in the law and in judicial and administrative practices to be incomplete, and the process of change to proceed slowly.[28] In this book, it is assumed that some private parties have an interest in using European law and court to subvert national regimes; national judges have the power to respond to these demands in various ways, and may pursue their own policy goals through their referral activities. But the

---

[27] For the most part, the question falls beyond the scope of this book, the main focus of which is on the impact of the legal system on the evolution of institutions—the governing rule structure—in the EC.

[28] The proposition is related to a "goodness of fit" variable that seeks to explain differences in the number and importance of compliance problems across the Member States (see Börzel 2002; Cichowski 2002; Green Cowles, Caporaso, and Risse (eds.) 2001).

extent to which litigators and judges actually do so surely vary across national jurisdictions and issue areas, in part because the potential benefits of litigating EC law varies.

Of course, it may also be that much of the variation found in Table 2.4 is, at least in part, explainable through mechanisms that operate in column-specific ways, rather than across the table as a whole. Consider the numbers in column A, which compare national referral activity in the area of free movement of goods. Of the 832 references filed in the area, 303 have attacked German laws for being in noncompliance. Indeed, Germany has the highest positive bold cell entry of any Member State in this domain, indicating that German judges disproportionately generate references in this domain, relative to all other domains and to their peers in other national systems. A number of propositions are immediately suggested. We may hypothesize that Germany has been more protectionist than the other Member States; or, more likely, that the relative size of national markets will determine references in this domain (a hypothesis considered further in Chapter 3; see also Stone Sweet and Brunell 1998a), but not necessarily in others. In addition, there is also an important literature, in comparative political economy, that emphasizes that Germany, compared with many of its EC partners, regulates the economy in ways that are relatively more "legalistic," with dense and relatively rigid rules structures more likely to generate litigation (Dyson (ed.) 1992). Whatever the explanation, the matrix of trade-relevant rules in place in Germany has provided the predominant context for the Court's decisionmaking; this matrix, one presumes, will partly condition the development of the Court's jurisprudence on one of the most important parts of the Treaty of Rome.

Or consider cross-national patterns depicted in column F, which is comprised mostly of references on equal pay for equal work and nondiscrimination. Among other things, EC rules in this area lay down certain minimal standards for treatment in the workplace; but these rules are presumably more or less advantageous to any given female worker, relative to national rules and practices, depending on where she lives and works (the first hypothesis above). But does the fact that UK judges generate far more than their share of Art. 234 activity in this area mean that women are subject to greater, and worse forms of, job-related discrimination in the United Kingdom than are women in every other Member State? Not necessarily. We would suggest that women workers in the United Kingdom may be better organized and better supported institutionally (by trade unions, the Equal Opportunity Commission, and judges on the labor courts) than are women elsewhere, and these factors make a difference (Kenney 1992; Tesoka 1999; Cichowski 2001, 2002). Thus, variance in references (in this and potentially other columns) may be explained, to some significant extent, by the relative capacities of potential litigants to organize themselves, differences in levels of resources that interest groups command, and the willingness of governmental organs to process social demands brought by private actors.

Other variables more internal to legal systems themselves also immediately come to mind, including differences in access to justice, in judicial administration, in organizational cultures embedded in specific courts or court systems, and so on. There is a striking absence of any systematic, comparative literature on the effects of such factors on the nature and scope of litigating EC law in national courts. Yet we have good reason to suppose that differences in the relevant rules of legal procedure for each national court system—such as rules of standing, and rules enabling or constraining judicial discretion to refer questions to the ECJ—may also help to explain differences across parts of the table, to the extent that judges, operating in different court systems according to different rules, process different kinds of cases. Finally, there exists no comparative research on the growth, networking, and activities of specialist law firms, the socialization of judges into the niceties of the ECJ's jurisprudence, or the development of EC law as an autonomous discipline in law faculties. Such research, however, will be necessary if we are to gain a more complete understanding of legal integration.

The information presented in Table 2.4 is used in Chapters 3–5, both as a testing instrument and as a spur to further research.

VI Conclusion

This chapter situates the development of the European legal system within the overall process of European integration. We have argued that the constitutionalization of the Treaty of Rome comprised a necessary condition for the forging of causal connections between transnational exchange on the one hand, and the various modes of supranational governance on the other. Moreover, as EC law expanded and became more effective, individuals and groups who were not directly engaged in transnational activity began to use litigation and the courts for their own private and public interests. Finally, we examined constitutionalization from multiple perspectives, showing that the process has not been neat, linear, or devoid of conflict. Nonetheless, the most challenging doctrinal problems associated with supremacy have been resolved, albeit in diverse ways.

The broad, macro-institutional perspective adopted in this chapter helps us to understand some of the major features of the EC's overall development. However, our analyses of aggregate data and innovation in formal doctrine tell only a part of the story, providing some of the necessary background for research undertaken at a much lower level of abstraction. Chapters 3–5 track and assess the impact of the legal system on integration in three different policy domains.

The Free Movement of Goods

With Margaret McCown

In the previous chapter, we showed how transnational activity, the adjudication of the European Community (EC) law, and EC lawmaking had developed symbiotically to determine much of what is important about European integration. We also provided evidence in support of our contention that, under the Court's tutelage, *negative integration* (the removal of barriers to transnational exchange) provoked, and helped to organize, *positive integration* (the development of common European policies to regulate transnational exchange). Here, we provide a more detailed sectoral account of how the adjudication of one class of trading disputes gradually, but authoritatively, undermined the intergovernmental aspects of the EC, while enhancing the polity's supranational, or federal, character.

It should come as no surprise that traders influenced, disproportionately in comparison to other private actors, the early development of the legal system. The Treaty prioritized the construction of a common market for goods, through rules that prohibited tariffs, quotas, discriminatory taxation, and other charges, as well as less obvious protectionist policies. Just as important, supremacy, direct effect, and related doctrines, once accepted by national courts, made it possible for private actors to activate the legal system in order to enhance the effectiveness of these same rules. Traders and producers had both the incentive and the resources to litigate; and trade litigation quickly generated much of the context for legal integration.

In this chapter, we assess the impact of adjudicating the free movement of goods provisions of the Treaty of Rome on integration and supranational governance. Although findings for the domain as a whole are reported, our focus is on the problem of non-tariff barriers, as governed by Arts. 28–30 (EC). No other part of the Treaty of Rome has been more implicated in the ongoing attempt to define the relationship between the scope and authority of European law, on the one hand, and the regulatory autonomy of the Member States, on the other. From its first preliminary ruling on Art. 28, *Dassonville* (ECJ 8/74, 1974), the Court began to convert these provisions into an expansive "economic constitution" (Poiares Maduro 1998). In the Court's reading of the Treaty, traders possess broad-based, judicially-enforceable rights. Further, private parties enjoy distinct advantages, relative to Member States, in any legal conflict in which a national law or administrative practice could be alleged to hinder trade. By 1980, it was clear to all of the key actors in the domain that no aspect of national regulatory policy fell beyond the reach of judicial scrutiny. As important, in the course of its review activities, the Court had gradually outlined a blueprint for completing the common market, which the Commission would champion and the Member States would later ratify in diverse ways, not least as part of the Single European Act (SEA, 1986).

The chapter proceeds as follows. First, we examine the treaty rules on intra-EC trade, derive hypotheses about how the domain could be expected to evolve, and contrast our argument with alternatives. Second, we track the emergence of the basic doctrinal framework governing the domain, analyze the aggregate data on adjudication in the sector, and trace the impact of the Court's case law on the decisionmaking of other actors, including the Commission and Member State governments. Third, we discuss the mutation of the framework in the 1990s, an event heavily conditioned by the endogenous development of the law itself. We conclude with an assessment of our findings in light of the pertinent scholarly debates about the legal system's impact on the greater course of market-building and political integration.

I Theoretical Issues

From the theoretical materials developed in the first two chapters, we derived a set of general expectations about how trading rights would likely evolve, given the constitutionalization of the treaty system.[1] One set of expectations concerned logics of litigating. Traders would use Art. 28 instrumentally, to remove national barriers to intra-EC trade, targeting—disproportionately—measures that hinder access to larger markets relative

---

[1] See also Stone Sweet and Brunell (1998*a*) and Stone Sweet and Caporaso (1998*a*).

to smaller ones. As negative integration proceeded (i.e. to the extent that the legal system sides with traders against national authorities), further litigation would be stimulated. A second set of expectations concerned the kinds of outcomes the legal system would be likely to generate. Given a steady supply of preliminary references, it would be the Court's case law, and not the preferences or decisionmaking of Member State governments, that would determine how the domain evolved. On the basis of assumptions about litigants' and judges' interests, we expected the Court to produce rulings that would (*a*) facilitate expansion of intra-EC trade; (*b*) undermine national control over such activity; and (*c*) press the EC's legislative bodies to extend the scope of the polity's regulatory capacities. A third set of expectations concerns precedent. As discussed in more detail below, we expected the Court to develop coherent argumentation frameworks that would enable it to govern effectively, and we expected these doctrinal structures to help to determine the paths along which trading rules would evolve. These expectations, of course, are heavily conditioned by the institutional setting in which free movement of goods adjudication takes place. The Court is a trustee of the Treaty, not an agent of national governments.

THE NORMATIVE STRUCTURE

Title 1 of the Treaty of Rome (*a*) establishes the EC as a customs union (Arts. 23–24); (*b*) lays down procedures for legislating a Common Customs Tariff (Art. 26); (*c*) prohibits the Member States from levying duties or direct charges on goods traded across borders within the EC (Art. 25); and (d) prohibits the Member States from adopting import quotas or other non-tariff barriers to imports and exports (Arts. 28–30). The European Court of Justice (ECJ), in Craig and de Burca's (1998: 544–5) words, has taken a "strident approach" to Art. 25, which they find "unsurprising and entirely warranted" given the importance of the Customs Union to the Common Market. Indeed, the Court (*Bresciani*, ECJ 87/75, 1975) has interpreted Art. 25 as capturing within its ambit "any pecuniary charge, whatever its designation and mode of application, which is . . . imposed on goods imported from another Member State by reason of the fact that they cross a frontier" (paragraph 9). The Treaty does not, the Court would stress here and elsewhere, provide for exceptions or a defense.[2]

---

[2] Under certain conditions, states may levy fees for services like health inspections, but only where such charges fund services required by EC secondary legislation.

Non-tariff barriers inherently pose greater challenges for those seeking to prohibit them. Compared with customs duties or border fees, they impede trade in less visible, more indirect ways, and they often can be justified as serving public policy purposes other than protectionism. The Rome Treaty seeks to ban protectionist policies while preserving the autonomy of the Member States to pursue legitimate public policy purposes. Art. 28 states that: "Quantitative restrictions on imports and all measures having equivalent effect shall be prohibited between member-states." The phrase, "measures having equivalent effect"—hereafter MEEs—refers to non-tariff barriers. Art. 29 lays down similar rules for the case of exports. Art. 30 permits a Member State to derogate from Art. 28, on grounds of public morality, public policy, public security, health, and cultural heritage, though derogations may "not . . . constitute a means of arbitrary discrimination or a disguised restriction on trade between Member States."

These provisions can, of course, be interpreted in different ways. How might actors—traders, litigators, judges, national legislators, and administrators—identify a national law or practice (an MEE) whose impact on trade is "equivalent" to an import quota? Could or must such "effects" be quantified, and what degree of equivalence is necessary for an MEE to be captured by Art. 28? What types of regulation, otherwise prohibited by Art. 28, could not be justified with reference to Art. 30? What would not count as a legitimate "public policy" exception, and how strictly must a defendant Member State be held to justify proposed derogations?

The basic rationale for delegating to the Court in this domain should be obvious. From the point of view of the Member States, the commitment problem associated with building a common market—a paradigmatic prisoners' dilemma situation—does not disappear with the creation of binding norms. On the contrary, the situation is immediately recast as a problem of governance: in the absence of authoritative mechanisms for interpreting, monitoring, and enforcing the rules, the dilemma is likely to persist. It follows that, in so far as the Member States perceive the problem, the demand for supranational governance will be a function of the strength of their underlying preferences for achieving a single market. Further, in the guise of Arts. 28–30, the Member States negotiated relatively open-ended (or incomplete) commitment rules. Normative indeterminacy supplements the demand for governance, and begs for insulating organizations from controls that might be easily activated by the contracting parties. In the absence of effective supranational governance, national authorities would be able to escape performing their obligations, say, through generating creative interpretations of Art. 30; and they might be tempted to do so as politically important domestic industries are increasingly exposed to competition from imports.

Although we have just invoked well-known, even mundane, functional logics, three points on the relevance of delegation theory to the market-building project deserve reemphasis (Chapter 1). First, because generic rationales for delegation (e.g. from "principals" to "agents" or "trustees") can appropriately inform *any* existing theory of regional integration, such logics cannot, in and of themselves, help us to discriminate *between* such theories. Second, notwithstanding the point just made, the size of the strategic "zone of discretion" in which delegated governance operates can help us to predict how effective supranational governance will, in fact, be. In our case, this is so only because we have elaborated a causal theory that relies on the agency of supranational organizations to account for some of the dynamics of integration. The third point, an empirical one, cannot be overemphasized: the Member States did not design the system of governance that entered into force on January 1, 1970.

The Treaty of Rome committed the Member States to eliminating national barriers to intra-EC trade by the end of 1969. They enlisted the help of the Commission. Ex-Art. 33 provides that:

The Commission shall issue directives establishing the procedure and timetable in accordance with which the Member States shall abolish, as between themselves, any measures in existence when this Treaty enters into force which have an effect equivalent to quotas.

The Member States meant Art. 28 and ex-Art. 33 directives to be binding, as a form of "international law-plus" that the Court could ultimately be asked to enforce. Judicial enforcement proceedings against a national government could be brought either by the Commission (through Art. 226), or by another government (through Art. 227). Trade liberalization at the national level, and reregulation of economic activities at the European level, were meant to go hand-in-hand. The Commission would propose legislation to governments sitting in the Council of Ministers; and the Council of Ministers would adopt this legislation under qualified majority voting (QMV), beginning in 1966.

The Member States did not provide for the supremacy or direct effect of Art. 28, or for any other provision of the Treaty of Rome; and they did not provide for the direct effect of directives.[3] Yet by 1970, the Court—in

---

[3] See Chapter 2.

collaboration with national judges—had authoritatively revised the Treaty, significantly expanding the legal system's capacity to respond to the demands of market actors and to control political outcomes. With constitutionalization, governments lost whatever pretense they might have had to being national gatekeepers to the Treaty of Rome. Individuals could now activate the EC's legal system on their own, against their own governments, through national judges. Constitutionalization thus increased the size of the legal system's zone of discretion, through enhancing the judiciaries autonomy vis-à-vis the Member States. It is an error to cast the Court as an "agent" of the governments, in a piece written by governments, from the standpoint of principal–agent theory. The Court must be modeled as a "trustee" of the Treaty, with fiduciary powers. When it comes to interpreting and enforcing the Treaty, the Court, not national governments, holds the relevant political property rights. Governments can seek to curb the Court, or to overturn its rulings on the Treaty, but only through revising the Treaty.

Constitutionalization and the Court's fiduciary status are necessary causal elements of our theory, and they undergird all of the hypotheses developed in this book. We have predicted that the system of governance built by judges (through constitutionalization) rather than the system built by States (through intergovernmental bargaining) would provoke and sustain the market-building project. In the free movement of goods domain, we have proposed that the Court's case law would become the focal point of institutional evolution, and that the legal system would operate to expand market opportunities for private, transnational actors, and to reduce the scope of national regulatory authority. These broad expectations are derived from a theory of integration that stipulates the underlying causal dynamics of an expansive system of supranational governance. Put simply, the more traders can activate the legal system, and the greater is the zone of discretion enjoyed by the Court, the more likely it is that the feedback loops (or mechanisms of spillover) theorized in Chapter 2 would emerge and become entrenched.

Positive and negative integration

Those who sought to build a European common market had assumed that negative and positive integration would reinforce one another. To take a first scenario: the more the EC's legislative bodies succeed in producing Euro-wide market regulations, the less costly it is for national governments to eliminate their own protectionist laws and administrative practices. Conversely, national governments are more likely to maintain their own idiosyncratic market rules in the absence of harmonization at the European level. In either case, the key issue is the extent to which each Member State trusts that the others would abandon protectionist policies. Positive integration provides such assurance, and therefore facilitates negative integration. This scenario is the one imagined, more or less, by the Member States when they negotiated the Treaty. The Commission would propose legislation to harmonize market rules under Art. 94,[4] and the Council would adopt it.

In Chapter 2, a rather different scenario was proposed. Negative integration through adjudication, in so far as it is effective, raises the costs of maintaining national systems of governing markets, and puts pressure on governments to Europeanize market regulation. Market actors have every reason to use litigation strategies to extend the reach of Art. 28 into national regimes, in order to undermine national hindrances to trade. Governments could seek to reassert regulatory control over markets, but only through legislative action, in EC fora. Put differently, as negative integration proceeds, it gradually but inevitably reduces the capacities of national authorities to manage the negative externalities produced by growing economic interdependence. At the same time, negative integration, by definition, expands opportunities for traders; and more trade means more legal challenges to national regulatory authority. Some costs of negative integration through adjudication are even more direct. When governments lose in court, they also lose reputation with their EC partners and with the growing numbers of domestic actors seeking to expand European markets; at the same time, national judges have the power to punish national governments, including providing compensation to traders for damages. This second scenario relies, in the first place, on traders litigating their disputes with national governments in national courts. They are far more likely to do so the more that the first scenario does not bear fruit.

This second—judicial—route proved to be the more important, precisely because it could not be blocked by recalcitrant governments.

---

[4] Art. 94 (ex-Art. 100):

The Council shall, acting unanimously on a proposal from the Commission and after consulting the European Parliament and the Economic and Social Committee, issue directives for the approximation of such laws, regulations or administrative provisions of the Member States as directly affect the establishment or functioning of the common market.

ALTERNATIVE VIEWS

Various strains of integration theory deserve at least summary discussion, to the extent that alternative propositions can be derived from them. A first strain is the strong intergovernmentalism developed by Moravcsik and Garrett. Strong intergovernmentalists (Moravscik 1991) argue that integration is a product of national interests, which is given agency through heads of government, and the relative bargaining power of the Member States in the EC, as conditioned by the EC's decision rules; private, "transnational actors" are of no relevance, and the EC's organizations play only a secondary role. For Garrett (1992) the decisionmaking of EC organizations follows more or less directly from the preferences of the Member States, and particularly those of the dominant Member States, such as France and Germany. The proposition has the virtue of being testable, although Garrett offered little in the way of supporting evidence.[5]

In a follow-up piece, Garrett (Garrett 1995: 178–9) proposed that the Court seeks to enhance its own legitimacy by pursuing two, sometimes contradictory, goals: (*a*) to curry the favor of powerful states, and (b) to ensure Member State compliance with its decisions. The ECJ, he argued, will sometimes censure "powerful governments," but only in "unimportant sectors" of the economy, while "accepting protectionist behavior" in more important sectors, since such governments are unlikely to comply with adverse decisions. Apparently, no stable predictions are derivable when it comes to "less powerful governments," since the Court will at times be concerned with noncompliance (the ECJ defers to the Member State), and will at times seek the goodwill of "Northern" governments that desire "trade liberalization" (the ECJ attacks protectionism). The Member States, for their part, continuously balance the short-term costs of complying with adverse decisions against the long-run benefits of trade liberalization through adjudication.

This analysis is flawed for two reasons. First, Garrett leaves out litigants and national judges entirely, actors that are crucial to both process and outcome; the omission is left undefended. The vast majority of Art. 234 references in this area are provoked by claims, brought forward by traders in national courts, that a specific national rule or practice is inconsistent with obligations announced in Art. 28. If the Court responds to a reference by

---

[5] Moravcsik, who initially had little to say on the topic, later admitted (1995) that his framework could not explain the construction of the legal system. He then treats the Court, constitutionalization, and the legal system as anomalies that somehow do not weaken his theory.

suggesting or insisting that the national judge refuse to apply the national measure in question (the Court renders an adverse decision from the point of view of the Member State), the choice—to comply or not to comply—rests with the national judge of reference, not the government. If the judge follows the ECJ's preliminary ruling, the government could still seek to enforce the censured measure in subsequent trading situations. This, apparently, is what Garrett means by a decision of noncompliance.[6] At this point, the government would face an intractable problem, namely, how to enforce an invalid rule. Traders adversely affected by any such enforcement could either refuse to accept the legality of the measure, or attack it in court, where effective remedies—including compensation for losses—are available. In either case, the ultimate site of decisionmaking would be the judiciary, not the government.[7] In other words, Garrett assumes what cannot be assumed: that a Member State government can make a decision of noncompliance stick without the support of the legal system. Second, given the ECJ's broad fiduciary powers, there would appear to be no valid basis for the assumption that the ECJ fears offending a powerful Member State, or even a consortium of powerful Member States, when it enforces Art. 28. In any event, we predict exactly the opposite: the preferences of defendant Member States will have no systematic effect on outcomes produced by the Court. Instead, in our view, the Court will work to enhance the effectiveness of EC law and to expand the scope of supranational governance, which will benefit the interests of traders, not to comfort the positions of Member States, powerful or not.

The weak intergovernmentalism of Moravcsik (1998) does not generate testable propositions about the kinds of outcomes that the legal system—or supranational organizations, more generally—will produce (see Chapter 1). Instead, Moravcsik stipulates some underlying functional need of the Member States for supranational governance, and then interprets outcomes produced by the EC's organizations in light of these needs—and a prior act of delegation—thereby "explaining" outcomes. Since the Member States established the authority of the Commission and the Court through purposive acts of delegation, supranational governance operates, presumptively, to fulfill the Member States' grand designs. By our reading, Moravcsik only makes one claim, a negative one concerning "unintended consequences,"

---

[6] Garrett does not define noncompliance or discuss the consequences of a refusal to comply with a decision of the Court, as applied by a national judge.

[7] It may be useful to recall the obvious: governments, parliaments, and administrators are dependent on judges to enforce their rules.

that is testable. He insists (1998: 482–90), that while governments set the agenda for the EC's organizations, the EC's organizations have *never* operated to "alter the terms under which governments negotiate new bargains." Moravcsik (1998: ch. 5) repeats these arguments in his analysis of the process leading up to the SEA, which we will take up shortly. If he is right, then our theory must be abandoned.

PRECEDENT

A final set of issues concerns the course of judicial lawmaking, that is, how the EC's trading institutions are likely to evolve through practices associated with precedent.

In Chapter 1, it was argued (*a*) that legal norms are fundamentally indeterminate and (*b*) that adjudication functions to reduce normative indeterminacy through the propagation and successive refinement of argumentation frameworks, or doctrinal structures. Such structures are judicially-curated as precedents. They emerge cumulatively, through analogical reasoning, under the meta-norm that similar disputes should be resolved similarly. Argumentation frameworks are institutions that enable judges to structure their (decentralized and noisy) political environments, to enhance the effectiveness of their decisions, and to legitimize accreted judicial rulemaking with reference to pre-existing normative materials. Such frameworks also help lawyers refine litigation strategies, thereby organizing the "market for litigation" (Shapiro and Stone Sweet 2002: ch. 2). One purpose of the chapter is to assess the extent to which the free movement of goods domain comes to be governed by judge-made institutions. If it does, then a second issue is raised: the extent to which doctrine helps to determine the path along which the law, and thus market integration, develops. We expect, at the very least, litigating and judging, at any given moment, to be meaningfully structured by how prior trading disputes had been sequenced and decided.

Chapter 1 also argued that the Treaty of Rome constituted a paradigmatic example of an "incomplete," or "relational," contract; that the size of the zone of the discretion in which the Court operates would favor judicial modes of governance; and that certain parts of the Treaty, if reconstructed as rights provisions, would lead the Court to develop balancing, proportionality, and "least-means" tests. Defending rights through least-means tests places a heavy burden on public authorities to defend their activities. Where a least-means proportionality standard is in place, government may be allowed to restrict the rights of individuals, but *only* to the extent necessary to achieve some separate, lawful, and socially beneficial good. Based on research on other legal systems, Shapiro and Stone Sweet (2002: 371–2) and Stone Sweet (2000: 97–9; 141–3; 203–4) have claimed that balancing typically, even inevitably, leads to the elaboration of least-means tests. Just as inevitably, judges who enforce such standards behave as relatively pure policymakers, in that they use their discretion to evaluate and control the lawmaking of others.

Articles 28–30 of the Rome Treaty create the conditions not only for sustained conflict between traders and national regulatory regimes, but for the development of balancing standards to resolve such disputes. If such standards stabilize as least-means tests, then the ECJ—given a steady caseload— will become the primary source of EC trade rules. The Court will also, necessarily, generate a normative discourse on the scope of national regulatory autonomy. The emergence of strict proportionality tests would empower traders and the Commission, while placing Member State governments on the defensive. In response the Member States could seek to curb the Court, or to renegotiate trading rules. But given the Court's trustee status, and the fact that traders have access to national courts, it is far more likely that governments will be induced to master the intricacies of the doctrines governing the sector. That is, if governments are rational actors, they will learn to pursue their pertinent "national interests" in doctrinally defensible ways. In so far as they do, governments will participate in reinforcing the centrality of legal argumentation and judicial process to the evolution of the EC's trade institutions.

Our view of precedent and judicial governance contrasts sharply with the models of many other political scientists, in particular those who have worked on the EC's legal system. Speaking directly to Arts. 28 and 30 of the Treaty of Rome, Garrett (1995: 178–80) asserts, for example, that "in most cases pertaining to the free movement of goods . . . there is no coherent legal basis to inform Court behavior. The reason for this [legal incoherence] is the coexistence of contradictory Arts. in the Rome Treaty." In a subsequent Article, Garrett, Keleman, and Schultz (1998) argued that the ECJ at times follows its own precedents, in order to legitimize its authority over the Member States, and at times defers to powerful governments, for fear of being punished. These analyses proceed from the assumption that the EC law "game" is played only by the governments of the Member States, on one side, and the ECJ, on the other. Litigants and national judges are nowhere to be found.

In response, we suggest that Arts. 28 and 30 have a reciprocal, rather than a "contradictory" relationship: each provision helps to define the scope of the other. Traders will rely on Art. 28 in their disputes with national authorities, while national authorities will defend themselves with reference to Art. 30. We expect the Court to elaborate a comprehensive argumentation framework, incorporating both sets of provisions, in order to allow it to decide such cases in principled, rather than strictly arbitrary, ways. Through use, the framework will gradually reduce normative uncertainty and organize the politics of market-building in the EC. To the extent that the Court engages in precedent-based rulemaking, the domain will exhibit enhanced "coherence" (see Bengoetxea 2003) by which we mean the development of an internal and self-reinforcing structure to litigation and adjudication. Although we now repeat ourselves, we do not expect the Court to face any recurrent situation in which it would be more concerned with Member State noncompliance than it would be in enhancing the effectiveness of the legal system and trader's rights through principled, precedent-based decisionmaking.

DATA AND METHODS

In order to help us evaluate these propositions, we gathered the following data for the free movement of goods domain as a whole: (*a*) preliminary reference activity; (*b*) type of national regulation being challenged, in preliminary references, as a potential violation of Art. 28; (*c*) the dispositive outcome announced in the ECJ's preliminary rulings, where such decisions pertain to violations of Art. 28; (*d*) the citation practices of the ECJ for the domain as a whole; and (*e*) the outcomes of infringement proceedings, under Art. 226, brought against Member States by the Commission, for alleged violations of Art. 28. For each of these data-sets, the information is comprehensive through at least mid-1998. We present our findings at various points below, in the context of our discussion of the impact of specific doctrinal outcomes.

II Judicial Governance and Market-Building

On the eve of the entry into force of free movement of goods provisions, the system of governance designed by the Member States to achieve the common market was in deep trouble. Member States had made no systematic effort on their own to remove non-tariff barriers, and the Commission's legislative agenda on behalf of regulatory harmonization faced a fearsome hurdle. In January 1966, the French had succeeded—the "Luxembourg Compromise"—in blocking the move to QMV in the Council of Ministers. The compromise allowed any government to demand, after asserting that "very important interests [were] at stake," that legislation be approved under unanimity rather than QMV. The kaleidoscope of disparate national regulations that producers and traders of goods confronted, including myriad "national measures having effects equivalent to quotas," remained in place. As important, the rapid building of uniform, or "harmonized," EC regulations looked unlikely, given that any government could veto the Commission's proposals in the Council.

In late December 1969 the Commission issued Directive 70/50 to jump-start matters. Recall that ex-Art. 33 charges the Commission with issuing directives "establishing the procedure and timetable" for the removal of MEEs by the Member States. But with Directive 70/50, the Commission had pushed far beyond its remit, giving Art. 28 an expansive reading. First, it listed nineteen types of rules or practices that Member States were to rescind, including discriminatory policies on pricing, access to markets, advertising, packaging, and names of origin. Pushing further, it announced what we will refer to as a "discrimination test": measures that treated domestic goods differently than imported goods—say, by limiting the availability or the marketing of imports, or by giving "to domestic products a preference" in the domestic market—were prohibited under Art. 28. Second, the Commission raised the very sensitive question of the legality of measures that States applied to domestic and imported goods equally, but were nonetheless protectionist. The Directive proposed that such "indistinctly applicable measures" [IAMs] ought to be captured by Art. 28 if they failed a test of proportionality. Where the "restrictive effects of such measures . . . are out of proportion to their [public policy] purpose," and where "the same objective can be attained by other means which are less of a hindrance to trade," IAMs constitutes an illegal MEE. With Directive 70/50, the Commission had exceeded its authority. The Member States (through ex-Art. 33) had not delegated to the Commission the task of defining the legal concept of the MEE, nor had they ever meant for Art. 28 to apply to IAMs.[8]

---

[8] Indeed, in ECJ 249/81 (1982), Ireland argued that this part of the Directive was *ultra vires*, and the Advocate General agreed. The Court chose not to respond to the argument.

Note, however, that the Commission, while being an agent of the Council of Ministers in the harmonization process, is a trustee of the Treaty under ex-Art. 33.

We now turn to the case law of the Court, which immediately superseded Directive 70/50, rendering it all but obsolete.[9]

THE EMERGENCE AND CONSOLIDATION OF THE "DASSONVILLE FRAMEWORK"

The basic doctrinal structure governing free movement of goods developed quickly, in a series of cases decided in the 1975–9 period. The crucial elements of the framework are the following: First, trader's rights are conceived broadly and expansively, while the prerogatives of national governments are conceived restrictively. Second, there exist no clear limits to the reach of judicial authority into national regulatory regimes. Third, through the enforcement of a least-means, proportionality test, the framework makes judges the ultimate masters of trade law. Thus, the structure encourages traders to use the courts as a means of negative integration, while denying that national authorities possess secure political property rights when it comes to the regulation of market activities. Perhaps most importantly, since the framework authoritatively organized the relationship between Arts. 28 and Arts. 30, it also *per force* organizes a discursive politics on the nature of European constitutionalism and the limits of national sovereignty (see Poiares-Maduro 1998).

Dassonville: hindrance to trade, direct or indirect

The *Dassonville* case (ECJ 8/74, 1974) provided the Court with its first important opportunity to consider the meaning of free movement of goods provisions.

In 1970, Mr. Dassonville imported a dozen bottles of Johnnie Walker Scotch Whiskey into Belgium, after having purchased it from a French supplier. When Dassonville put the whiskey on the market, he was prosecuted by Belgian authorities for having violated customs rules. The rules prohibited

---

[9] There exist no good a priori reasons to think that Directive 70/50, absent the support of the Court, could have been sustained as an authoritative interpretation of what is or is not prohibited as a non-tariff barrier to intra-EC trade. Given the constitutionalization of the Treaty system (i.e. supremacy, direct effect, and the fact that Arts. 28–30 trump secondary legislation), we have better reason to think that the Court, not the legislator, will be the key source of institutional innovation.

the importation from an EC country, in this case France, of spirits that originated in a third country, in this case Britain, unless French customs rules were substantially similar to those in place in Belgium. Mr. Dassonville was also sued by a Belgian importer who possessed, under Belgian law, an exclusive right to market Johnnie Walker. In his defense, Dassonville claimed that Art. 28 meant that (*a*) goods entering France legally must be allowed to enter Belgium freely and (*b*) exclusive rights to import and market goods were invalid. The Belgian court appeared to agree and requested guidance from the ECJ.

Dismissing the objections of the United Kingdom and Belgium, whose counsel argued that such rules were not prohibited by Art. 28, the Court found for Dassonville. Much more important, the Court declared the following:

All trading rules enacted by the Member States, which are capable of hindering, directly or indirectly, actually or potentially, intra-Community trade are to be considered as measures having an effect equivalent to quantitative restrictions.

Thus, with no supporting argument, the Court had repudiated the two rival understandings of Art. 28 then current. In its official brief to the Court, the United Kingdom had argued that only measures that actually result in a "quantitative reduction in the movement of goods" might be caught by Art. 28. The UK's position, which would have placed the burden on the trader–plaintiff to show that a given national measure had caused direct and deleterious effects on trade, had wide support among the Member States and legal scholars at the time (see Oliver 1996: 90–2). With Directive 70/50, the Commission had sought to destroy this interpretation. The Court replaced the Commission's discrimination model with its own, even more rigorous, "hindrance to trade test" (Gormley 1985: 22). If put to a vote, the ECJ's interpretation of Art. 28—more expansively integrationist than any in circulation at the time—would certainly not have been accepted by the Member State governments.

The Court had, after all, placed no limits to the reach of Art. 28: all national laws or administrative practices that negatively impact the activities of traders, including those that do so only "indirectly or potentially," are presumptively prohibited. This Court had thus raised a delicate political issue, which proved inseparable from how the law would come to develop. The wholesale removal of national regulations would strip bare legal regimes serving otherwise legitimate public interests, such as the protection of public health, the environment, and the consumer. Further, where the

Council was unable to produce harmonized legislation in a timely fashion, this lack of protection might not only endure, but could weaken public and political support for integration down the road. In response, the ECJ announced, in *Dassonville* and subsequent decisions, that the Member States could, within reason, continue to regulate the production and sale of goods in the public's interest, pending harmonization by the EC's legislator. The Court stressed that: (*a*) the condition of "reasonableness"[10] would be controlled strictly; (*b*) such regulations—as with national measures justified under Art. 30 grounds—could not "constitute a disguised restriction on trade between member states"; and (*c*) the European judiciary would review the legality of these exceptions to Art. 30, on a case-by-case basis.

Thus, not only did the *Dassonville* decision define the scope of the Art. 28 prohibition of MEEs as broadly as possible, it laid the foundations for balancing, and therefore for judicial dominance over trade policy within the EC.

De Peijper: least-means proportionality

The ECJ's ruling in *Dassonville* showed traders that litigation of Art. 28 in the national courts could be an effective means of subverting national laws that hurt them, and of shaping the evolution of EC institutions in their favor. At the time, the legal establishment (in Brussels, Luxembourg, and the academy) still clung to the idea that the appropriate way to review breaches of Treaty law by the Member States was through infringement proceedings brought by the Commission (Art. 226 EC). The Court, however, had made it clear that the rights of traders must be defended by national judges, and that national judges must do so in particular ways. Most important, *Dassonville* requires national judges to assess the reasonableness of national measures that might affect trade. In *De Peijper*, the Court (ECJ 104/75, 1976) demonstrated that such a requirement entails the judicial review of the decisionmaking of national lawmakers, in micro-detail if necessary.

The case concerned criminal charges brought by Dutch prosecutors against an importer of the pharmaceutical, Valium. Mr. De Peijper had distributed the drug to a hospital and pharmacy, after having purchased it from an English wholesaler and repackaged it under his own company's name. He was accused of violating a law that prohibited the marketing of medicinal products without the prior consent of the Public Health

---

[10] Reasonableness as a criterion for legality is common in European administrative and constitutional law. The rule normally implies proportionality: a law or administrative act is unreasonable if it produces effects that are out of proportion to its purpose.

Inspector, in the absence of certain documents, to be verified by the Inspector, certifying the origin and composition of imported medicines. In his defense, Mr. De Peijper pleaded Art. 28. He could do so since the files and reports required by the Public Health Inspector could be completed only by designated "experts" who, in practice, were pharmacists employed by a company that was also the official importer of Valium into the Netherlands. Since Mr. De Peijper's company sold Valium at a lower cost than the official importer, he did not believe he could obtain the latter's help in completing the required documents. The national court of referral asked the ECJ if the measures in question, as applied to parallel imports, constituted an MEE under Art. 28 and, if so, whether the measure could be justified on Art. 30 grounds, namely, under the heading of "public health." Once the oral proceedings before the ECJ had been completed, the Commission instituted infringement proceedings against the Netherlands, under Art. 226.

The Advocate General sided with the importer, noting that Valium circulated lawfully in other Member States, under various licenses and other public controls, which could in principle be used by national authorities to trace origin. The Dutch and British governments defended the measures in question, first as nondiscriminatory, then on Art. 30 grounds. But they also argued, joined by the Danish government, that the measures simply implemented existing EC directives, and thus were presumptively valid under EC law. These directives prohibited the marketing of "medicinal products" in the absence of "a prior authorization issued by the competent authority in the Member State"; and they obliged distributors of imported medicines to show to this authority documents, to be completed with the aid of designated "experts," certifying the product's "composition and the method of preparation." In response, the Advocate General argued that the case implicated only the relationship between Arts. 28 and 30, and that EC secondary legislation could not expand the scope of "the residuary powers left to the Member States by Art. 30."

A final issue concerned the judicial function of the preliminary reference procedure, relative to infringement proceedings. In his report, the Advocate General stated that:

Although it is not within the scope of the Court's jurisdiction under Art. 234 to give a ruling on the compatibility of the provisions of a specific national law with the Treaty, it acknowledges . . . that it has jurisdiction to provide the national court with all the factors of interpretation under Community law which may enable it to adjudicate upon this compatibility.

"There is no doubt," the Advocate General continued, "that the normal way of testing the compatibility of national laws [with EC law] is by means of . . . Art. 226," rather than through a reference from a national court. Yet, he argued, "if the Court wishes to give a helpful answer to the national court," it would be "impossible for it . . . to avoid examining this problem of compatibility." Further, given his expressed view on how the case ought to be decided, "the question then arises how Netherlands law should be adjusted in order to encourage free trade to the greatest possible extent while complying with the well-known requirements of public health." The Advocate General suggested that the Court could avoid the question for now, leaving it to be resolved through the Commission's infringement proceedings.

The Court ruled that the Dutch measures fell within the purview of Art. 28, taking care to restate the *Dassonville* formula. It then proceeded to balancing, generating an explicit least-means test:

National rules or practices do not fall within the exception specified in Art. 30 if the health and life of humans can be as effectively protected by measures which do not restrict intra-Community trade so much.

The ECJ then insisted that the national court apply such a least-means formula to resolve the case.

The Court could have ended the matter there. Instead, it chose to evaluate the proportionality of the Dutch measures on its own, showing how a Member State might secure the public's interest in ways that would hinder trade less than the Dutch rules at hand. Among other solutions, the Court suggested that national authorities "adopt a more active policy" of helping importers acquire necessary information, rather than "waiting passively for the desired evidence to be produced for them," or making traders dependent upon a competitor. More broadly, a Member State could hardly claim to be acting to protect public health, the Court declared, if its policies discouraged the distribution of lower cost medicines. Finally, the Court ruled that the various EC directives harmonizing regulation of pharmaceuticals had no effect on the scope of Arts. 28 and 30.

De Peijper illustrates some crucial aspects of the dynamics of judicial balancing under least-means proportionality tests. Courts do not enforce such tests without reenacting the decisionmaking processes of those whom they are being asked to control. That is, "they . . . put themselves in the latter's shoes, and walk through these processes step-by-step" (Stone Sweet 2000: 204). Inevitably, judges speak to how governmental officials should have behaved, if the latter had wished to exercise their authority lawfully. In doing so, judges lay down prospective rules meant to guide future decision-making. Lawfulness, balancing courts are telling policymakers, entails reasoning through the legal norms as judges do, as balancers of rights with respect to an opposed public interest. Not surprisingly, ongoing enforcement of least-means tests tends to generalize judicial techniques of governance, inducing other public officials, if they hope to defend their interests adequately, to engage in the style of argumentation developed in the pertinent case law.

The *De Peijper* ruling supplemented *Dassonville* in ways that quickly locked in these dynamics with respect to European market integration. The Court served notice to the Member States that national regulations bearing on trade could only be justified under the most restrictive of conditions. It demonstrated to potential litigators and the Commission that the preliminary reference procedure comprised an effective means of reviewing the conformity of national with EC law, parallel to, but not restricted by, the infringement procedure. And the ECJ ordered national judges to engage in least-means testing, while promising to instruct them exactly how to do so, where necessary.

Cassis de Dijon: mutual recognition and strict scrutiny

A third seminal ECJ decision, *Cassis de Dijon* (ECJ 120/78, 1979), completed the construction of a comprehensive framework for adjudicating trade disputes under Art. 28. With Directive 70/50, the Commission had sought to bring within the ambit of Art. 28 those national measures—IAMs—that did not, on their face, discriminate between domestic and imported goods, but which nonetheless restricted market access to imports, or otherwise disadvantaged them relative to domestic goods. In *Cassis de Dijon*, the Court extended the *Dassonville* principles and least-means testing to such "equally applicable" measures. The Court interpreted Art. 28 as prohibiting a Member State from applying national regulations to any imported good that has been lawfully produced under the production or marketing rules of another Member State. Put very differently, the Court had decided that traders should not be asked to bear the costs of the Member States' failure to produce harmonized EC market rules.

In 1976, the German federal agency that regulates the marketing of spirits denied a request to import the French liquor, Cassis de Dijon, a black currant syrup typically mixed with wine as an aperitif. It did so because the syrup's alcohol content fell below a minimum that would, under German law, allow it to be sold on the German market as a liquor. The national judge, in effect, asked the ECJ if Art. 28 covered national laws that fixed different "mandatory requirements" for the marketing of products relative to those in place in other Member States. In its defense, the German agency claimed that mandatory requirements—when they are applied indistinctly to domestic and imported goods—do not constitute MEEs under the Treaty; it referenced Commission Directive 70/50 in support of the contention. In the absence of harmonization through EC directives, counsel for the German agency asserted, "each Member State retains full legislative juris-diction over the technical characteristics upon which the marketing of bev-erages and foodstuffs is made conditional." As a second line of defense, the agency dutifully trotted out arguments to the effect that its rules on alcohol content served various public interests, covered under various headings of Art. 30. The Advocate General rebutted each of these arguments in his report, stating, notably, that the Court had rejected the more "limited interpretation" of Directive 70/50 being relied on by the Germans.

The Court agreed with the agency that, where harmonized rules were not in place, "it is for the Member States to regulate all matters relating to the production and marketing of . . . alcoholic beverages . . . on their own territory." However, it also ruled that "disparities between the national laws" that hinder trade in such products would be "accepted only in so far as [such laws] may be recognized as necessary . . . to satisfy mandatory requirements relating in particular to the effectiveness of fiscal supervision, the protection of public health, the fairness of commercial transactions, and the defense of the consumer." After rehearsing and dismissing each of the justifications given by the German agency, the Court then declared that it could not divine: "[any] valid reason why, provided that they have been lawfully produced or marketed in one of the member states, alcoholic beverages should not be introduced into any other member states."

With these *dicta*, the Court floated a new principle: that of the "mutual recognition," on the part of each Member State, of the national production and marketing standards ("so called mandatory requirements") in place in the other Member States.

The Court's judgment extended the logic of *Dassonville*, while innovat-ing in several important ways. With *Cassis de Dijon*, the Court extended Art. 28's coverage to IAMs: henceforth, no aspect of national regulatory policy touching on the market for goods could be considered, a priori, to be exempt from judicial scrutiny. The ruling required national judges to attend to the effects, on traders, of "disparities" between national legal regimes, thus making them supervisors of the politics of harmonization. At the same time, the Court made available to the Member States a new set of justifications for derogating from Art. 28, although these are valid only in the absence of harmonization.[11] In subsequent cases, the Court imposed a least-means proportionality test to scrutinize such claims, which it taught to national courts by way of example.

OUTCOMES

The Court's case law on Art. 28 combined with the doctrines of supremacy and direct effect to give traders rights that were enforceable in national courts. The argumentation framework produced gave very wide scope to Art. 28, placed a heavy burden on Member State governments to justify claimed exceptions to Art. 28, and directed national judges to enforce trader's rights where governments could neither prove reasonableness nor necessity. This structure encouraged traders to use the courts as makers of trade law. Although important, the production of favorable doctrines does not conclude the story. The more the legal system actually removes barriers to markets, the more subsequent litigation will be stimulated. That is, positive outcomes will attract more litigation, negative outcomes will deter it. Further, the more effective the legal system is at enforcing Art. 28, the more pressure adjudication puts on the EC's legislative organs to harmonize market rules. The data we have collected allow us to examine the various relationships between litigation, doctrine, and outcomes on a number of dimensions. These aspects include the dynamic impact of this doctrinal structure on the greater integration process, culminating in the Single European Act.

We begin with Art. 234 reference activity for the free movement of goods domain as a whole. Figure 3.1 depicts the annual number of preliminary references in the domain as a whole, and for Art. 28, through mid-1998. References have steadily increased since *Dassonville*, and spike upward after *Cassis*.

---

[11] In *Cassis*, the Court generated four "mandatory requirements" (fiscal supervision, the protection of public health, the fairness of commercial transactions, and the defense of the consumer), which were later supplemented by two other headings: the improvement of working conditions (ECJ 155/80, 1981), and the protection of the environment (especially ECJ 302/86, 1988, discussed at length in Chapter 5). Although the Court treats the source of the mandatory requirements as Art. 28, they are nonetheless subject to exactly same judicial standards of scrutiny as are justifications claimed by the Member States under Art. 30 (see Oliver 1996: 181).

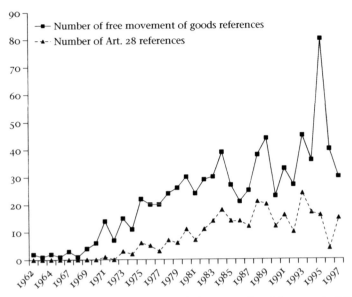

Figure 3.1. Annual Number of Preliminary References—Free Movement of Goods

Source: Alec Stone Sweet and Thomas L. Brunell Data Set on Preliminary References in European Law, 1958–98, Robert Schuman Centre for Advanced Studies, European University Institute (San Domenico di Fiesole, Italy: 1999). See Stone Sweet and Brunell (2000).

Table 2.4 (see Chapter 2) shows that one country—Germany—dominates reference activity in the sector, far beyond expected rates. Further, only two countries of the original EC-6 or the first EC-12, France and Germany, show positive values in the "percentage difference" cell; that is, only French and German judges have generated a disproportionate number of references in this legal domain. Of the original EC-12 (i.e. excluding references from Austria, Finland, and Sweden), the legal systems of France, Germany, Italy, and the United Kingdom have produced 73 percent (591/805) of all references in the domain. Thus, we find strong support for our hypothesis: trader-litigators, in fact, do target large markets, relative to smaller ones. The finding seems unsurprising. Traders have a far greater interest in opening larger markets relative to smaller ones; and higher levels of cross-border trade, strongly correlated with larger markets, will generate relatively more trading disputes than would smaller markets (see Stone Sweet and Brunell 1998*a*). In contrast, however, Garrett (1992, 1995) claimed that the ECJ and the legal system only worked effectively against the smaller and less powerful Member States. Yet if the ECJ is much more likely to vindicate trader's rights against smaller countries, compared with larger ones, why would traders be devoting far greater resources to bringing cases before the courts of the larger states?

Analysis of the dispositive outcomes produced by the Court provides a more direct test of such claims. We examined all of the ECJ rulings pursuant to Art. 234 references that expressly invoked Art. 28; $n = 254$. For each ruling, we coded for whether the Court either (*a*) declared the type of national rule or practice at issue to be a violation of Art. 28 or (*b*) found it not to be contrary to Art. 28. The ECJ ruled in favor of the traders in exactly half of all decisions in which such a determination was clearly made (108/216). Traders have a higher success rate in France, Germany, and Italy—well over 50 percent—than they do in Belgium, the Netherlands, and the United Kingdom; and they enjoy the best success rate (60 percent) in Germany.

These results are supported by Kilroy (1996), who produced the first relatively systematic empirical study of legal outcomes in the free movement of goods area. Her sample included both preliminary rulings and decisions pursuant to infringement proceedings brought by the Commission under Art. 226. Kilroy found that in eighty-one decisions, two-thirds of her pool, the Court struck down national rules as treaty violations; and that in forty-one cases, one-third of her pool, the Court upheld national rules as permissible under the EC's trading rules. She also assessed the relationship between *observations*—the briefs filed by the Commission and the Member States in pending cases—and the ECJ's rulings. She found that in 98 of 114 cases in which the Commission intervened, the Court sided with the Commission. The Commission's position therefore "predicted" the Court's decision 86 percent of the time. Member State briefs to the Court—revealed state preferences on how the Court should decide cases—failed to presage, or influence, the Court's rulings; and German interventions were found to be particularly ineffectual in generating outcomes. Following Garrett's logic, Kilroy (1996: 23) found it "surprising that Germany has a relatively lower impact on the Court." It is clear that the Court and the Commission work to make EC law effective and to enhance transnational activity, not to codify or give legal comfort to the preferences of dominant Member States. Similarly-designed studies of adjudicating EU social provisions and environmental protection confirm these results (Cichowski 1998, 2001, 2002; Chapters 5 and 6 of this book).

The evidence refutes Garrett's various hypotheses to the effect that the Court defers to the preferences of the larger Member State in its case law. Indeed, when it comes to interpreting Art. 28, there is no evidence that governments constrain the Court in any important, let alone systematic, way. The data also tell us a great deal about why litigating EC law has been so attractive to private actors.

We also examined the types of national rules and practices that have come under attack in preliminary references, as a supplementary means of assessing some of the arguments related to spillover discussed in earlier chapters. We expected to find that traders would begin by targeting the most obvious and direct barriers to trade; to the extent that the legal system succeeded in eliminating these barriers, traders would find themselves confronting new layers of national regulation, which they would attack in court. In this way, the shadow of the law would gradually cover the whole of national regulatory regimes (see Chapter 2). Our findings support these claims. In the 1970s, the vast majority of references attacked national measures that required special certification and licensing requirements, border inspections, and customs valuations for imports. After *Cassis*, a host of IAMs, such as those that impose purity or content requirements, came onto the Court's agenda. By the end of the 1980s, traders were attacking an increasingly broad range of national rules, such as those related more to the marketing—rather than the cross-border trading or production—of goods: minimum pricing, labeling and packaging requirements, Sunday trading prohibitions, requirements concerning distribution and warehousing, and advertising. The absence of any clear limit to the reach of *Dassonville-Cassis* made these dynamics—which progressively extended the reach of Art. 28 to more and more indirect hindrances to trade—possible.

Precedent

The founding cases in this legal domain—*Dassonville, Cassis*, and *De Peijper*—produced a set of doctrinal principles that governed it until its partial mutation in the 1990s (discussed below). We have analyzed citations patterns, that is, how judges have actually built precedent across all the free movement of goods decisions. Over a third of the Court's decisions on MEEs under Art. 28 cite at least one of these three judgments. These rulings continue to be the main building blocks for doctrinal evolution, even as the Court builds increasingly sophisticated argumentation frameworks. Of rulings that combine clusters of statements found in past ECJ decisions, half cite at least one of the founding trio.

As the adjudication of Art. 28 proceeded, litigants and judges refined doctrine, in order to deal with particular problems. Litigants learned to build arguments from rulings involving situations that most closely resembled those in which they found themselves. The Court, in turn, treated these arguments, and its own previous case law, as sectorally based. For example, intellectual property rights decisions tend to draw on previous cases dealing with trademarks and patent questions, rather than advertising or labeling requirements, even where the legal question at issue deals with rather general balancing rules that are otherwise applied similarly in all free movement of goods disputes. At the same time, a precedent-based discourse on the various justified exceptions to Art. 28 developed. These frameworks vary subtly across the Art. 30 headings and the mandatory requirements of *Cassis de Dijon*.

The Court confronted the "incompleteness" of the Art. 28–30 normative structure by building explicit sets of rules for identifying legitimate national derogations to free movement principles and for evaluating proposed derogations. Early in the ECJ's case law on IAMs, *Dassonville, Cassis de Dijon*, and an Art. 226 case brought by the Commission pursuant to *Cassis*—the famous German "Beer Purity" case (ECJ 178/84 *Commission* v. *Germany*, 1987)—comprised a framework for dealing with the public health derogation. This framework established a balancing standard—an "in the absence of harm" variation on the proportionality test—to evaluate national measures governing the labeling of food products. This framework is applied in subsequent rulings (e.g. ECJ 269/89 *Bonfait*, 1990; ECJ 298/87 *Smanor*, 1988) that probe the boundary between Art. 28 and the public health derogation. This framework constitutes the essential structure of the ECJ's explicit commitment to strictly review IAMs that impose labeling and contents requirements on food. Subsequent cases are gradually incorporated, creating a more precise framework for argumentation in specific situations. Thus, a cluster of cases emerges as stable doctrine governing the litigating of national regulations on food additives and preservatives (e.g. ECJ 42/90 *Höfner*, 1990; ECJ 13/91 *Debus*, 1992).

We could go on. The essential point should by now be clear. Far from being incoherent and unstructured as Garrett (1995) or Garrett, Keleman, and Schulz (1998) imply, the rule system produced by the Court is richly differentiated; it has, moreover, evolved speedily in response to the needs of those who use the system.

FROM NEGATIVE TO POSITIVE INTEGRATION

In adjudicating trading disputes under Art. 28, the Court exercises lawmaking and constitution-building powers. Given the nature of least-means balancing, the ECJ and national judges inevitably came to play a powerful lawmaking role. By providing detailed reasons for why a given measure does or does not infringe upon the treaty-based rights of traders, the Court gives guidance on how positive integration ought to proceed. The menu of policy options available to the EC legislator, at any given moment in time, may contain those types of measures that the Court had deemed acceptable under Art. 28, but not those that it has censored. As important, the doctrinal structure developed by the Court heavily implicates the legal system in the process through which the relationship between national sovereignty and supranational governance is determined. As we have seen, the *Dassonville* framework, as completed by *Cassis*, reconstituted the rules of the game that governed interactions between national governments, the Commission, and market actors. How important these changes were, to the course of European integration, is a crucial question to which we now turn.

We begin with the Court's legislative role. There is compelling evidence that the ECJ possessed, right from the beginning, a sophisticated under-standing of both its quasi-legislative powers and the strategic context in which these powers would operate. Recall that the Court's aggressively inte-grationist reading of Art. 28 was predicated, or justified, on the grounds that traders should not be required to bear the costs of intergovernmental inac-tion at the EC level. In the absence of harmonization, the logic of *Cassis de Dijon* goes, the legal system determines if and what kinds of regulation are acceptable, for the EC as a whole, under Art. 28. The ECJ insisted that it would do so through controlling the reasonableness and proportionality of the actions of individual Member States. Given this balancing structure, it is unsurprising that the ECJ and the national courts would perform a pow-erful lawmaking role, not least by providing templates of what is or is not lawful government action. In its Art. 28 case law, the Court routinely gener-ated such templates, which could have become harmonized, European law in one of two ways. National regimes could adapt themselves to the Court's case law, in order to remain competitive and to insulate themselves from litigation. Or, more efficiently, the Commission could propose legislation of the kind that had passed review by the Court, enabling the Member States to reassert some modicum of control over the process, and providing the latter with legal shelter.

Both routes were facilitated by how the Court actually decided cases. In a very important piece of research, Poiares-Maduro (1998) examined how the ECJ balances (*a*) trading rights against (*b*) derogations from Article 28 claimed by Member State governments, in that part of the domain governed by *Cassis* (i.e. the review of the conformity, with Art. 28, of IAMs). The data show that the judges engage, systematically, in what he calls (1988: 72–8) "majoritarian activism." When the national measure in question is more unlike than like those equivalent measures in place in a majority of Member States, the ECJ strikes it down as a violation of Article 28. (We found that the Court began, in the early-1980s, to ask the Commission to provide such information on a regular basis). Poiares-Maduro found no exceptions to this rule. On the other hand, he found that the Court tends to uphold national measures in situations in which no dominant type of regulation exists, although there are important exceptions. In this way, the Court generates a "judicial harmonization" process. Majoritarian activism undermines the logic of minimum common denominator outcomes asserted by intergovernmentalists. At the same time, the Court would have little to fear in the way of reprisals, since a majority of Member States would likely be on its side on any given case.

No systematic research on the relationship between the Court's Art. 28 case law and legislative harmonization in the EU has been undertaken. It is, however, routinely noted that the Court replaced the Council of Ministers as a force for positive integration prior to the Single European Act (Oliver 1996: ch. 6; Craig and De Burca 1998: ch. 14), and a smaller literature (Empel 1992; Berlin 1992) focuses on how the Court's case law required or provoked governments to act legislatively. In any case, dozens of EU directives adopted prior to the Single European Act codified, as secondary legislation, the key holdings of specific rulings of the Court. Much more attention has been paid to the constitutional impact of *Cassis de Dijon*, from which the Commission developed a new strategy for achieving market integration.

The *Dassonville–Cassis* framework deserves to be considered as a constitutional innovation in that it implies a mode of integration neither foreseen nor anticipated by the Member States. In the Treaty of Rome, intergovernmental control over course of positive integration was seemingly assured by the dominance of the Council of Ministers over the legislative process, control that was upgraded by the Luxembourg Compromise. With Commission Directive 70/50, the Member State's governments had been told that Art. 28 would cover national measures that discriminated, on their face, between domestic and imported goods, although even this interpretation was controversial among at least some governments. In *Cassis*, the Court extended the *Dassonville* principles to the whole of domestic law and administrative practice (that is, to IAMs), and generated a new principle capable of being legally enforced: the mutual recognition of national standards. In doing so, the Court recast the relationship between negative and positive integration. Prior to *Cassis de Dijon*, the responsibility and authority to reduce the negative effects of divergent national regulatory regimes on EC production and trade rested with the EC legislator, acting through Art. 94. *Cassis de Dijon* obliterated the separation between Art. 28 and ex-Art. 94, extending the reach of the former into the purview of the latter.

Floating the doctrine of mutual recognition placed the relationship between negative and positive integration in the shadow of the law. The legal system had shown that the market could, at least in theory, be completed through adjudication. At the same time, mutual recognition created a powerful incentive to harmonize the most important market rules. It was readily apparent to governments, the Commission, and business that, if mutual recognition were actually introduced, a race to the bottom could follow: investment, production, and jobs might move to the states with lowest regulatory costs of production.

Following the Court's ruling in that case, the Commission took the unusual step of issuing a "Communication," in the form of a letter sent to the Member States, the Council, and the Parliament (reproduced in Oliver 1996: 429–31). The letter asserted that the Court had effectively established mutual recognition as a constitutional principle, which the Commission went on to interpret in the broadest possible manner. The Court had shown how states might retain their own national rules, capable of being applied within the domestic market, while prohibiting states from applying these same rules to goods originating elsewhere. Reliance on mutual recognition could obviate the need for extensive harmonization. Indeed, the Commission announced, it would henceforth focus its harmonization efforts on IAMs, particularly those "barriers to trade . . . which are admissible under the criteria set by the Court." Almost immediately, the large producer groups and associations of European business proclaimed their support for the initiative, and the new strategy—mutual recognition, minimal harmonization, concern for the transaction costs of producers and traders within Europe—came to dominate the discourse on how best to achieve market integration.

Concurrently, the Commission (contrary to the analysis of Alter and Meunier-Aitshalia 1994: 548) began to use Art. 226 more aggressively—for the first time—in order to increase pressure on governments. Markus Gehring and Alec Stone Sweet have collected the data on infringement proceedings brought, withdrawn, and decided by the Court. Prior to *Cassis*, the Court produced only two Art. 226 rulings on Art. 28. From the date *Cassis* was rendered to the date the Single Act was signed, the ECJ ruled on forty-six enforcement actions concerning Art. 28 brought by the Commission. Member States lost 90 percent of these cases. During this same period, the Commission filed an additional thirty-six more Art. 28 suits against Member States that did not go to the Court, because Member States agreed to settle. In the crucial 1980–4 period, free movement of goods cases comprised more than one-in-three of all Art. 226 rulings, and nearly 30 percent of all such rulings concerned Art. 28.

The literature on the sources of the Single European Act—which bundled together mutual recognition, a return to qualified majority voting, and the establishment of a binding timetable for harmonizing in the most important regulatory areas—has sufficiently demonstrated the extent to which transnational business elites and the Community's supranational organizations were ahead of governments in the process of "relaunching" Europe (Alter and Meunier-Aitsahalia 1994; Dehousse 1988, 1994; Egan 2001; Fligstein and Mara-Drita, 1996; Sandholtz and Zysman 1989; Stone Sweet and Caporaso 1998; Weiler 1991; but Moravscik 1991, 1995, 1998, disagrees). Governments acted, of course, in the form of a Treaty that codified integrative solutions to their own collective action problems, including the renunciation of the Luxembourg compromise. But these solutions had emerged from the activities of the EC's organizations and transnational actors, against the backdrop of pent-up demand for more, not less, supranational governance. Of course, the process was not only to do with transnational activity, law, courts, and trusteeship. It was propelled forward by a growing sense of crisis, brought on by globalization, the failure of go-it-alone policies to sustain economic growth, and an accumulation of legal precedents that empowered traders and the Commission in legal disputes with national administrations.

We expected that the adjudication of trading disputes would, among other things, serve to expand the domain of supranational governance, to reduce the EC's intergovernmentalism, and to reconstruct the contexts in which intergovernmental bargaining takes place. We believe that the Court's free movement case law on integration and the European polity did each of these things. Intergovernmentalists, however, would presumably tell this story differently, highlighting the putatively proactive role of governments. In his most recent account of the SEA, Moravcsik (1998: ch. 2) denies all of this, declaring that the EC's organizations "generally failed to influence the distribution of gains" that could have had an effect on the preferences of governments to negotiate.

With respect to the impact of the Court and the legal system, what evidence does Moravcsik (1998: especially 353–5) marshal to support this view? None, in our view. First, he does not discuss the sources and consequences of litigating Art. 28 and related provisions, and thus is not in the position to address if or how adjudication "influence[d] the distribution of gains." During the crucial 1979–84 period, levels of Arts. 226 and 234 litigation under Art. 28 rose sharply; rulings of noncompliance proliferated; and national regulatory frameworks were placed in a creeping "shadow of the law." Second, Moravcsik (based on an error made by Alter and Meunier-Aitshalia 1994[12]) wrongly claims that *Cassis de Dijon* was actually a "retreat from previous ECJ jurisprudence," but he does not explain or defend the assertion. In fact, *Cassis de Dijon* extends *Dassonville* to IAMs, a deeply controversial area that governments had not contemplated being covered by the treaty until the Commission's 1970 directive. Third, he argues that mutual recognition "was not a new innovation," but had been floated as early as the late 1960s. Yet, if by Moravcsik's own admission, the governments knew of this proposal, they did not adopt it. Instead, they pursued an intergovernmental politics that failed miserably. In the end, they adapted to the Court's case law, for obvious, "rational" reasons, partly due to the fact that the Court had constructed Art. 28 in ways that redistributed resources away from the Member States and towards transnational actors and supranational authority.

Last, Moravcsik argues that (*a*) governments fulfilled their own "demand" for mutual recognition and majority voting and (*b*) "Cassis, at most, accelerated the single market program," but "was not a necessary condition." Since he nowhere specifies the conditions necessary for the SEA, it is not obvious how one might assess or respond to this claim. We have argued, in effect, that (*a*) the Member States' "demand" for an accelerated market-building project was heavily conditioned by two (inseparable) factors: the course of market integration through the mid-1980s, and (*b*) outcomes produced by the legal system. Moravcsik does not show otherwise. As Egan (2001: 59–60) stresses, larger, more open markets do not develop without altering "the alignment of interests" within affected industries, "which will, in turn, affect policy preferences and corporate strategies." She then goes on to show that the Court's evolving case law shaped the strategies of large corporations, the Commission, and ultimately governments. In fact, the Court's steady and expansively integrationist interpretation of Art. 28

---

[12] Alter and Meunier-Aitshalia (1994) emphatically claim that, beyond the *dicta* on mutual recognition, the Court's ruling does not innovate on the basic *Dassonville* framework. The error is critical, and it undermines their analysis of the ruling's impact.

undermined national regulatory sovereignty, enhanced the role of trans-national actors and national judges to participate in market integration, and empowered the Commission, in both legislative and judicial processes. Clearly, the *Cassis de Dijon* jurisprudence raised the cost of intergovern-mental inaction, and made the benefits of intergovernmental cooperation more attractive. The "distribution of gains," by any reasonable measure, had indeed been altered.

A broader point deserves emphasis. To take imperfect commitment and delegation in the EU seriously requires us to abandon an exclusive focus on governments, and to examine the dynamics of trusteeship empirically. In this story, the Member States did *not* design the EU's trading institutions, nor did they design the mode of governance that best served to enforce them. The Court did. When *Cassis* was rendered, the Legal Service of the Council of Ministers actually produced a finding that rejected the ruling's main principles, asserting the viability of the Commission's (pre-*Dassonville*, Directive 70/50) discrimination test![13] Here, as before, govern-ments adapted themselves to rules that had emerged earlier, through the actions of the EC's organizations, while remaining several steps behind what the Court and the Commission were in fact doing. A simple counter-factual might provide the best test: in a world without direct effect and supremacy, in a world in which the Member States actually controlled the evolution of Europe's trading institutions, how far would market integra-tion have gone after the Luxembourg compromise?[14]

III Mutation of the Framework

The *Dassonville* framework remained remarkably stable until 1993, when, in *Keck* (ECJ 167/1991), the Court removed national regulation of certain "selling arrangements" from the corpus of IAMs covered by Art. 28. We view the *Keck* decision as an adjustment dictated largely by the evolution of adju-dication in the domain, that is, with factors endogenous to the adjudication of Art. 28. The aggressively interventionist approach taken by the Court in *Cassis de Dijon* ultimately generated four sets of interrelated problems.

---

[13] Which some, and perhaps all, governments opposed at that time.

[14] Scholars disagree on the question of whether the EC's legal system, on its own, would have been able to impose mutual recognition as authoritative law in the EC. We have reason to think that it could, given the Court's subsequent decisionmaking, while Alter and Meunier-Aishalia (1994) disagree. Whether the Court could have, on it own, "completed" the common market, is quite a different matter.

First, as noted above, in the 1980s firms that were *not* primarily involved in intra-EC trade began to make use of Art. 28 to attack national regulations they did not like. This led to a great deal of doctrinal soul-searching about the absence of limits to the reach of *Cassis de Dijon* (Mortlemans 1991; Rawlings 1993; Steiner 1992), worries that we have good reason to think were shared by the Court (Advocate General Van Gerven in *Torfaen*, ECJ 145/88). Indeed, in the end, the Court adopted the solution proposed in a beautifully argued article (White 1989) produced by a lawyer in the legal affairs department of Commission.

Second, by the early-1990s, the Court's docket had become overloaded. With *Keck*, the ECJ was, in effect telling litigators, "litigators have pushed us far enough; it's time to back them off."

Third, the Court was responding to signals from their most important interlocutors: the national courts. Many national judges had all but refused to subject IAMs to least-means proportionality testing and, partly in consequences, the ECJ had produced a handful of obviously inconsistent decisions. Stone Sweet examined, for the *Cassis* through *Keck* period, every national decision on IAMs reported by courts in three EC Member States (France, Netherlands), UK. Most judges, at least implicitly, used a discrimination test, not the "actual or potential, direct or indirect" hindrance to trade test announced by the European Court in *Dassonville*. In all three Member States, national judges often showed themselves unwilling to find for litigants not directly involved in moving goods across borders (Jarvis 1998; Rawlings 1993). *Keck* formally reduced the political exposure of judges, by restricting the range of national policies subject to supervision through proportionality balancing.

Fourth, the marginal returns to market integration of an aggressive approach to IAMs had, by the time *Keck* was decided, fallen virtually to zero (see also Shapiro 1999, Weiler 1999). In our view, the approach was a victim of the Court's more general successes. After the Single Act, the legislative process opened up (Chapter 2), and harmonization proceeded steadily, thereby withdrawing, prospectively, whole classes of cases from the Court's docket. The court's role in market regulation has necessarily become lower profile since.

Keck and its Aftermath

In *Keck*, the Court announced that the legal system would (*a*) continue to monitor and enforce Art. 28 rules against one class of IAMs—mandatory requirements related to the characteristics of products[15]—but would (*b*) greatly reduce or abandon altogether the review of national measures that restrict "selling arrangements," conceived as the circumstances (the time, place, and manner) of selling goods.

The dispute involved the prosecution of a retailer for selling goods at a loss in order to attract customers, a practice forbidden by a long-standing French law most recently renewed in 1986. In defense, the retailer alleged that the law fell foul of Art. 28, since its effect was to reduce the quantity of imported goods sold and, therefore, imported. Bearing in mind Poiares-Maduro's "majoritarian activism" thesis, it is worth mention that the ECJ stated in its decision that a majority of the Member States had enacted similar rules. The Court then limited the scope of its Art. 28 jurisprudence on IAMs:

It is not the purpose of national legislation [prohibiting] resale at a loss to regulate trade in goods between Member States.

Such legislation may, admittedly, restrict the volume of sales, and hence the volume of sales of products from other Member States . . . But the question remains whether such a possibility is sufficient to characterize the legislation in question as [an MEE].

In view of the increasing tendency of traders to invoke Art. [28] of the Treaty as a means of challenging any rules whose effect is to limit their commercial freedom, even where such rules are not aimed at products from other Member States, the Court considers it necessary to re-examine and clarify its case law on this matter.

[The Court restates its holding in *Cassis de Dijon*.]

However, contrary to what has previously been decided, the application to products from other Member States of national provisions restricting or prohibiting certain selling arrangements is not such as to hinder directly or indirectly, actually or potentially, trade between the Member States in the meaning of the *Dassonville* judgment . . . provided that those provisions apply to all affected [concerns] operating within national territory and provided that they affect in the same manner, in law and in fact, the marketing of domestic products and of those from other Member States . . .

Accordingly, the reply to be given to the national court is that Art. [28] of the Treaty is to be interpreted as not applying to legislation of a Member State imposing a general prohibition on resale at a loss.

With *Keck*, the Court took a first step to limit explicitly the reach of Art. 28. The ruling, however, did not delineate the scope of "selling arrangements," beyond the statement that these included the national

---

[15] That is, of the kind dealt with in *Cassis de Dijon*.

statue under review. Instead, the Court indicated what remained within the purview of Art. 28. IAMs that "lay down requirements to be met by [traded] goods—such as those relating to designation, form, size, weight, composition, presentation, labeling, and packaging—constitute measures of equivalent effect prohibited by Art. 30." Clarification would have to await further adjudication.

Nearly a decade's time allows us to examine *Keck's* impact on the evolution of a new argumentation framework for this part of the domain. A review of rulings in which the decision has been applied demonstrates the importance of the Courts' pre-*Keck* jurisprudence to its interpretation of "selling arrangements." This influence flows in two directions: where pre-*Keck* argumentation frameworks were relatively clear, these continue to shape and define the legal issues. Where the jurisprudence was, before 1993, relatively ambiguous, the application of *Keck* has, at best, incrementally improved coherence, although problems may always remain.

Generally, the case law does not "reverse," but reclassifies, the Court's pre-*Keck* jurisprudence. A few months after *Keck*, for example, the Court decided *Huenermund* (ECJ 292/92, 1993), a dispute involving a challenge to a German law that limited the promotion of para-pharmaceutical products. The ECJ held the German measure to be a "selling arrangement," and thus beyond the reach of Art. 28. Prior to *Keck*, the Court had curated a long line of decisions upholding, as permissible derogations to Art. 28, national measures governing the sale of such quasi-pharmaceuticals (e.g. ECJ 227/82, ECJ 266/87, ECJ 60/89, ECJ 369/88, ECJ 347/89). These types of cases are now covered by the *Keck* doctrine. In such areas, dispositive outcomes will be patterned as before, although the formal process for reaching those outcomes will have changed. What has already changed is not purely a matter of rhetoric. On the contrary, from the point of view of the Court and the national judge, *Keck* eliminated a form of review that had been mandatory, intrusive, and politically delicate: of the proportionality of national measures having little to do with trade, per se.

Applying *Keck* to well-established derogations thus removed whole classes of regulation from the coverage of Art. 28, while maintaining a semblance of continuity with prior practice. In these areas, the old case law constrains the range of permissible arguments available to litigants and judges. In *Belgapom* (ECJ 63/94), for instance, the Court found that legally mandated minimum prices at retail fell under "selling arrangements." A decade before it had bluntly declared that similar measures "[did] not constitute quantitative restrictions on imports," under Art. 28 (ECJ 80/85), so the ruling hardly constituted a break with previous interpretations. Previous interpretation had, however, drawn a distinction between regulations governing prices which it decided were caught by Art. 28, such as price freezes on agricultural goods (as in ECJ 5/79 and ECJ 16/79), and those which, like minimum set retail prices, are not. The ruling in *Belgapom* reinforced and clarified the distinction.

A review of the case law on derogations to Art. 28 (Art. 30 and mandatory requirements under *Cassis*) shows the Court working assiduously to reclassify permissible derogations, where possible, as "selling arrangements." *Keck* thus enables the Court to do what White and other legal academics had advocated. It provides a clarifying explanation of the scope of Art. 28, and a more uniform taxonomy of IAMs.

Where the *Cassis–Dassonville* framework had broken down, *Keck* had perhaps more potential to push the law in new directions. One important group of such disputes concerns national laws establishing opening hours for retailers, including Sunday openings. The Court's rulings in these cases generated heavy criticism for being unclear (reviewed in Rawlings 1993). In post-*Keck* rulings that include *Punto Casa* (ECJ 69/93) and *Tankstation* (ECJ 401/92), the Court could simply announce that such measures comprised "selling arrangements," and thus were no longer subject to challenge under Art. 28.

On the other hand, some classification problems seem to be intractable, by their very nature; in such cases, *Keck* may not succeed in reducing indeterminacy. The most obvious example concerns the national regulation of product advertising. Restrictions on advertising can affect how goods are labeled and packaged; labeling and packaging were traditionally covered by *Cassis de Dijon*, under Art. 28; but the Member States could defend their packaging requirements under the heading, "consumer protection." Prior to *Keck*, lawyers prepared arguments from two positions. Simplifying somewhat: (*a*) one line of cases had it that the Member States possess significant discretion to restrict labeling and packaging, to protect the consumer (e.g. *Oosthoek*, ECJ 286/81; *Buet*, ECJ 382/87); (*b*) another line of cases had it that the legal system strictly scrutinizes national measures on advertising (*GB INNO BM*, ECJ 362/88; *SARPP*, ECJ 241/89). How the case was classified—labeling or advertising—could determine the outcome. Academic commentators, too, complained that the Court did not use consistent criteria for classifying and then deciding these cases (Jarvis 1998: 58–63).

Post-*Keck*, the Court, notably in *Leclerc-Siplec* (ECJ 412/93), announced that advertisements, which are designed to promote products, are "selling arrangements." *Keck* and *Leclerc* have since been used in tandem, to create a specific argumentation framework defining the relationship of advertising to Art. 28 (e.g. *KO*, ECJ 405/98). In *Mars* (ECJ 470/93) and *Familiapress* (ECJ 368/95), however, the problem of distinguishing labeling from promotion resurfaced. Governments continue to defend national measures under the consumer protection heading; when the Court accepts the defense, it does not apply the *Keck/Leclerc* framework. Academic commentators disagree on how successful the Court has been in reducing indeterminacy with respect to labeling and advertising. Weatherill (1996) argues that the case law is both inconsistent and unclear, and proposes various ways to improve the situation. Others claim that the Court is developing different rules for different modes of product promotion. "Where the method of advertising is an intrinsic part of the product itself, as in *Mars*, the *Cassis* rule applies," Greaves argues (1998: 310), citing the case of *Familiapress*.

In summary, *Keck* showed the Court to be sensitive to the concerns of the national judges and the legal epistemic community. "Contrary to what has previously been held," the ruling began, but *Keck* did not initiate anything like a doctrinal revolution. Its primary virtue has been to help the Court preserve the *Cassis–Dassonville* framework, by pruning it of its most controversial elements. In areas where *Keck* has failed to reduce indeterminacy, the situation, compared to the pre-*Keck* era, is made no worse.

IV Conclusion

With supremacy and direct effect, the Court of Justice put into place the basic instruments for the judicialization of the trade regime in Europe. The subsequent entry into force of Art. 28 assured the dominance of the legal system over the evolution of trade institutions, given a steady caseload. The Court successful imposed its vision of the common market for three basic reasons. First, the Member States had failed to make progress on market integration, according to the plans they themselves had designed. Second, the Court's efforts were broadly supported by transnational business, the Commission, and national judges. And third, the Court maintained a principled, precedent-based discourse on Art. 28.

Through compulsion and persuasion, the Member States adapted to the judicial construction of Art. 28. In the 1970s, the Member States argued that Art. 234 references could not be used as a general instrument for reviewing the conformity of national law with Art. 28. They lost. Then they lost arguments, almost continuously made, to the effect that the Commission and the Court had exceeded their respective authority, notably by generating unacceptably broad interpretations of Art. 28. In 1970, governments claimed that the Commission, in Directive 70/50, had gone too far; but they would later invoke Directive 70/50 to defend their actions, given that the Court had pushed even further with *Dassonville*. After *Cassis de Dijon* was decided, governments still continued to claim, before the ECJ and through their own Legal Service, that Art. 28 did not mean what the Court said it meant in *Dassonville* and after. Ultimately, against a backdrop of rising levels of trade-oriented litigation, governments developed proficiency in defending their decisionmaking in light of the Court's rulemaking. In doing so, the Member States served to legitimize the Court's Art. 28 jurisprudence.

The Member States neither anticipated nor welcomed the Court's jurisprudence on the free movement of goods; and academic observers were taken by surprise by *Dassonville* and *Cassis de Dijon*. Yet there was nothing unintentional about this case law or its effects. Indeed, the overarching coherence of the Court's activities in this domain is striking. It seems to us that the members of the Court of Justice proved to be far better political economists—with a better and more subtle understanding of the varied purposes of delegation and self-binding, and of the logics of incrementalism—than have many of the social scientists who have sought to explain market integration in Europe.

In the next chapter, we move from negative to positive integration, and examine the judicialization of lawmaking in the social provisions field.

4

Sex Equality

With Rachel Cichowski

In Chapter 3, we saw how the commitment logics of federalism gradually came to infuse the politics of judicially-governed market-building under the Treaty of Rome. The outcome can only partly be understood in terms of original Member States' decisions to delegate to the Court and the Commission. After all, the legal system itself generated the necessary conditions for some of the most important outcomes produced, and it did so in the absence of Member State authorization. Most important, the European Court of Justice (ECJ) interpreted Art. 28 so as to confer, upon traders and other private actors, rights enforceable in the national courts. In doing so, the Court went far beyond what any purely functionalist theory of judicial governance within federalism would require for market integration to proceed.[1] In developing a rights-based jurisprudence, the Court enhanced the effectiveness of free movement of goods provisions, and constrained the Member States further than they had ever considered necessary or appropriate. The ECJ's position as trustee made such a jurisprudence possible, while an aggressive rights posture further reinforced the Court's fiduciary powers, in partnership with national judges.

This chapter charts the evolution, through adjudication, of rules governing a quite different domain of European Community (EC) law: sex equality. In 1976, the Court (*Defrenne II*, ECJ 43/75) recognized the direct effect of Art. 141, which provides that male and female workers shall receive equal pay for equal work. It also announced that Art. 141 "forms part of the social

---

[1] Indeed, standard rational choice and game theoretic "explanations" of constitutional judicial review are openly hostile to rights and to rights-based adjudication (e.g. Brennan and Buchanan 1985), not least because such politics have the capacity to unravel the constitutive bargains upon which the legitimacy of the polity is alleged to rest. Further, game theorists have not yet developed techniques of modeling changes in constitutional rules provoked by judicial rulemaking (see the exchange between Stone Sweet 1998*b* and Vanberg 1998*a*, *b*).

objectives of the Community, which is not merely an economic union, but is at the same time intended . . . to ensure social progress and seek the constant improvement of the living standards and working conditions of [its] peoples." By 2000 (Schröder, ECJ C-50/96), the ECJ could remind its audience that "the Court has repeatedly held that the right"—contained in Art. 141—"not to be discriminated against on grounds of sex is one of the fundamental human rights whose observance the Court has a duty to ensure." The founding Member States conceived Art. 141 as a means of discouraging social dumping; over the course of twenty-five years, private litigants and national judges helped the Court transform the provision into a basic right to sex equality in the workplace.

During this period, the legislative politics of this domain were comprehensively judicialized. As the legal system developed into a privileged site of policy innovation in the area, national governments routinely found themselves playing catch-up with the Court's case law. The underlying dynamic of this process should by now be a familiar one:

1. The constitutionalization of Art. 141, and of the principle of equal treatment for men and women, encouraged private parties, primarily women, to activate the legal system; they did so for private reasons, but also in order to challenge existing national rules considered discriminatory, and to replace these rules with law whose source was supranational.
2. In response, the Court steadily developed a rights-oriented interpretation of the Treaty (and of relevant secondary legislation), which further empowered women, vis-à-vis national governments, within processes governments could not directly control.
3. This progressive (re)construction of the EC's sex equality law served to enhance supranational governance, to organize the work of the EC legislator, and to erode the capacity of governments to use veto powers to block change.

The institutionalization of judicialized, rights-oriented deliberation proved to be crucial to the outcomes generated by the system. Claims of discrimination placed governments on the defensive (rights trump infraconstitutional interests and values); and a stream of such claims provoked virtually continuous per se judicial policymaking on the part of the Court. As we shall see, the Court found that certain types of policies not only inhered in primary EC law, but that legislators were positively required to adopt these policies as secondary law.

The chapter also addresses two other theoretical issues raised earlier in this book. The first concerns the extent to which supranational organizations like the Court and the Commission produce "unintended consequences" from the perspective of the Member States, a possibility that Moravcsik (1998) and Tsebelis and Garrett (2001) deny. As in Chapter 3, we provide overwhelming evidence to the contrary. The second concerns the relationship between positive and negative integration. Some scholars, most notably Scharph, have argued that while supranational organizations have been effective in provoking negative integration, they have been less successful when it comes to positive integration. This chapter shows that the argument cannot be sustained (see also Stone Sweet, Sandholtz, and Fligstein (eds.) 2001), at least not without significant modification.

The chapter proceeds as follows. Part I provides an overview of the Treaty rules and secondary legislation that constitute the domain of sex equality. Part II examines how Art. 141 evolved once it had been constitutionalized by the Court. Part III focuses on the relationship between the Court, and its case law on sex equality, and the production of directives by the EC legislator. We also briefly discuss the impact of the Court's rulemaking on national judicial and legislative processes. In Part IV, we analyze the aggregate data on litigation and adjudication in the field, focusing on how precedent-based lawmaking has organized the development of the field. We address a range of theoretical issues in the conclusion.

I The Normative Structure

In contrast to the principles of free movement of goods and of workers, the founding Member States did not consider the principle of equal pay for equal work to be one of the "fundamental objectives" of the Community. In the original Treaty of Rome, ex-Art. 119 came under Title VIII—"Social Policy, Education, Vocational Training and Youth." In ex-Arts. 117 and 118, the Member States asserted their desire to "promote improved working conditions" and standards of living, "so as to make possible [the] harmonization" of both in the future; and they invited the Commission to help them achieve closer "cooperation" in the "social field," by "making studies," and "arranging consultations." Of the provisions contained in Title VIII, however, only ex-Art. 119 employed the language of legal obligation:

Ex-Art. 119. Each Member State shall during the first stage [i.e. January 1, 1962] ensure and subsequently maintain the application of the principle that men and women should receive equal pay for equal work.

For the purpose of this Article, "pay" means the ordinary basic or minimum wage or salary and any other consideration, whether in cash or in kind, which the worker receives, directly or indirectly, in respect of his employment from his employer.

Equal pay without discrimination based on sex means: (*a*) that pay for the same work at piece rates shall be calculated on the basis of the same unit of measurement; (*b*) that pay for work at time rates shall be the same for the same job.

The Member States adopted ex-Art. 119—hereafter referred to as Art. 141—primarily for economic reasons (Collins 1975; Warner 1984; Hoskyns 1996): in an emerging common market, discriminatory wage structures, if left unchecked, would distort labor markets to the advantage of those who discriminated. To be sure, the implementation of equal pay for equal work rules at the national level would also have the effect of reducing gender inequality, at least in the workplace. But the Member States assumed that broader goals of social justice were to be pursued, at least for the foreseeable future, through national—rather than supranational—legislation.[2]

Indeed, the Member States designed the provision with relatively limited purposes in mind: they expected it to apply only to "pay," as that word was defined in the Treaty, and only to workers performing virtually identical tasks. Although Art. 2.1 of Convention No. 100 (1951) of the International Labour Organization (ILO) served as the template for Art. 141, the Member States amended the former in a crucial way. The ILO Convention proclaims that men and women shall receive equal pay for work of "equal value," in order to extend the law's reach to practices that segregate women into jobs paying less than those typically held by men. The Member States did not intend to cover such discrimination with Art. 141, although it was pervasive throughout the Community.

Nonetheless, read as binding law, Art. 141 contained intriguing ambiguities. It was to apply not only to wages and salaries, but also to "any other consideration, whether in cash or in kind, which the worker receives, directly or indirectly, in respect of his employment from his employer." Does "any other consideration . . ." include vocational training, sick leave, pensions, and so on? Does the reach of equal pay rules extend to a company's promotion policies, if such policies lead to wage structures that discriminate on the basis of sex? If full-time and part-time workers perform the same tasks, are they working the "same job," at least for purposes of comparing pay between

---

[2] The French delegation proposed the provision, as a means of protecting its own rules on equal pay for equal work. France also sought but failed to achieve broader harmonization of labor costs, in the face of strong German opposition (Cichowski 2002: ch. 3).

male and female workers? In hindsight, we see that, once the Court recognized the direct effect of Art. 141, adjudication became the central mechanism for answering questions like these, and for raising a host of new and subsidiary issues that would be steadily litigated.

In addition to Art. 141, the sex equality domain is structured by a small but important body of secondary legislation.

THE DIRECTIVES

The EC legislator became active in the area in the 1970s, producing three foundational directives, on equal pay, equal treatment, and social security, each under unanimity voting rules. The Equal Pay Directive (EC Directive 75/117) prohibits sex discrimination in matters of pay and job classification: men and women shall receive "equal pay" both for "equal work" and for "work of equal value." Member States also agree to abolish statutes and administrative rules that permit pay discrimination, and to ensure that the principle is honored in collective agreements and private contracts. The Equal Treatment Directive (EC Directive 76/207) extends the principle of nondiscrimination between men and women to vocational training, access to employment and promotion, and working conditions. Art. 2.1 defines "equal treatment" broadly: "the principle of equal treatment shall mean that there shall be no discrimination *whatsoever* on grounds of sex *either directly or indirectly* by reference in particular to marital or family status [emphasis added]." Certain legal regimes are exempted from the directive's scope of application, including social security, the protection of pregnancy and maternity, and affirmative action policies. The purpose of the Social Security Directive (EC Directive 79/7) is to further "the progressive implementation" of the "principle of equal treatment for men and women" in the area of social security. The legislation covers social security schemes—but only those established through national legislation—that provide pensions to retired workers, benefits to the unemployed, and assistance to those who cannot work due to illness, invalidity, or accident. The directive explicitly excludes occupational-based social security schemes—those constituted through collective bargaining or private contracts—from its coverage. The ECJ would later recognize the direct effect of the core provisions of each of these directives.

After this initial flurry, legislative activity in the domain stalled. Most importantly, the UK government (joined periodically by others) sought to block the extension of EC's competences into social policy. After a long delay, the Council finally adopted the Occupation Social Security Directive in 1986 (EC Directive 86/378, amended by Directive 96/97), which applies the equal treatment principle to social security benefits, including pension plans, provided by employers to employees. Since 1986, the Council has also adopted: legislation clarifying equal treatment for self-employed (EC Directive 86/613), pregnant (EC Directive 92/85), and part-time (EC Directive 97/81) workers; and directives establishing rules governing burden of proof in indirect discrimination cases (EC Directive 97/80), and conferring rights to parental leave (EC Directive 96/34, extended to the United Kingdom by EC Directive 97/75).

II The Constitutionalization of Article 141

In the rest of this chapter, we focus on analyzing outcomes that would not have been produced had the Court declined to recognize the direct effect of Art. 141. Put differently, the direct effect of Art. 141, which the ECJ announced in 1976, constitutes a necessary causal condition for the institutional evolution of the domain of sex equality. It bears emphasis that no Member State government—in 1957 or 1976 or at any time in between— went on record in support of the direct effect of Art. 141. On the contrary, national governments actively sought to delay the implementation of the equal pay for equal work provision, and to maintain intergovernmental control over how the provision would be implemented in national legal systems. With one broad stroke, the Court began a process that would destroy that control.

DEFRENNE II: THE DIRECT EFFECT OF ARTICLE 141

A series of preliminary references from Belgian courts gave the ECJ its first opportunities to interpret Art. 141. The references involved different aspects of one case, that of Gabrielle Defrenne, a flight attendant with the Belgian national airline, Sabena. Until 1966, Sabena paid higher wages to stewards relative to stewardesses, required women attendants to retire at age forty, fifteen years earlier than male counterparts, and provided men with statutory-based pension benefits that were denied to women. The job responsibilities of male and female attendants were, nonetheless, identical. In 1968, after having been forced into age-based retirement, Ms. Defrenne

challenged these inequalities before various Belgian courts, on the grounds
of Art. 141.[3] In its first preliminary ruling on her situation (*Defrenne I*, ECJ
80/70, 1971), the ECJ held that Art. 141 did not cover statutory social security schemes, notwithstanding the fact that the Belgian scheme tied levels
of pension payouts to wage levels. The second preliminary reference
(*Defrenne II*, ECJ 43/75, 1976) concerned Ms. Defrenne's attempt to recover
arrears in salary, calculated as the difference between her wages and that of
male stewards, for the period in which she worked for Sabena as a flight
attendant. Our focus here is on the crucial point of law decided by the Court
in this second proceeding: that Art. 141, on its own, could confer rights on
individuals that national judges must protect.

With the *Defrenne* cases, the Court confronted a long record of Member
State indifference and Commission negligence. According to Art. 141, the
Member States were to have completed the implementation of the "princi-
ple of equal pay for equal work" by January 1, 1962. In July 1960, the
Commission sent a letter to national governments, reminding them of this
obligation. The Member States responded by establishing a new timetable.
In a resolution dated December 31, 1961, they promised that Art. 141 would
be implemented by January 1, 1965. This new deadline also passed, but
virtually no concrete action had been taken. As important, at the time
Defrenne II was being argued before the Court, the Commission had not
brought a single Art. 226 infringement proceeding in the domain. Instead,
the Commission drafted, and the Member States adopted, the Equal Pay
Directive of 1975. Thus, in 1976, no one could deny that the Member States
had defaulted on their duties with regard to Art. 141. The issue of the provision's direct effect, however, was a separate matter, governed by its own
doctrinal framework.

In their observations to the Court, the United Kingdom and Ireland
argued that Art. 141 failed to satisfy the criteria on direct effect set by the
Court (see Chapter 2), that of normative (*a*) precision; (*b*) unconditionality;
and (*c*) completeness—the absence of a need for implementing measures.
In our view, the claim had a good deal of merit. Art. 141 declares equal
pay for equal work to be a "principle" that Member States take subsequent
measures "to ensure and maintain." As the United Kingdom pointed out,
principles of law, by definition, are typically the most general, even vaguest,
of norms, and thus the criteria of normative precision could not be met.

---

[3] *Defrenne* was represented by Elaine Vogel-Polsky, a labor lawyer and activist for women's
rights who saw the case as a test of the applicability of Art. 141 in national legal systems.

Further, since Art. 141 explicitly calls for implementing measures, the provision must also fail the third criteria. Ireland, too, asserted that Art. 141 had been "deliberately worded ... so as to avoid direct effects." The provision addresses the Member States, rather than announcing an individual right to be free of pay discrimination. In any case, the governments argued, implementing measures had been taken, in the guise of the Equal Pay Directive. Once the directive had been transposed into national law by national legislatures, the measures could be recognized and enforced by national judges.

The ECJ prefaced its ruling with the announcement that "the principle of equal pay for equal work forms part of the foundations of the Community." It then went on to consider Art. 141's direct effect. The Court agreed with the Member States that the provision was incomplete, in that its underlying purpose could only be properly achieved through associated legislative action:

It is impossible not to recognize that the complete implementation of the aim pursued by [Art. 141], ... the elimination of all discrimination, direct or indirect, between men and women workers, not only as regards individual undertakings but also entire branches of industry and even of the economic system as a whole, may in certain cases involve the elaboration of criteria whose implementation necessitates the taking of appropriate measures at Community and national level.

These and related dicta appeared to indicate that Art. 141 would not apply to certain circumstances, and in particular, to indirect discrimination and equal pay for work of equal value (discussed below). Such problems, the ruling suggested, must be dealt with through legislative not judicial action. Nonetheless, it then quickly went on to hold that Art. 141 had direct effect in "at least" one type of situation: where "direct discrimination can be identified [by the national judge] solely with reference to the criteria laid down by Art. 141." Ms. Defrenne's situation—wherein a woman is paid less than a man doing exactly the same job—fit these criteria. The Court also addressed arguments to the contrary. It noted that the word "principle" is used in the Treaty "to indicate the fundamental nature of certain provisions" (e.g. Title I), and not simply to introduce "vague declarations." And it rejected the claim that Art. 141 was aimed at Member States, but not individuals, in these terms:

As the Court has already found in other contexts, the fact that certain provisions of the Treaty are formally addressed to the Member States does not prevent rights from being conferred at the same time on any individual who has an interest in the performance of the duties thus laid down. ... The effectiveness of [Art. 141] cannot be affected by the fact that the duty imposed by the Treaty has not been discharged by certain Member States and the [Commission has] not reacted sufficiently energetically against this failure to act.

The referring judge had also raised a secondary question that was crucial to the resolution of Ms. Defrenne's claims: from what date was Art. 141 directly effective? The Court held that the date mandated by the Treaty—January 1, 1962—was the operative one, firmly stating that neither the Member State resolution of December 31, 1961, nor the Equal Pay Directive of 1975, could in any way modify the Member States' Treaty obligations. The ECJ, however, carefully considered the financial implications of its ruling. Recall that directly effective Treaty provisions can be invoked by private parties against other private parties before national judges, whereas directives may produce only vertical, but not horizontal, effects (see Chapter 2). Left unmodified, the Court's holding would have opened the gates to a flood of claims, by women against their employers, for backpay for the 1962–76 period. During the proceedings, the Court had asked (an unusual request at that time) the participating Member States to assess the costs of a ruling in Defrenne's favor, whereupon the United Kingdom and Ireland produced data demonstrating, in effect, that pay discrimination was extensive in certain industries. If such a decision were to be applied retroactively, the governments argued, many businesses would be forced into bankruptcy, leaving thousands of women unemployed. These arguments swayed the ECJ. Invoking the principle of "legal certainty," the Court held that "the direct effect of Art. 141 [could not] be relied upon to support claims concerning pay periods prior to the date of this judgment, except as regards those workers who have already brought legal proceedings." In effect, the judges were unwilling to punish companies—whose wage practices were lawful under national, but not EC, law—for the malfeasance of the Member States. The ECJ also took pains to scold the Commission. In the Court's view, the Commission's decision not to bring infringement proceedings had helped to "consolidate the incorrect impression as to the effects of [Art. 141]," on the part of both public officials and private companies.[4]

---

[4] The Commission must have known that a day of reckoning was imminent, which makes its failure to act surprising, if not indefensible. In *Defrenne I*, the Advocate General, prompted by counsel for the plaintiff, had raised the question of the direct effect of Art. 141, although the Court chose not to address it. Two years later, in 1973, the Commission produced a report detailing the failure on the part of the Member States to provide for equal pay for equal work, and promising to bring infringement proceedings in the immediate future. The ECJ referred to the 1973 report, and the Commission's hollow threat, in *Defrenne II* (recital 51).

The breakdown of the "international law-plus" legal system designed by the Member States did not require the Court to constitutionalize Art. 141. The determination of the direct effect of a Treaty provision is invariably an exercise in judicial lawmaking, one that follows from prior acts of lawmaking, traceable back to *Van Gend en Loos* (see Chapter 2). In our view, *Defrenne II* must be understood in light of the Court's prior posture on the direct effect of other Treaty provisions, that is, as part of a more general strategy to enhance the effectiveness of EC law through a jurisprudence of individual rights. Not surprisingly, the ruling resulted in a steady flow of Art. 227 references from national courts, allowing the Court to determine progressively the meaning, scope, and application of equal pay rules.

We now turn to how Art. 141 has evolved through use, post-*Defrenne II*. We focus on how the Court has (*a*) defined "pay"; (*b*) provided coverage for work of "equal value"; and (*c*) addressed the issue of indirect discrimination. In these areas, the Court produced outcomes—both substantive and doctrinal—that advantaged women, and encouraged further litigation in the national courts.

THE MEANING OF PAY

Article 141 defines "pay" not only in terms of wages and salaries, but also as "any other consideration, whether in cash or in kind, which the worker receives, directly or indirectly, in respect of his employment from his employer." With one important exception, the ECJ has given this latter phrase "a broad and purposive" construction (Ellis 1998: 64), covering virtually "all perks provided for employees by their employers." That exception deserves to be noted up-front. In *Defrenne I* (ECJ 80/70, 1971), the Court ruled that social security schemes, and "in particular retirement pensions," fell outside the scope of Art. 141, where such schemes are "directly governed by legislation without any element of agreement within the undertaking," and where they are "obligatorily applicable to general categories of workers." The holding was justified, in part, on the grounds that legislatively-governed pension plans are "determined less by the employment relationship between the employee and the worker, and more by considerations of social policy." In his report, the Advocate General had put it more boldly: statutory social security benefits are more analogous to a "road, water main, or sewer" than to a wage or salary.

Defrenne I was the Court's first decision on Art. 141, and it remains good law, but only as regards a narrow range of statutory social security schemes. Subsequently, the ECJ "has given a very wide scope" (Craig and De Burca

2002: 865) to the term, "pay," inevitably blurring boundaries separating the remuneration of workers from social policy. In *Bilka* (ECJ 170/84, 1986), the Court formally rejected the view—held by at least some Member States—that *Defrenne I* had effectively excluded, from the scope of Art. 141, all legislatively-mandated benefits provided by employers to their workers. The decision provoked a flood of litigation, to which the ECJ responded favorably. Today, virtually all such benefits are considered "pay" for the purposes of applying Art. 141. Equal pay rules now cover both privately-contracted and statutorily-governed: compensation and benefits for part-time (see *Nimz*, ECJ C-184/89, 1991) and overtime work (e.g. *Stadt Lengervich*, ECJ C-399, joined, 1994); bonuses (*Commission* v. *Luxembourg*, ECJ 58/81, 1982); access to promotion and pay raises, even during leave periods (*Gillespie*, ECJ C-342/93); compensation payments for training programs (*Bötel*, ECJ C-360/90, 1992), sick pay (see *Rinner-Kühn*, ECJ 171/88, 1989); severance packages and other redundancy benefits (e.g. *Kowalska*, ECJ C-33/89, 1990); and retirement plans, including pensions provided by employers (*Barber*, ECJ C-262/88, 1990).

EQUAL PAY FOR EQUAL VALUE

Determining the juridical relationship between Art. 141 and the foundational directives in the field has been an important, but politically difficult, task of the Court. In *Defrenne II*, the ECJ described the 1975 Equal Pay Directive as following from the underlying social objectives of Art. 141. The Directive "was intended to encourage the proper implementation of Art. 141," and could not modify the latter's material or temporal "effectiveness." On the other hand, the Court acknowledged that the Directive, which "establishes the principle of equal pay for work of equal value," went beyond the "the narrow criterion" of "equal pay for equal work" contained in Art. 141. It thus implied that the Directive reached further than the Treaty, and that the latter could not cover equal pay for work of equal value. Today, it is clear that Art. 141 subsumes the Directive in every important respect, including this one.[5]

Commission vs. the UK: work of equal value

In 1981, the Commission brought an infringement case against the United Kingdom for improper implementation of the Equal Pay Directive. Art. 1.1 of

[5] Ellis (1998: 148–9) writes: "If the Directive merely spells out the detail of [Art. 141], without in any way undermining its scope, it follows that its chief practical effect today is to shed light on the more obscure aspects of [Art. 119]."

that Directive calls for the "elimination of discrimination on grounds of sex" for "the same work" or "for work to which equal value is attributed." The relevant UK rules then in place defined "equal work" restrictively, as "like work," as when a man and a woman perform essentially the same job. Art. 1.2 of the Directive then goes on to state that job classification schemes *may* be used to determine when "unlike work" might nonetheless be of equivalent value. British statutes on the matter recognized a woman's right to equal pay for work of "equal value," but only after, first, her employer had commissioned a study of the sources and effects of job classification in the workplace and, second, after such a study had determined that women were being systematically segregated into lower paying jobs. Under British law, however, women employees could not require their employers to commission such a study. In the Council of Ministers, the United Kingdom worked to preserve this situation, pending changes in the British law that might be initiated by the UK government itself. Indeed, during the negotiations on the Directive, the United Kingdom insisted on writing into the Council's minutes its understanding of the relationship between Art. 1 of the Directive and British law, namely that the latter would conform to the former once the Directive had been transposed.

In 1982, the Court ruled on the lawfulness of the UK rules (*Commission* v. *UK*, ECJ 61/81, 1982). In its defense, the United Kingdom presented a literal reading of the Directive: according to Art. 1.1, "equal value" must be "attributed" by some means; the only means to attribute equal value that is recognized by the legislation is that which is in fact found in British practice—the evaluation of job classification practices. The Directive does not explicitly confer a right on employees to demand, or an obligation on employers to commission, such an evaluation. Indeed, as the United Kingdom noted, its vote for the Directive was contingent on the reading just given, and referenced the Council's minutes on the matter. The Court rejected these arguments, declaring that the situation under UK law "amount[ed] to a denial of the very existence of *a right to equal pay for equal of equal value* where no [evaluation of] classification has been made" [emphases added]. The ECJ then ruled that, in national law, "a worker must be entitled to claim . . . that [her] work has the same value as other work and, if that is the case, to have [her] rights under the Treaty and the Directive acknowledged by a binding decision." (Denmark lost a similar case [*Commission* v. *Denmark*, ECJ 143/83, 1985].)

In phrasing the ruling in this way, the Court effectively (*a*) conferred a judicially enforceable right on individuals (to have the value of their work evaluated for the purpose of determining the existence of discrimination in pay), *and* (*b*) anchored that right in the Treaty (although Art. 141 says nothing about equal pay for work of equal value). Interpreting the provisions of secondary legislation in light of overlapping, and normatively superior, Treaty rules is a common technique in sex equality law. The technique displaces the Council of Ministers as the site of reversal. To overturn this decision, and many others like it, the governments of the Member States can only reassemble as a constituent assembly to begin the process of Treaty revision.[6] In this case, the Member States did act, but only to codify the Court's approach. With the Treaty of Amsterdam (signed in 1997, entered into force on May 1, 1999), they rewrote Art. 141. The Treaty now reads: "Each Member State shall ensure that the principle of equal pay for male and female workers for equal work or work of equal value is applied."

INDIRECT DISCRIMINATION

Making a case for sex discrimination in pay normally entails comparing the situations of two employees, one male and one female, or two classes of employees, men and women (but see the discussion of pregnancy, below). The so-called direct discrimination in pay exists if male and female workers are paid unequally for the same job, or for work of equal value. The so-called indirect discrimination exists if the difference in pay between men and women is based on criteria that, while being gender-neutral on their face, nonetheless negatively impact one sex more than the other to some significant degree. If courts are to adjudicate indirect discrimination cases, they will be led to probe the underlying logic of workplace procedures and policies. If judges are to be effective at this task, they will evolve, *inevitably*, a highly intrusive form of judicial review and lawmaking.

In *Defrenne II*, the ECJ took pains to distinguish (*a*) "direct discrimination," which it defined as situations that could be judicially established and controlled through Art. 141, on its own, without implementing measures, from (*b*) "indirect discrimination," situations that could "only be identified by reference to more explicit implementing provisions of a Community of national character." The distinction, the Court strongly implied, yielded a juridical difference: Art. 141 could be used to challenge direct, but not indirect, discrimination in the national courts. The doctrine survived a first

---

[6] The United Kingdom amended its law to conform to the Court's ruling by the 1983 Equal Pay Regulations, although Ellis (1996) reports further problems of implementation.

challenge (*Macarthy's*, ECJ 129/1979, 1980), before the second (*Jenkins* ECJ 96/80, 1981) all but destroyed it.

In *Jenkins*, a UK court asked the ECJ if Art. 141 required companies to pay part-time workers the same hourly wage as full-time workers, where women made up the bulk of the part-time staff in question. The Court accepted that lower pay for part-time workers might be "objectively justified," meaning defensible with reference to criteria unrelated to the sex of workers. However, it also held that where "a considerably smaller percentage of women than of men" work part-time, not least for reasons of family obligations, then "the pay policy of the undertaking in question cannot be explained by factors other than discrimination based on sex." The Court then declared that "it is for the national courts to decide in each individual case whether, regard being had for the facts of the case, its history, and the employer's intention," to determine if the "pay policy" is unlawful under Art. 141.

The decision extended the coverage of Art. 141 to one type of indirect discrimination, while setting the legal system down a path that would gradually place virtually all such discrimination under the control of judges. Today, women can challenge, on the basis of the direct effect of Art. 141, any situation in which they can make a prima facie case of indirect discrimination as regards pay and benefits (see *Danfoss*, discussed below). Defendant parties to a case—whether an employer or a Member State government representing the national legislature or administration—are required to justify their remuneration policies, usually on the so-called objective, economic grounds, that is, on criteria unrelated to sex. National judges, for their part, have a duty to scrutinize these justifications under least-means, proportionality tests. We now examine how this framework emerged, focusing on two decisions, post-*Jenkins*.

Bilka: occupational social security

In 1984, after several years of litigation in German courts, the Federal Labor Court asked the ECJ for guidance in a discrimination suit brought by Ms. Weber, a sales assistant, against her employer, Bilka, a department store chain. Pursuant to German labor law, Bilka paid a supplementary pension—"topping-up" the ordinary statutory pension—to its employees, provided that they had worked at least twenty years for the company, fifteen of which at full-time. Ms. Weber left Bilka in 1976 with fifteen years, of which twelve years at full-time service to her credit; in accordance with the law, management denied access to the company pension. Ms. Weber sued, claiming that the plan discriminated against women, in so far as women were far more likely than men to work part-time, given family responsibilities. The department store defended the scheme on what it claimed were purely economic grounds: part-time workers entail higher marginal costs, relative to full-time workers, and Bilka hoped to reduce costs through discouraging part-time work, not least by taking advantage of the law to deny supplementary pensions to part-timers. Bilka also was able to show that female workers received more than 80 percent of the pension payout, although they made up only 72 percent of the pool of pensionable workers. The Federal Labor Court asked the ECJ to assess these arguments, given its recent decision in *Jenkins*. The referring court did not hide the fact that it considered the Bilka plan to be discriminatory, noting that the store's part-timers were ten times more likely to be female than male.

The United Kingdom again weighed in against extending the scope of Art. 141. In the Thatcher government's view, secondary legislation (the 1976 Equal Treatment Directive) rather than the Treaty governed access to a pension plan. Further, the argument went, if the Court were to consider that the case more properly concerned *benefits*, rather than *access* to bene-fits, then a piece of legislation currently pending in the Council of Ministers applies. If the situation were otherwise, why had the Commission submitted to the Council its draft of a Directive on Occupational Social Security (adopted in 1986)? Citing *Defrenne I*, the United Kingdom asked the Court to remove any ambiguity surrounding the issue of pensions, by ruling explicitly that Art. 141 did not cover any employment-related, retire-ment pension scheme. These arguments were defensible ones, given that the Court had yet to hold that occupational social security schemes could constitute pay under Art. 141. The United Kingdom also claimed that Art. 141 "does not apply to indirect discrimination" which, coming on the heels of *Jenkins*, sounded like a last-gasp attempt to avert the inevitable.

The Court (ECJ 170/84, 1986) held that supplementary pensions of the kind offered by Bilka did indeed constitute "pay" for the purposes of apply-ing Art. 141. Although "adopted in accordance with the provisions laid down by German legislation," it was nonetheless "based on an agreement between Bilka and a staff committee," and thus fell within the scope of Art. 141. Citing *Jenkins*, the Court declared that:

Art. [141] is infringed by a department store company that excludes part-time employees from its occupational pension scheme, where that exclusion affects a far greater number of women than men, unless the undertaking shows that the exclusion is based on objectively justified factors unrelated to any discrimination on grounds of sex.

The ECJ then refined the argumentation framework it had begun to erect in *Jenkins*. The Court withheld reference to an employer's "intention" as a criteria of evaluation, and focused instead on the logic of giving "objec-tively justified economic" reasons for pay practices that negatively impact on women, relative to men. The Court did so discretely, tailoring its ruling to the case at hand:

under Art. [141] a department store company may justify the adoption of a pay policy excluding part-time workers, irrespective of their sex, from its occupational pension scheme on the ground that it seeks to employ as few part-time workers as possible, where it is found that the means chosen for achieving that objective cor-respond to a real need on the part of the undertaking, are appropriate to achieving the objective in question, and are necessary to that end.

The ruling in *Bilka* demonstrated that Art. 141 reached beyond pay packages governed by purely private contractual arrangements, to state-sponsored social benefits provided by employers to their workers. It also suggested that giving "objective economic" justifications for allegedly dis-criminatory pay practices constituted the only line of defense available to employers, and that such a defense would be subject to strict scrutiny by national judges. Least-means testing—based on assessments of "real need," "appropriateness," and "necessity"—had appeared. In subsequent deci-sions, the Court would treat these elements as self-evident, generalizable, and legally binding components of a stable argumentation framework, with least-means testing at its core.

Rinner-Kühn: social policy and the workplace

In *Rinner-Kühn* (ECJ 171/1988, 1989), the ECJ extended the *Bilka* framework to the judicial review of statutory-mandated social policy. At issue was a challenge to a German statute requiring employers to pay up to six weeks of annual sick leave for employees who worked more than ten hours per week, or more than forty-five hours per month. Ms. Rinner-Kühn sued her employer, an office cleaning company for whom she worked ten hours per week, after her request for eight hours of sick pay had been refused. Her claim was that, if Art. 141 covered statutory-mandate sick pay provisions, the German legislation discriminated indirectly against women. The clean-ing company based its defense on the statute, leading the presiding judge to ask the ECJ if the situation violated Art. 141, given that "the proportion of women adversely affected . . . is considerably greater than that of men."[7]

---

[7] During the proceedings, the Commission, pursuant to a request made by the Court, col-lected figures on part-time work in the Community. The data showed that women made up 89% of the part-time labor force in Germany, 83% to 88% in the Netherlands, the United Kingdom, Spain, and France, 62% in Italy, etc.

The case thus raised the specter of judicial review, under Art. 141, of national legislation in the field of social policy. In their submissions to the Court, Denmark and Germany urged the Court not to transpose its *Bilka* jurisprudence to public social welfare schemes. Advocate General Darmon took up these arguments with unusual vigor, warning the Court not to use *Bilka* as a template for the case at hand. To do so, he counseled, would place national judges in the delicate position of reviewing the decisionmaking of national parliaments, an inherently complex matter.

There is an essential difference between an employer, for whom wages policy is one of the most important areas of [the] undertaking, and a legislature, which is responsible for the common weal, and which must take into account a large number of social, economic, and political circumstances amongst which the respective number of men and women workers are just one factor.

He suggested that the law address this difference by weighting the burden of proof more heavily on plaintiffs who challenged social legislation. The Court, the Advocate General advised, should give the following answer to the referring judge:

a legislative provision that excludes part-time workers from the continued payment of their wages in the event of illness, thereby affecting a much greater number of women than men, is compatible with Art. [141], *unless it is proved before a national court that the provision was based on objectives related to discrimination on grounds of sex* (emphasis added).

Had the proposed ruling become law, it would have substantially reduced the political exposure of judicial review in the area of sex discrimination. On the other hand, it would have reduced the chances of women prevailing in such cases virtually to nil.

In the event, the ECJ did not follow its counsel. Instead, the Court held that Art. 141 covered sick pay, and that consequently the statute "must, in principle, be regarded as contrary to the aims of Art. [141]," unless the German government could muster an argument to the contrary. During the proceedings, the Court had pointedly requested the government to justify its statute on sick pay with regard to the criteria elaborated in *Bilka*. The government's response was that, compared to full-time workers, part-timers "were not as integrated in, or as dependent on, the undertaking employing them," and thus an employer's responsibility toward the latter was reduced. The Court formally rejected this submission, declaring that "these considerations, in so far as they are only generalizations about certain categories of workers, do not enable criteria which are both objective and unrelated to any discrimination on grounds of sex to be identified." It then announced a variation of the least-means proportionality test developed in *Bilka*. To mount a successful defense, Member States must convince a judge that the legislative "means chosen meet a necessary aim of its social policy," and that these means "are suitable and requisite for attaining that aim." The national judge has a duty to apply this test.

Summary and assessment

Bilka and *Rinner-Kühn* established the foundations of a highly invasive form of judicial review, organized by a doctrinal framework that requires judges to review the policy decisions of both private economic actors and public authorities. Just as in the case of Art. 28 and the free movement of goods, the ECJ quickly made least-means balancing a general, obligatory technique of litigating indirect discrimination suits where national public policy was involved. Further, as with Art. 28, it is probably impossible to establish fixed limits to the reach of the Treaty, given the expansive, rights-based, construction the Court has given to Art. 141. One can celebrate or decry this development, as being "good" or "bad" for the women's movement, business, the courts, or representative democracy. But there is no denying that the Court's move to require the legal system to tackle direct discrimination has bolstered the authority of judges to participate in the making of social policy, within processes that national governments and legislatures can not directly control.

III Judicialization: The Court and the Legislator

In the most general sense of the term, the "judicialization of politics" refers to the process through which judicial authority over the institutional evolution of a polity is constructed. In Chapter 1, it was noted that levels of judicialization vary, across time for the polity as a whole, and across policy domains (see Chapter 1). And it was argued that judicialization was likely to proceed more extensively under the tutelage of a trustee court, activated by a steady caseload. The "judicialization of policymaking," a feedback effect, is measurable as the impact of a court's case law (judicial rulemaking) on how legislators take decisions and strategically interact with one another (see Stone 1989, 1992; Stone Sweet 2000). In the EC, several mechanisms of judicialization routinely operate. First, the Court may construe the Treaty of Rome in ways that enshrine, as "higher" constitutional law, a particular policy outcome that Member States had assumed to be a purely legislative matter. As discussed, the ECJ found that Art. 141 contained protection for equal work of equal value; fifteen years later, with the Treaty of Amsterdam, the Member States codified the Court's approach. Second, the ECJ may interpret secondary legislation as if the legislative provisions themselves express or contain values of a higher, constitutional status. In doing so, the Court carves out substantive legal positions, or guiding principles for law-making, that lie outside the EC legislator's—and the Council of Ministers'—direct control. In both situations, the EC legislator has little choice but to adapt to the Court's case law. The policies produced by the ECJ fall within the Court's zone of discretion, as a trustee of the Treaty; there is no exclusive legislative authority. The field of sex discrimination, as we will now seek to demonstrate, has been heavily judicialized.

INDIRECT DISCRIMINATION AND BURDEN OF PROOF

Under the Court's tutelage, a relatively comprehensive argumentation framework for the litigation of indirect discrimination emerged and institu-tionalized through sustained use. In the last section, we examined how the framework organizes the arguments of defendants: employers must "objec-tively" justify their pay systems, and governments are obliged to defend their social legislation in the same way. We now turn to how the Court has treated a threshold question: what plaintiffs must show in order to bring an indirect discrimination case in the first place. *Bilka* and *Rinner-Kühn* are representative of the first wave of such cases. The ECJ predicated its rulings on a presumed fact, namely, that plaintiffs had demonstrated that women suffered disproportionately, as a group relative to men, under work-place rules or procedures that were otherwise neutral with regard to sex. It was enough, the Court appeared to be saying, for a woman to make a prima facie case of unfavorable treatment—through the marshaling of pertinent statistical evidence—to trigger tight scrutiny of proposed justifi-cations from the state or employers. The ECJ simply followed the lead of the national court of reference: the judge had already determined that a prima facie case had been made, and the Court had no reason to review that determination.

Not all national judges shared the Court's position—left implicit and informal—since it effectively reversed "normal" burden of proof standards applying to discrimination cases. Indeed, we know that, in some national jurisdictions, judges operated under different standards. Further, even under the Court's presumptions, women still faced significant hurdles in mounting a prima facie case. They needed to know a great deal about the policies of their employers and be able to trace the effects of these policies on pay and benefits, information that employers might not know themselves, or hide.

In 1989, with *Danfoss* (ECJ 109/88, 1989), the Court explicitly addressed the problem, which we simply refer to as the question of burden of proof in indirect discrimination cases. The case, referred by a Danish Industrial Arbitration Board, concerned wage policies agreed between an employer's association and a union representing mainly clerical employees. The system established equal pay for equal work, but also allowed employers to grant pay supplements to individual workers according to their respective levels of "training" (i.e. skill), "mobility" (i.e. flexibility), and seniority. The trade union's original case rested on the evidence of two women, working in different job areas, each of whom was paid a lower wage than a male counterpart. The Arbitration Board dismissed the suit, declaring that two examples were not enough to prove systemic discrimination. The union then returned with new figures showing that, for a pool of 157 workers, the employer paid women 6.85 percent less than men, on average, over a span of five years. The employer claimed that this difference reflected the implementation of the pay supplement scheme, which was justified as an incentive. The Arbitration Board would normally have proceeded to examine how the scheme operated with respect to gender; yet it proved virtually impossible to do so, since it was the employer's policy not to inform workers how they were being assessed on any of the three criteria. The Arbitration Board agreed with the union that the pay system lacked transparency, and asked the ECJ if the Equal Pay Directive had anything to say about the matter.

The Court's reply was that Art. 6 of the Directive, which requires the Member States "to take the measures necessary to ensure that . . . effective means are available to ensure that [the principle of equal pay] is observed," includes making "adjustments to national rules on the burden of proof." It then held that where a business "applies a system of pay totally lacking in transparency," the following rule holds: "It is for the employer to prove that his practice in the matter of wages is not discriminatory, [once] a female worker establishes, in relation to a relatively large number of employees, that the average pay for women is less than that for men."

The Court did not say how great the pay difference would have to be, or how many employees would have to be surveyed, for such a finding to be made. However, it made it clear that the evidence brought forward by the Danish Employees Union was sufficient.

Somewhat curiously, the ECJ tied its ruling in *Danfoss* to Art. 6 of the Equal Pay Directive.[8] In the next burden of proof case, *Enderby* (ECJ C-127/92, 1993), the Court "proceeded to a more general statement of principle" (Ellis 1998: 120–121), this time grounding its position in Art. 141, thereby constitutionalizing it.

The case was brought by a speech therapist who claimed that the pay system of the British National Health Service (NHS) discriminated on the basis of sex. Dr. Enderby complained that, at her level of seniority, the NHS fixed the pay of her specialization lower—on the order of 20–40 percent—than the pay of comparable professions that had a higher ratio of men to women. Two courts, however, had sided with the government, finding that the difference in pay between speech therapists and, for example, pharmacists and psychologists resulted from a combination of the effects of the labor market and the separate collective bargaining agreements governing pay for each profession. On further review, the Court of Appeal decided to ask the ECJ if Art. 141 required the British government "to justify objectively the difference in pay between job A and job B" and, if so, had it done so? The German government intervened on the side of the UK, arguing forcefully that since "the jobs of a speech therapist and pharmacist [were] not comparable," the *Bilka/Rinner-Kühn* test did not apply.

In its ruling, the ECJ admitted, for the first time, that its case law had tended to recalibrate burden of proof in favor of plaintiffs in indirect discrimination cases. Citing *Bilka* and *Danfoss*, it justified the move as a means of enhancing the legal effectiveness of Art. 141:

It is normally for the person alleging facts in support of a claim to adduce proof of such facts. Thus, in principle, the burden of proving the existence of sex discrimination as to pay lies with the worker who, believing [herself] to be the victim of such discrimination, brings legal proceedings against [her] employer with a view to removing the discrimination.

However, it is clear from the case law of the Court that the onus may shift when it is necessary to avoid depriving workers who appear to be victims of discrimination of any effective means of enforcing the principle of equal pay.

Of course, the *Enderby* case was unlike *Danfoss* in the most significant way: the NHS's pay system was a model of transparency. The Court, however, appeared determined to issue a rule of broad potential coverage: "[I]f the

---

[8] Perhaps because the referring court posed its question with reference to that Directive.

pay of speech therapists is significantly lower than that of pharmacists, and if the former are almost exclusively women while the latter are predominantly men, [then] there is a prima facie case of sex discrimination . . ."

It then held that, in Dr. Enderby's situation, separate collective bargaining agreements could not justify differences in pay between professions; on the other hand, the interaction of supply and demand for different kinds of specialists might constitute an objective justification, but only to the extent that the national court is able "to determine precisely what proportion of the [difference] in pay is attributable to market forces."

It is easy to see how the ruling could be generalized: *Enderby* made it clear that once women were able to mount a prima facie case of pay discrimination, based on relevant and "significant" statistics, employers would lose unless they could prove that they had not discriminated on the basis of sex. *Bilka* requires that such "proof" come in the form of an "objective justification." *Enderby* has since been interpreted as covering all forms of employment discrimination, not just pay, including aspects covered by secondary legislation, such as the Equal Treatment Directive.

In 1997, the Council of Ministers adopted legislation on indirect discrimination and burden of proof (EC Directive 97/80). Art. 2 reads:

Indirect discrimination shall exist where an apparently neutral provision, criterion, or practice disadvantages a substantially higher proportion of the members of one sex unless that provision, criterion, or practice is appropriate and necessary, and can be justified by objective factors unrelated to sex.

The outcome registers judicialization, in that the provision codified, as secondary law, what the Court had already developed as constitutional law. The remainder of the directive reflects the Court's case law on burden of proof.

Indirect discrimination and the national courts

The argumentation framework developed to handle indirect discrimination cases is remarkably similar to the *Dassonville–Cassis* framework the Court fashioned to deal with Art. 28 cases. Both require litigants and judges to follow a step-by-step process of argumentation and deliberation that ends with the strict scrutiny of the defendant's justifications for presumptively illegal policies. As in the free movement of goods domain, there are important discrepancies between the ECJ's requirements and how the national judges actually decides cases. As discussed briefly in Chapter 3, some national judges have refused to use least-means proportionality testing when it comes to reviewing "indistinctly applicable measures": national regulations that do not discriminate against imports on their face, but which nonetheless put imported goods at a disadvantage relative to domestically produced goods. In the field of indirect discrimination, we find similar resistance to the framework built from *Bilka*, *Rinner-Kühn*, and *Danfoss*.

Outside of EC law, the concept of indirect discrimination per se was virtually unknown in the law of the Member States. Indeed, the United Kingdom alone recognized the concept, having imported it into the 1975 Sex Discrimination Act, following a seminal decision of the US Supreme Court.[9] Beginning with *Jenkins*, the ECJ formalized a slightly different conception of indirect discrimination. Today, most of the Member States have adopted legislation that forbids indirect discrimination, although in some countries, including Germany and Spain, it was the courts themselves that constructed this area of the law. In 1992, Vegter and Prechal edited a report surveying how national judges have applied the Court's framework for adjudicating indirect discrimination. They found, as one would expect, significant variation across court systems. Only in Germany, Ireland, the Netherlands, and the United Kingdom did judges explicitly make use of each step of the framework. The German, Dutch, and UK courts imposed lower thresholds on plaintiffs seeking to make a prima facie case, while French judges apparently refused to recognize claims of indirect discrimination at all. German judges engaged in strict review of the objective justification proffered by defendant companies and governments, while UK judges used only a "reasonably necessary" standard, rather than a strictly "necessary" one. In the majority of countries, fewer than a half-dozen decisions in the area had been reported, so it remained to be seen what judges would do.

In the 1990s, this part of the sex equality domain—social security and the problem of indirect discrimination—supplied a far higher proportion of references from the national courts than any other. Prodded by lawyers choosing from a large pool of potential litigants, national judges began to master the doctrinal niceties of indirect discrimination law. The 1997 directive on indirect discrimination has further facilitated the diffusion of the Court's jurisprudence in the field.

Even if national judges fully understand the Court's doctrines, and work faithfully to apply them to the facts of the cases that come before them,

---

[9] *Griggs v. Duke Power Co.*, 401 US 424 (1970).

significant crossnational variation in adjudicating indirect discrimination would, we think, still persist. Balancing and least-means testing always means that different sets of judges, even in the same court system, will not always arrive at the same conclusions about the relationship of means to ends, or of a policy's "necessity," or "suitability." The preliminary reference procedure is only a partial antidote to the "problem," if problem it is. The ECJ does not, and cannot, process all cases. Just as important, the Court's case law is not always consistent (see Ellis 1998: 130–1). There are two obvious reasons for inconsistency. First, the preliminary reference procedure organizes lines of intra-judicial communication that go both ways, not just top-down. The ECJ has every reason to be sensitive to the needs of the national courts, if it seeks to elicit their compliance (see Chapter 2). When national judges have made it clear that they accept proffered justifications of national social policy to be sufficient to override a case for indirect discrimination in pay, the Court may well defer.[10] At the same time, the ECJ invariably reiterates its balancing doctrines. Second, there is always a built-in degree of discretion to judges in determining the relationship between the facts of a case, which are always in some sense unique, and the norm to be applied. In balancing situations, it is the stability of the doctrine, rather than the consistency of substantive outcomes, that tends to count. In this area of the law, the doctrine has remained remarkably stable.

OCCUPATIONAL PENSIONS

As noted, the Council of Ministers has consistently sought to exclude various aspects of social security, in particular retirement pensions, from the reach of the EC's equal treatment rules. In *Bilka*, however, the Court ruled that private, supplementary pension plans were to be considered pay under Art. 141, throwing intergovernmental control over these issues in doubt. In July 1986, less than three months after *Bilka* was handed down, the Council adopted the Directive on Occupational Social Security. The Directive's declared purpose was to extend equal treatment rules to private social security benefits. Yet again, the Council carved out exceptions for key areas, the most important of which, for our purposes, was the determination of

---

[10] Compare *Bötel* (ECJ C-360/90, 1992) with *Lewark* (ECJ C-457/93, 1996), cases that involve the extent to which part-time workers ought to be compensated for attending training sessions, given that such sessions would enhance part-timers' participation on workplace councils. In *Lewark*, the Court defers to the German Federal Labor Court's argument in favor of narrowing the holding in the former case, *Bötel*.

pensionable age. Given *Bilka*, these derogations from the principle of equal pay were arguably unconstitutional, since they would deprive individuals of rights guaranteed to them under the Treaty. In October 1987, the Commission submitted draft legislation to revise the 1986 Directive, Art. 9 of which declared: "when the pensionable age is determined for the purpose of granting old age and retirement pensions, it shall be identical for both sexes." The United Kingdom and France, at least, promised to veto the proposal (Curtin 1990).

With its decision in *Barber*, the ECJ (C-262/88, 1990) effectively enacted the proposal on its own, as a matter of constitutional interpretation. The decision "had serious repercussions throughout the Community" (Craig and de Burca 2003: 873), in that it all but required the reorganization of national pension systems.

Barber: occupational pensions

The case reaches back to 1980, when Mr. Barber was laid off by his long-time employer, the Guardian Insurance company. Simplifying a complicated situation, Barber brought an action against the Guardian, requesting compensation for the loss of certain redundancy benefits, including pension pay, due to discriminatory rules that permitted women to retire earlier than men. He rested his claim on provisions of the UK Sex Discrimination Act (1975), Art. 141, and the directives on equal treatment and equal pay. The complaint was dismissed twice, the second time by an appellate court on the basis of a UK statute that explicitly excluded death and retirement benefits from the application of nondiscrimination rules. It was this exclusion that the United Kingdom had sought to protect through Art. 9 of the 1986 Directive on Occupational Social Security. The ECJ's decision in *Bilka* revived Barber's appeal. In 1988, a third court, the Court of Appeal, asked the ECJ to clarify the relationship between the various EC rules and private pensions. Recall that *Bilka* involved a supplementary pension that the employer made available to full-time, but not part-time, workers. The Guardian's pension, however, was a legislatively-authorized, "contracted-out" scheme designed to replace the ordinary state pension.

Oral arguments were dominated by the question of whether *Defrenne I* or *Bilka* best applied to the situation. The United Kingdom argued that a pension plan that comprehensively substituted for a state pension must, by analogy, be treated more as a public than a private supplementary pension, and therefore must be considered to fall outside the scope of Art. 141. The Commission and the Advocate General sided with Mr. Barber, pleading that the Court's recent case law had restricted *Defrenne I* to purely public pension schemes. Pursuing various policy arguments, the Commission advised the Court to rule that Art. 141 covered the entire range of occupational pensions, including rules governing access. To do otherwise, it warned, would "convey the impression of a retreat from the judgement . . . in *Bilka*"; as important, the 1986 Occupational Social Security Directive "might be understood as having modified" the Treaty. The United Kingdom had, in fact, asserted that Art. 9 of the 1986 Directive on Occupational Social Security—rather than Art. 141 of the Treaty—governed the matter.

The ECJ sided with Barber and the Commission, ruling that "all benefits granted to a worker in connection to his redundancy fall . . . within the concept of pay for the purposes of Art. [141]." It then turned to the Guardian's pension plan. Working methodically through the criteria laid down in *Defrenne I*, the Court held that equal pay rules applied to the scheme. This meant, for all practical purposes, that Art. 141 applied to all occupational pensions.

It is important to emphasize at this point that, prior to 1986, none of the Member States considered, nor had any reason to think, that Art. 141 applied to occupational social security. Likewise, businesses had every reason to assume that pensions—conceived not as "pay" under Art. 141, but as "social security" benefits governed by EC secondary legislation—were largely excluded from the application of sex equality rules. *Bilka* had provoked Member State governments into yet another round of legislating exceptions to equal treatment, in the form of the 1986 Occupational Social Security Directive; the *Barber* decision voided the Directive in all but name.

The Court knew that its ruling would be politically controversial, and costly to implement. In some EC countries, like the United Kingdom, the Netherlands, and Denmark, the use of "contracted out" schemes was extensive. In the Court's own words, the United Kingdom had "emphasized the serious financial consequences" of finding for Barber. For its part, the Commission had suggested that the proper solution would be to apply Art. 141 to the Guardian's pension, while limiting the ruling's retroactive effects: "so as to make it possible to rely on this judgment only in proceedings already pending before the national courts and in disputes concerning events occurring after the date of the judgment." The Court, invoking "overriding considerations of legal certainty," declared that, in view of the relevant secondary legislation adopted by the Council of Ministers:

[T]he Member States and other parties concerned were reasonably entitled to consider that art. [141] did not apply to pensions paid under contracted-out schemes and that derogations from the principle of equality between men and women were still permitted in that sphere.

It must therefore be held that the direct effect of Art. 141 of the Treaty may not be relied upon in order to claim entitlement to a pension with effect from a date prior to that of this judgment, except in the case of workers . . . who have before that date initiated legal proceedings or raised equivalent claims under the applicable national law.

In response to the *Barber* decision, the Member States adopted the so-called Barber Protocol, which they attached to the Maastricht Treaty on European Union, signed in 1992. The Protocol states:

For the purposes of Art. [141] of this Treaty, benefits under occupational social security schemes shall not be considered as remuneration if and in so far as they are attributable to periods of employment prior to May 17, 1990 [the date of the ECJ's ruling in *Barber*], except in the case of workers . . . who have before that date initiated legal proceedings or raised an equivalent claim under the applicable national law.

The Barber Protocol did not attempt to reverse the Court's ruling. On the contrary, the Member States selected, from among several possible interpretations of the decision, one way to understand its temporal effects. They hoped to freeze their preferred interpretation of the "*Barber* limitation," through Treaty revision.

The *Barber* limitation could be read in multiple ways (Honeyball and Shaw 1991: 56–7; Whiteford 1996). Simplifying, the ruling was ambiguous on at least two crucial points. First, the Court could have meant that Art. 141 applied to pension benefits accrued after May 17, 1990. Workers whose pensions discriminated on the basis of sex could not, however, recover any pension pay that would have accrued between April 8, 1976 (the date on which, according to *Defrenne II*, Art. 141 could be relied upon in legal proceedings) and May 17, 1990. The *Barber* Protocol sought to mandate this interpretation. But the Court could also have meant that workers affected by the judgment were entitled to have their pension payments adjusted upward, but only after May 17, 1990, to reflect service periods going back to April 8, 1976. This second interpretation, obviously, would entail a greater financial burden on firms. Second, did the Court mean for the *Barber* limitation to apply to (*a*) all facets of occupational pensions, or (*b*) only to pension payouts? With the Protocol, the Member States had selected the first interpretation (Whiteford 1996).

Even before the Member States signed the Protocol, a new wave of references on occupational pensions poured into Luxembourg. Each asked whether Art. 141 covered some particular aspect of a private social security scheme, and queried the precise scope of the *Barber* limitation. In *Ten Oever*

(ECJ C-109/91, joined, 1993), the Court reiterated its stance on occupational pensions, this time bluntly stating that "it is settled law" that such pensions are covered by Art. 141, including survivor's benefits. It then announced that "given the reasons explained in . . . the *Barber* judgement, it must be made clear that equality of treatment in the matter of pensions may be claimed only in relation to benefits payable in respect of periods of employment subsequent to May 17, 1990." Seemingly, the Court had adopted the Member States' preferred interpretation. In their submissions, both the Commission and the Advocate General had counseled the Court to proceed in this way, arguing that such a ruling would simply reiterate what the Court had stated in the first place. They were joined by the governments of five Member States.

A second wave of cases tested the material scope of the *Barber* limitation further. Did the limitation apply to all aspects of rules governing occupational pensions, as the Member States seemed to believe? If so, then the Court's major finding in *Bilka*—that pension benefits are pay under Art. 141—would also be limited in time. *Vroege* (ECJ C-57/93, 1993) raised both questions directly. The case concerned the right of a part-time worker to join a Belgian contracted-out pension plan, with retroactive effect dating from the *Defrenne II* judgment. The Commission and the Advocate General claimed that the Barber limitation, being an "exceptional" point of law, must be construed narrowly, essentially to "factually-identical" situations. The United Kingdom and Belgium governments maintained that the Barber limitation applied, not only to this case, but also to "every kind of discrimination based on sex which may exist in occupational pensions." Invoking the Court's own arguments on legal certainty, they argued that neither governments nor businesses could have guessed, pre-*Bilka*, that equal pay rules applied to the field, given the relevant secondary legislation. The ECJ explicitly repudiated this reading of the Barber Protocol, supported in part by the Commission and the Advocate General. It distinguished *Barber* from *Bilka*, finding that the right of access to an occupational pension plan, which had been settled by *Bilka*, was left untouched by *Barber*, since the latter only concerned the provision of benefits under occupation pensions. Since the *Bilka* judgment "included no limitation in time," the Court continued, "the direct effect of Art. [141] can be relied upon in order retroactively to claim equal treatment in relation to the right to join an occupational pension scheme . . . as from April 8, 1976."

In a joined case, *Fisscher* (ECJ C-128/93, 1994), the Court confronted a Dutch pension scheme that had first been negotiated between employers and labor unions, before being declared compulsory for the industry as a whole by the government. The rules of the scheme excluded married women from joining the plan until January 1991, whereupon the same were allowed to buy into it retroactively, but only from January 1988. Ms. Fisscher argued that those who had been excluded were entitled to membership in the pension as from April 8, 1976. The Court found for Fisscher, repeating the reasons given in *Vroege*.

In both rulings, the Court addressed the *Barber* Protocol in the same way:

There have been divergent interpretations of the *Barber* judgment which limits, with effect from the date of the judgment . . . the effect of its interpretation of Art. [141] of the Treaty. Those divergences were removed by the judgment in *Ten Oever* . . . which was delivered before the entry into force of the Treaty of European Union. [The Barber Protocol] essentially adopted the same interpretation of the *Barber* judgment as did the *Ten Oever* judgment. It did not, on the other hand, any more than the *Barber* judgment, deal with, or make any provision for, the conditions of membership of such occupational schemes.

The question of membership is thus governed by the judgment in *Bilka* . . . which . . . does not limit the temporal effects of its interpretation of Art. [141] of the Treaty.

It is clear that, notwithstanding the *Ten Oever* line of cases on the actuarial calculation of pension payouts, the *Barber* Protocol did not induce the ECJ to abandoned its pre-*Barber* case law (Whiteford 1996). On the contrary, *Bilka*, now hardened as "settled law," organizes a continuous flow of litigation in the national courts, while the *Barber* limitation itself has been limited to the determination of pensionable age.

In 1997, the Council of Ministers enacted a revised Directive on Occupational Social Security (EC Directive 46/20). The Directive "reflect[s] the substance of the Court's ruling in *Barber* and its later jurisprudence on pensions equality" (Ellis 1998: 88). In EC law, however, the main source of such equality is Art. 141, not secondary legislation, an outcome that reflects the high degree of judicialization one finds in the field.

PREGNANCY

To this point, we have focused on the Court's Art. 141 jurisprudence, and how its case law on equal pay undermined the Member States' control over the evolution of the sex equality domain. The Member States designed Art. 141 with limited purposes in mind. It turned out, however, that the principle of equal pay, enshrined in the Treaty, overlapped with the more general equal treatment rules contained in the various foundational directives adopted during the second half of the 1970s. Indeed, by the early 1990s, the Court could hold, without generating controversy, that "a breach of the rule of equal treatment . . . is caught by Art [141]" (e.g. *Vroege*, recital 29). It is clear that the progressive judicialization of EC sex equality law was in part due to the "constitutionalization" of general principles that could not be found explicitly in the Treaty.

Determining the precise juridical relationship between the Treaty of Rome and the 1976 Equal Treatment Directive has never been an easy task. The Directive, after all, seeks to ban sex discrimination in work conditions, while Art. 141 commands the Member States to ensure respect only of the "principle of equal pay for equal work." Since *Defrenne II*, however, the Court has emphasized that Art. 141's true purposes were more extensive and grand, namely, to "eliminate all discrimination between men and women workers." In *Defrenne III* (ECJ 149/1977, 1978), the ECJ held that Art. 141 could not be extended beyond the question of remuneration, while also announcing that:

The Court has repeatedly stated that respect for the fundamental personal human rights is one of the general principles of Community law, the observance of which it has a duty to ensure. There can be no doubt that the elimination of discrimination based on sex forms part of those fundamental rights (recitals 26–27).

For its part, the Equal Treatment Directive has been interpreted as not applying to pay, which is covered by Art. 141 (*Gillespie*, ECJ C-342/93, 1996). On the other hand, in *P* v. *S* (C-13/94, 1996) the Court held that the Directive "is simply the expression, in the relevant field, of the principle of equality, which is one of the fundamental principles of Community law." *P* v. *S* involved the dismissal of a worker who had decided to undergo a sex change operation. The Court found for the employee on the basis of the Directive, while making it clear that an underlying, constitutional norm governed the matter: "The right not to be discriminated against on grounds of sex is one of the fundamental human rights whose observance the Court has a duty to ensure."

Thus, the ECJ's position is that the prohibition of sex discrimination is governed by norms that rise to constitutional status, notwithstanding the Equal Treatment Directive's formal rank as secondary legislation. The Directive ought to be considered as a kind of "constitutional directive." There is another, purely institutional, sense in which the Directive deserves to be analyzed as one would analyze the Treaty. The Directive was adopted under unanimity voting rules and thus can only be revised under unanimity. For most practical purposes, the Court's interpretations of the instrument are insulated from intergovernmental reversal, just as are its interpretations of the Treaty. It bears emphasis, in this regard, that the Court has interpreted the Directive expansively with respect to individual rights, and restrictively as regards exceptions to the equal treatment principle that the Directive makes available to the Member States (see Ellis 1998: ch. 3).

Here we examine the impact of adjudicating the Directive in one area of the law: workplace rules regarding pregnant workers. The Directive mentions maternity in order to permit derogations for social policies such as maternity leave. In the mid-1980s, the Commission developed draft legislation to deal more explicitly with maternity issues in the workplace, but the directive stalled in the Council of Ministers under the veto of (at least) the United Kingdom. In a string of rulings beginning with *Dekker* (ECJ C-177/88, 1990), the Court again preempted the EC legislator, enacting some of the core features of the stalled directive. The Court interpreted the Equal Treatment Directive as prohibiting employers from either (*a*) refusing to hire or (*b*) firing women due to their pregnancy, an essentially "negative right." The Court subsequently found that EC law also contained a "positive right" to paid maternity leave, being a social benefit that the Member States must require employers to provide to their female employees.

Dekker and Hertz: maternity rights

The first of two leading cases on maternity rights was brought by a Dutch woman denied a teaching position at a youth training center. The Center's hiring committee had explained to Ms. Dekker, three months pregnant at the time, that although she was the best candidate for the job, they did not have the funds to hire her. After inquiries, the Center had been told by its insurance provider that its coverage did not extend to "sick leave" for "illnesses" that might occur during the first six months of employment, if these illnesses could be anticipated at the time of hiring. The Dutch decree governing this particular part of the insurance industry treated pregnancy and sickness as similar conditions in that they leave an employee "unfit to work." Dekker rested her case on Art. 2 of the 1976 Equal Treatment Directive, the most general of the Directive's provisions, which prohibits employment discrimination on the grounds of sex, marital, or family status. Supported by the Commission, she argued that the insurance rules, the decree they were based upon, and thus the Center's decision constituted direct sex discrimination, since only women, but not men, could become pregnant. The Supreme Court of the Netherlands agreed to refer the matter to the ECJ.

In its observations to the Court, the United Kingdom advocated the adoption of its own traditional approach to discrimination. The proper test, the United Kingdom claimed, was whether or not employers would treat a woman as they would a hypothetical "comparable man." Thus, if the employer would have refused to enter into a contract with a prospective male worker, knowing that he would soon become unable to work for health reasons, then sex discrimination was not involved in a case like Dekker's. The proposed test would be an appropriate one, the United Kingdom explained, since "the Directive does not require that a woman be treated more favorably because of her pregnancy . . . than a man would have been treated in similar circumstances." On this issue, the Commission, the Dutch government, and the Advocate General sided with Ms. Dekker. Each took the position that the comparative approach would be ill-suited to deal effectively with pregnancy discrimination, since, in the Commission's words, "only women can become pregnant."

The ECJ agreed, issuing a ruling of broad legislative scope:

[Since] only women can be refused employment on the grounds of pregnancy . . . such a refusal . . . constitutes direct discrimination on grounds of sex. A refusal of employment on account of the financial consequences of absence due to pregnancy must be regarded as based, essentially, on the fact of pregnancy. Such discrimination cannot be justified on grounds relating to the financial loss which an employer who appointed a pregnant woman would suffer for the duration of her maternity leave.

The Court thus implied that it preferred to treat pregnancy as a condition that is both unique to women and analytically incomparable to other "conditions," such as illness.

In its answer to a subsequent question posed by the Dutch Supreme Court, the ECJ took up the appropriateness of the comparative approach more directly. The defendant had argued that "when an employer chooses from among exclusively female candidates, [that] choice cannot be attributable to discrimination on grounds of sex, because in such a case the employer is guided by other considerations of a financial or administrative nature." The Court replied that when pregnancy is the reason for the rejection of a prospective employee, "then the decision is directly linked to the sex of the candidate," even where no male candidates had been considered.

The same day *Dekker* was announced, the Court also rendered its judgment in a Danish case, *Hertz* (C-179/88, 1990). The case involved the firing of a part-time cashier, Ms. Hertz, for recurrent absences due to health problems related to giving birth. These problems, however, did not appear until six months after Hertz had exhausted her maternity leave and resumed a normal work schedule. The ECJ found that, under the Equal Treatment Directive, that "the dismissal of a female worker on account of pregnancy constitutes direct discrimination . . . as is a refusal to appoint a pregnant woman [citing *Dekker*]." It then turned to the questions raised by the referring court, namely, whether the Directive protected women against dismissals "as a consequence of absences due to illness . . . attributable to pregnancy or confinement." Reviving the comparative approach as a way of dealing with such situations, the Court ruled that a woman may be laid off for such absences, if a man would have been treated likewise in such circumstances. Thus, the comparable man test comes into play where illness is the reason for inability to work, even where childbirth caused the illness. In important *dicta*, however, the Court implied that this part of its decision followed from the fact that Hertz's health problems appeared after the expiration of her maternity leave. "It is for every Member State," the ECJ ordered, "to fix periods of maternity leave in such a way as to enable female workers to absent themselves during the period in which the disorders inherent in pregnancy and confinement occur." The *Hertz* judgment thus extended the protection afforded by *Dekker* to dismissals, and suggested that women have a positive right to maternity leave.

Following these judgments, the Council of Ministers adopted the 1992 Pregnancy Directive (Directive 92/85), under qualified majority voting. The legislation guarantees at least fourteen weeks of maternity leave, two weeks of which are compulsory, with pay not to be lower than that fixed by national statutory sick pay levels.[11] It also requires Member States to prohibit employers from dismissing workers on the basis of pregnancy. On these points, at least, the Directive enhanced the legal protection of pregnant women in Ireland, Portugal, Sweden, and the United Kingdom (Kenney 1994: 14; Cichowski 2004).

Since the adoption of the Pregnancy Directive, national courts have produced a continuous flow of references on the relationship of Art. 141, the Equal Treatment Directive, and the Pregnancy Directive to disputes involving maternity rights. In 1996, the ECJ held that "the benefit paid by an employer under legislation or collective agreements to a woman on maternity leave . . . constitutes pay within the meaning of Art. [141]" (*Gillespie*,

---

[11] The fact that the Pregnancy Directive equates maternity with sickness in this and other respects has been controversial (Ellis 1998: 261), given the ECJ's position to the contrary.

ECJ C-342/1993, 1996); it further suggested that the amount of such a benefit could not be "so low as to jeopardize the purpose of maternity leave, namely the protection of women before and after giving birth." This ruling, like others on the scope of protection for pregnancy and motherhood (see Cichowski 2002: 163–74), will generate further litigation.

Remedies, equal treatment, and maternity

This chapter provides a wealth of evidence for one of the core arguments of the book, namely, that the progressive elaboration of European Union (EU) institutions through adjudication tends to organize the activities of the EC legislator in ways that reinforce the legal system's capacity to control policy outcomes. Given the supremacy doctrine, it should not be surprising to find that the Court's case law also regularly influences outcomes registered at the national level of governance. In the sex equality field, a large body of scholarship has shown that the impact of the ECJ's case law on national law has, in fact, been pervasive. This literature, however, does *not* show that the Court's impact proceeds automatically, say, from a "bold" ECJ decision ordering the dismantling of discriminatory practices to frictionless and routine national implementation and adaptation. Instead, this research shows that the "Europeanization of national law" is a complex, messy, conflict-laden process, occurring, if at all, through painful negotiation and adjustment.

The Court's interaction with the Member States at the supranational level, and its impact on national law and politics, are of course related processes. The reader may have noticed, for example, that the United Kingdom intervened as a respondent in virtually every major case examined here. It did so hoping to maintain the control of the EC legislator, and to block judicial supremacy, over the evolution of sex equality law. At the same time, the United Kingdom constituted *the* crucial veto point in legislative deliberations within the Council of Ministers on social provisions (Pillinger 1992: 85–101). Indeed, that government has hardly wavered in its intention, publicly declared, to veto any European proposal that would enshrine, as EC law, rules not already present in existing parliamentary statutes (Kenney 1992). Our data on preliminary references (analyzed further below) show that adjudication in the sex equality domain has been driven by litigation originating in the UK courts. In this area of EC law, the legal system has disproportionately targeted the national rules and practices of the Member States representing a lowest common denominator position in the Council of Ministers. As we have shown, judicial authority quickly overcame legislative control of the domain, and lowest common denominator bargains produced in the Council did not stick. Instead, the Court has—systematically—ratcheted Member State obligations upward, in a pro-integrative direction.

The Court's sex equality case law affects national law in diverse ways. Kenney, who examined the relationship between EC and British sex discrimination law in great detail, showed that by the mid-1980s "the EC [had] eclipsed the British parliament as the arena of innovation" in sex discrimination law (Kenney 1992: ch. 3), primarily due to intra-judicial interaction. On successive occasions, British Conservative governments have been forced to ask Parliament to amend British statutes to conform to the ECJ's evolving case law. The Court's impact on the UK judiciary has been deep and profound (Levitsky 1994), despite the entrenched dogma of parliamentary sovereignty (Craig 1991).

To illustrate these points, we now examine the combined impact of two different lines of sex discrimination cases on the work of British courts. The first of these concerns remedies for breaches of EC law under the 1976 Equal Treatment Directive. As discussed in Chapter 2, the ECJ's rights-oriented approach to sex equality led it to insist that national systems make available "effective" judicial remedies. In the case of the Directive, the Court tied this requirement to Art. 6, which requires the Member States "to introduce . . . such measures as are necessary to enable all persons who consider themselves wronged by failure to apply to them the principles of equal treatment . . . to pursue their claims by judicial process."

The *Marshall* saga raised the issue of how Art. 6 applied to one type of remedy: compensation for damages. *Marshall I* (ECJ 152/84, 1986) concerned an alleged violation of Art. 5 of the Equal Treatment Directive, which provides for nondiscrimination as to "conditions governing dismissal." Ms. Marshall, a dietitian working for a British Health Authority, had been forced to retire at sixty years of age, whereas the statutory-governed, mandatory, retirement age for male employees was fixed at sixty-five. The retirement deprived Ms. Marshall of certain pension benefits. The UK government claimed that since Art. 1.2 of the Directive expressly excludes social security matters from the scope of the Directive, its own statutes on the matter were insulated from review under European law. The UK legislation, in fact, excluded all social security benefits related to "retirement and death" from the reach of the 1975 Sex Discrimination Act. In its decision, the Court announced that the exception for social security in the Directive "must be interpreted strictly [i.e. narrowly], in view of the fundamental importance of the principle of equal treatment." It then held that: "the dismissal of a woman solely because she has attained the qualifying age for a state pension, which age is different under national legislation for men and women, constitutes discrimination on grounds of sex, contrary to [the] Directive."

Having won rights guaranteed under European law, Ms. Marshall then returned to the courts to fight for compensation. Compensation, however, proved to be a difficult task. Applying the ECJ's judgment, an industrial tribunal assessed damages at £19,405, which included lost earnings, pension entitlements, injury to feelings, and interest. The British Sex Discrimination Act, however, set a ceiling for such reparation at £6,250, and excluded interest awards. An appeal—on the question of the legality under EC Law of these limits—reached the House of Lords, which forwarded the matter to Luxembourg.

The UK and German governments argued to the Court that EC law did not preclude fixing a ceiling on damages, as long as compensation was "adequate."[12] In 1993, the Court ruled (*Marshall II*, ECJ C-271/91) that individuals who have been unfairly dismissed under the Equal Treatment Directive possess "rights which that person must be able to rely upon before the national courts as against State authorities"; in protecting these rights, the national judge must "set aside a national provision which imposes limits on the amount of compensation recoverable by way of reparation"; and EC law requires "full and complete compensation," which must include "the award of interest."

The second line of cases followed the *Dekker* and *Hertz* decisions. In *Webb* (ECJ C-32/93, 1994), the ECJ reiterated its main holding in these cases, bluntly repudiating several entrenched orthodoxies of litigating sex discrimination in the British courts. In 1987, Mrs. Webb was hired by an air cargo company to replace a female clerk who was scheduled to take maternity leave. During her training period, Webb discovered that she too had become pregnant. The company dismissed her, on the grounds that she was no longer able to do the job for which she was hired. Webb lost a series of appeals, including a unanimous judgment of the House of Lords. These decisions deserve brief comment (for extended analysis, see Kenney 1995: 392–401).

The question before the appellate courts was whether Webb's dismissal constituted direct sex discrimination, to which they replied in the negative, contrary to the *Dekker–Hertz* jurisprudence. Simplifying, judges on the

[12] In 1984, the Court had held in *Von Colson* (ECJ 14/83) that although the Member States had considerable discretion in the area of remedies, compensation must be available and "be adequate in relation to the damage sustained." For further discussion of remedies, see Chapter 2.

various courts analyzed the case along two related dimensions. First, they used (what was for them) the "normal" approach to sex discrimination, which proceeds from a comparison between a man and a woman, using a "hypothetical man" as a surrogate if necessary. The first appeal—rendered by the Employment Appeal Tribunal prior to *Dekker-Hertz*—rejected Webb's petition on the grounds that the employer could have been expected to fire a male comparator if suddenly he, too, could no longer fulfill his contract. After *Hertz* had been handed down, the Court of Appeal upheld the Tribunal's decision, declaring that the British Sex Discrimination Act "expressly required a comparison to be made between the dismissal of the . . . pregnant woman, and what would have happened to a male employee in the nearest comparable situation."[13] In its decision, the Court of Appeal interpreted *Hertz* as evidence that at least some kinds of dismissals related to the pregnancy of the worker could be considered lawful. Second, British judges considered that justice would not be served by applying *Hertz* to the facts of the Webb case. The employer, after all, had shown sensitivity to maternity issues, hiring to replace, rather than firing, a pregnant worker. Under the comparative approach, *Dekker-Hertz* seemed to mandate "special treatment" for women—"treatment that would amount to discrimination against men" (Kenney 1995: 395–6).

In its decision,[14] the House of Lords distinguished Webb's case from *Dekker-Hertz*, declaring that: "The ECJ did not [in these cases] have to consider the situation where a woman, on account of her pregnancy, will not be able to carry out, at the time when her services are required, the particular job for which . . . she has been engaged."

Citing irreconcilable conflicts between the British Sex Discrimination Act and the Court's recent judgments, the Law Lords decided to refer the matter to the ECJ.

The European Court, in a terse decision, found for Webb, implying that the core issues of the case had already been decided.

There can be no question of comparing the situation of a woman who finds herself incapable, by reason of pregnancy discovered very shortly after the conclusion of the employment contract, of performing the task for which she was recruited with that of a man similarly incapable for medical or other reasons.

Furthermore, contrary to the submission of the United Kingdom, dismissal of a pregnant woman recruited for an indefinite time period cannot be justified on grounds relating to her inability to fulfill a fundamental condition of her employment contract.

---

[13] Reported in Industrial Relations Legal Information Bulletin (1992: 116).
[14] Reported in Industrial Cases Reports (1993: 175).

On the other hand, the Court left open the question as to whether the same protection would be afforded workers hired other than for "indefinite time period." Three months later, the Law Lords reversed themselves, finding for Webb on the basis of the ECJ's ruling (Kenney 1995: 398). In *dicta*, the Lords indicated that their decision might "not necessarily" apply to a situation in which the plaintiff had been hired on a fixed-term contract.

The *Dekker* and *Webb* line of cases, coupled with the *Marshall II* requirement for full compensation, produced a flood of claims from women discharged from the British armed forces. In the 1978–90 period, some 5,500 women had been forced into retirement on the grounds that their pregnancy had made them unable to perform their duties. *Hertz* led many of these women to pursue compensation. Prior to the *Marshall II* judgment, the Defense Ministry began settling claims at £3,000 per woman. In settlements reached under the *Marshall II* doctrine, courts awarded one woman £33,000 plus pension rights, and an air force pilot £173,000. By the spring of 1994, 1,800 compensation claims remained pending (Current Survey 1994: 221). These outcomes, and the underlying changes in practice that produced them, are concrete evidence of Europeanization. In this episode, EC sex equality rules were rendered effective for women in national courts, but national judges had to be dragged along in the process.

IV Adjudicating Sex Equality Law

The aggregate data on adjudicating social provisions are patterned in ways that reflect the Court's concern for giving an expansive, rights-based reading of the Treaty and secondary legislation. The data provide strong support for the narrative presented in this chapter.

Figure 4.1 plots the annual number of Art. 234 preliminary references and rulings in the legal domain coded by the ECJ as "social provisions," the vast majority of which concern sex equality rules. The first reference in the domain was received by the Court in 1970. By the 1990s, national courts sent an average of nearly twenty-five such references per year. Today, references in the area of social provisions make up nearly one-in-twelve of all preliminary references; most of these are sex discrimination cases.

Table 2.4 (see Chapter 2 for a discussion of the purposes of this table) shows that, of the EC-12, only Denmark and the United Kingdom show positive values in the "percentage difference" cell; that is, judges from only

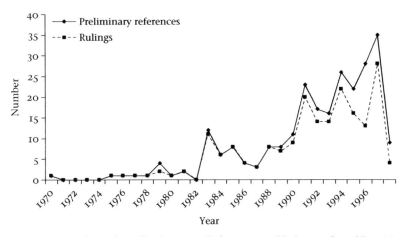

Figure 4.1. Annual Number of Preliminary References and Rulings—Social Provisions
Source: Alec Stone Sweet and Thomas L. Brunell Data Set on Preliminary References in EC Law, 1956-98, Robert Schuman Centre for Advanced Studies, European University Institute (San Domenico di Fiesole, Italy: 1999). See Stone Sweet and Brunell (2000).

these countries have generated a "disproportionate" number of preliminary references in this domain. The UK's percentage, 17.35 percent, is the second highest figure of any Member State in any legal domain. Indeed, litigation originating in the United Kingdom accounts for more than one-quarter of all references. While we cannot offer a simple or parsimonious explanation of the crossnational variation in references in this domain, we would emphasize several factors. First, sex equality litigation in the United Kingdom has been supported by labor unions, by a stable and growing network of labor lawyers who specialize in this area of the law, and by state structures (like the Equal Opportunities Commission) that serve as clearinghouses for information and other litigation resources (see Kenney 1992; Tesoka 1999; Alter and Vargas 2000; Cichowski 2001). Labor unions in Denmark and Germany have similarly provided legal services to individual women, and have sometimes brought cases in the interests of women in the abstract (e.g. *Danfoss*, discussed above). Second, although the matter is understudied, some crossnational variation in references is a function of the magnitude of disparity between existing national rules and new EC rules in a given domain (Cichowski 1998, 2002; Stone Sweet and Caporaso 1998*a*, *b*; Stone Sweet and Brunell 2000).[15] In the case of the United Kingdom, these factors are easily combined: British women are highly

---

[15] There exists a related research on national implementation of EC law more generally (Börzel 1999, forthcoming; Green Cowles, Caporaso, and Risse (eds.) 2001).

mobilized, can access legal resources relatively easily, and have a great deal to gain from litigating in the domain, given the UK government's remarkably stable position as the main veto point in the Council of Ministers.

Obviously, the more the EC legal system produces the kinds of outcomes desired by those who have activated it, the more subsequent litigation will be stimulated. Put differently, to the extent that intra-judicial interaction enhances the effectiveness of EC law within national legal orders, private actors will be encouraged to use litigation to pursue their own goals and policy objectives. Other things equal, positive outcomes attract more litigation, whereas negatives ones deter it.

We examined all ECJ decisions pursuant to Art. 234 references in the domain of sex equality. As in Chapter 3, we sought an answer to the question: what has been the success rate for those whose cases have been sent to Luxembourg by national judges? Second, we examined the relationships between the arguments contained in the observations filed by the Commission and the Member States, for each case, and the Court's ultimate decisions. We sought an answer to the question: to what extent do *amicus* briefs presage (or perhaps influence) the Court's ruling? Given our theory and earlier findings, we assumed that the Commission and the Court would exhibit a joint interest in enhancing the effectiveness of EC law within national legal orders, and in expanding the scope of supranational governance. We also expected to find that private litigants would win enough to attract subsequent litigation, given its cost, and that the preferences revealed by Member State governments in their briefs would not have a significant impact on outcomes.

In the period for which we have comprehensive data (1970 to mid-1998), private litigants invoking EC sex equality rules had a success rate of 55 percent, 107 of 187 rulings in which the Court had made it clear that a given national rule or practice (*a*) constituted a violation of EC law, or (*b*) did not violate EC law. Success rates rise to 60 percent when the "defendant state" is one of the big three, France, Germany, or the United Kingdom.

Table 4.1 summarizes our data on observations submitted to the Court during proceedings pursuant to an Art. 234 reference in the area of social provisions through 1993 (the date after which the arguments in *amicus* briefs are no longer systematically reported). It breaks the data down, by Member State, into five categories: rulings; observations submitted in *all* cases; observations that successfully and unsuccessfully presage the ECJ ruling; and the rate at which a given Member State intervenes in proceedings *other than those involving references from its own courts* (labeled, "participation rate"). Table 4.1 also includes data on the Commission.

Table 4.1. *Amicus* Briefs Observations Pursuant to Art. 234 Proceedings—Social Provisions

	Total rulings	Total observations	Successful observations	Unsuccessful observations	Participation rate
Belgium	11	7	4	3	0
Denmark	10	16	13	3	7.7
France	2	6	4	2	4.7
Germany	15	17	9	8	2.7
Ireland	4	6	2	4	2.4
Italy	3	9	5	4	7.1
Netherlands	18	26	9	17	11.4
Portugal	0	2	1	1	2.3
Spain	1	1	0	0	0
United Kingdom	24	52	29	23	43.8
Commission		88	80	8	

Note: N = 88. An observation was coded as "successful" if the written briefs filed by either Member State governments or EU institutions were successful at predicting the ECJ's final ruling and "unsuccessful" if the brief was unsuccessful at predicting the ECJ's ruling. Participation rate denotes the rate at which a given Member State intervenes (by submitting an observation) in cases beyond those involving its own legal system. This rate is calculated as the number of observations submitted by a country in cases not directly involving their legal system as a percentage of the total number of rulings not directly involving the country that they could have filed observations. For example, Italy submitted two observations beyond cases originating from Italian courts, and the total number of rulings not directly involving Italian law was eighteen, thus they participated in 11.1% of preliminary ruling cases that did not directly involve their national practice.

Source: Cichowski (2002).

As Table 4.1 shows, the Commission submitted observations in all cases, while the Member States vary widely in their propensity to intervene. The Netherlands, for example, participated in 11 percent of the Court's rulings on reference from courts of other Member States, whereas Belgium never did (indeed, it chose not to submit observations in one-third of its own cases). The UK government has been extraordinarily active, intervening in 44 percent of cases referred by the judges of other Member States. As we have seen, the United Kingdom has done so to defend its own national practices, and to persuade the Court not to extend the scope of EC competence in social policy further than it already has. Although its success rate is 57 percent, the United Kingdom lost nearly all of the most important cases. The Commission's rate of success is more than 90 percent. We also examined the relationship between (*a*) the number of Member States submitting observations, which we take as one surrogate for assessing the political or financial importance of a given case, and (*b*) the Court's propensity to declare a national rule or practice contary to EC sex equality law. The relationship is actually negative: the greater the number of governments intervening in a case, the more likely it is that the Court will render an adverse ruling. In cases where four or more Member States participate in the argument stage of the proceedings, the Court has found for the plaintiff 60 percent of the time; in cases where only one Member State intervenes, the Court does so only 52 percent of the time.

Our findings on the success rates of private litigants and on the influence of *amicus* briefs are remarkably similar to those reported for the free movement of goods domain in Chapter 3. The data refute Garrett's (1992, 1995) theory of judicial deference to the preferences of the larger Member States, and cast doubt on intergovernmentalist accounts of how supranational governance operates, more generally. We also examined each of the Art. 226 enforcement actions in the social provisions. The Commission prevailed in thirty-two of thirty-three infringement proceedings brought against Member States. Of fourteen cases brought against Member States for failure properly to transpose directives in the area of sex discrimination, or for a breach of such directives, Member States lost all but one.

PRECEDENT AND PATH DEPENDENCE

We now examine our data on citation practices, as one means of assessing how precedent has organized the path dependent evolution of the sex equality domain. Figure 4.2 plots the average number of prior ECJ rulings cited by the Court in its decisions in the domain of social provisions. The Courts cites more in this domain than in any other. One reason may be that the field of sex equality has been constituted by judicial rulemaking. The law of this domain is judge-made law. Practices associated with precedent enable actors to understand and to use of the doctrines and principles developed by the court.

In any area of law built principally by judicial rulemaking, one finds that some decisions comprise critical junctures in that law's evolution. These are rulings that constitute the necessary causal conditions for subsequent doctrinal developments. Thus, *Defrenne II*, which is doctrinally dependent upon *Van Gend en Loos* (ECJ 26/62, 1963), proclaims the direct effect of Art. 119. Absent the direct effect of Art. 119, the domain could not have developed into the differentiated, dense, and technical body of law it later became. It turns out that in EC sex discrimination law, we can identify critical cases simply by counting how many times they have been cited by other cases in the domain. The more a prior decision is cited by the Court in subsequent cases, the more likely it is that the decision furnished core

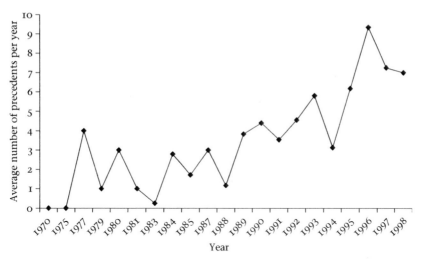

Figure 4.2. Average Yearly Number of Citations Per Preliminary Ruling—Social Provisions

Source: Data compiled by Margaret McCown and Alec Stone Sweet. See Stone Sweet and McCown (2003).

normative elements later used to refine an argumentation framework. Sex equality law is constituted by an interlocking web of such frameworks.

Our data basically retell the various stories told in this chapter. *Defrenne II*, cited in twenty-four rulings, is the second most cited case in the domain. However, its main holding (as to the direct effect of Art. 141) is today taken for granted by all of the actors in the system, so it is cited less and less in this regard as time goes on. In the social security field, *Barber* leads with thirty-one cites, followed by *Bilka* (twenty-two), *Ten Oever* (twelve), and *Rinner-Kühn* (eleven). In the field of maternity rights, either *Dekker* or *Hertz* are cited by every subsequent case (*n* = 12 in our data-set, which ends in mid-1998); after only two years, *Gillespie* had already been cited five times. We could go on. What is clear is that certain kinds of decisions—including those that expand individual rights, or extend the judicial protection of rights to new area—have begat new domains of law. As argumentation frameworks emerge, are refined, and diffuse throughout the system, they go on to organize new lines of legal activity. Each new branch of the law tends to develop its own relative autonomy from previously institutionalized activities, as argumentation frameworks take their own path of development.

The data show that categories of sex equality law, and then further differentiation within such categories, have evolved in both incremental and path-dependent ways. Judicial rulemaking (including doctrinal innovation) opens up new opportunities for litigation, which in turn enables the Court to recognize and then consolidate new domains of law. Responding to requests to clarify the meaning of "equal pay," the Court brought occupation pensions, end-of-year bonuses, vocational training schemes, maternity benefits, and so on within the protection of Art. 141. As discussed at length above, in *Jenkins*, the Court began to develop a test for indirect discrimination in pay policies, which it then extended and refined in *Bilka*. From this trunk, distinct branches of law grew. Each of these branches, in turn, can also be traced to a seminal ruling that furnished the necessary normative materials for litigating certain kinds of cases. *Rinner-Kühn* thus constructs the conditions necessary for the strict review of legislatively-mandated, occupational social security benefits, and *Nimz* (cited ten times) does the same for systems of promotion. Maternity rights are today heavily litigated only because *Dekker* and *Hertz* established these rights under EC law, while judicializing the legislative process at both supranational and national levels of governance.

New branches of the law can be said to be institutionalized when the Court no longer makes use of the normative materials found on other branches but, rather, refers only to those cases that have branched together. We find branching occurring in every sector of sex equality law, as litigation in that sector proceeds. Although we will not dwell longer on this matter here, the data show that, as sex equality law has expanded in density and scope through adjudication, the structure of precedent has become more "coherent," as coherence is conceived in Chapter 2 (see also Stone Sweet and McCown 2003).

What has made EC sex equality law path dependent? Without rehearsing all of the argument laid out in Chapter 1, three factors deserve emphasis. First, EC sex discrimination law is judge-made law. The nature and scope of rights to be found in Art. 141 and the 1976 Equal Treatment Directive have been determined by the Court, albeit in processes in which other actors actively participate. Because the ECJ exercises trustee powers over both instruments, its dominance over the institutional evolution of the domain is virtually assured. For most purposes, it makes no sense to consider the Court an "agent" of the Member States: operating in a huge zone of discretion, the ECJ enforces sex equality rules against the Member States themselves. Second, judicial dominance makes the outcomes produced by the Court relatively "inflexible," as defined in Chapter 1. Given (*a*) the constitutionalization of the legal system; (*b*) the Court's trustee status; and (*c*) the Court's propagation of relatively stable doctrinal frameworks to explain and justify its ongoing decisionmaking, adjudication comprises virtually the only means of changing the institutions governing sex discrimination. Private actors can therefore be expected to generate a continuous flow of litigation; for their part, the Member States have little choice but to participate in the domain's development, thereby helping to legitimize the Court's authority over that development. Third, adjudication in the domain has exerted powerful feedback effects. This chapter has documented some of these effects, focusing on the dynamics of judicialization. We now turn to how the Court's sex equality jurisprudence provoked and helped to sustain the development of transnational "civil society," whose central purpose is to enhance the Europeanization of sex discrimination law.

There is a small but important literature on the relationship between the development of sex equality law after *Defrenne II* and the construction of networks of lobby groups, union officials, law professors, and litigators (e.g. Warner 1984; Kenney 1992, 1994, 1996; Mazey 1998; Cichowski 2004). These networks lobby and consult with the Commission for the expansion of women's rights; and they monitor compliance with the ECJ's rulings, and sponsor new litigation in the national courts. Since the late 1970s, these activities have gradually been institutionalized, indeed, the Commission even organizes and funds legal action groups in this domain. This dynamic interaction can be traced over time.

While the ECJ heard few sex equality cases in the 1970s, the effects of the *Defrenne* litigation were transformative. The litigation, and the Court's decision as to the direct effect of Art. 141, created new rights for women, which they used to help expand the scope of EC sex equality law within national regimes. At the same time, the 1970s marked the beginning of Community legislative action in this area, and a Brussels-based infrastructure to support this policy expansion.

In 1976, the Commission established the Women's Information Service as part of the Directorate General for Information and Communication. This office represented a progressive innovation at the time, being the first official Brussels-based organization to promote information exchange between national women's organizations and the EC (Deshormes 1992). Among other things, the Service gave women's groups formal access to the Commission. In the same year, the DG for Employment and Social Affairs created a Women's Bureau, a policymaking unit established by the women civil servants and employment experts that were brought together to negotiate and develop the 1976 Equal Treatment Directive.

With these structures in place, activists working within the Commission were able to carve out a European space for the concerns and issues facing women. The work of Fausta Deshormes, founder of the Women's Information Service, is an important example. The Service's original purpose was to provide information to women's organizations throughout the Member States, through a news bulletin—*Women of Europe* (first published in 1976)—and the organization of conferences and informational activities at the national level. Under Ms. Deshormes's leadership, the newsletter quickly took on a central role in networking women's groups throughout Europe, notably through gathering information on the changing position of women in the workplace and in politics, and through reporting national failures in properly implanting EC sex discrimination law. In the 1970s, the newsletter was the main instrument for the dissemination of the Court's judgments to women's organizations, unions, and labor lawyers. In the 1980s, the *Women of Europe* contained a series of Special Supplements on Community Law and Women. These publications served as "major reference works" on EU equality law, were widely read throughout the EU, and subsequently fostered collaboration between national legal experts (Deshormes 1992: 51).

The Court's rulings also provoked and sustained activism outside EC organizations, in the form of informal networks and grassroots meetings. The Women's Organization for Equality (WOE) is one such example (Hoskyns 1996). The group originally formed as a consciousness-raising group in 1971 and by the end of the 1970s had a large membership and a monthly newsletter. In reaction to ECJ decisions and expanding EU competence in the area of sex equality, WOE decided to create a special subgroup in 1978 dedicated to "finding out how the European institutions work, what they do (and don't do) for women, and how women get into politics." This group, now the Women's European Action Group (WEAG), became increasingly formalized and powerful in the 1980s.

The legacy of the Court's *Defrenne* decisions carried over into the next decade. As the word spread through informal organizations such as WEAG and through the Women's Information Service, women and the groups that supported them brought new discrimination claims to the Court through the preliminary reference procedure. As the Court's case law became more dense and sophisticated, so did the network of women rights activists at the supranational level. Operating through non-governmental organizations and in Commission sponsored networks, this activism became a crucial link between national courts, the EC, and the Brussels complex.

The Centre for Research on European Women (CREW), which grew out of the WEAG, exemplifies this relationship. By the end of the 1980s, the Commission had institutionalized the process of consulting CREW on policy papers (white and green), and on sex equality legislation (CREW 1993). The CREW office in Brussels provided women with information about their European rights, and helped to coordinate the efforts of national women's organizations, notably through a monthly publication. The Reports, which were published between 1985 and 1995, became a crucial reference point for up to date information on ECJ case law and national legal action taking place in the area of sex equality.[16] They provided a wide audience across the Member States with information about the concrete effects of the ECJ rulings for women, and suggested how new rulings could be used to ground future litigation in various national contexts.

The Commission overtly supported this type of activism. In 1982, the Directorate General for Employment created a Legal Experts Network On the Application of the Equality Directives. The Network—a multinational group of lawyers, academics, and trade unions—provides country reports and updates on the implementation of EU sex equality law, and on the Commission's proposals for new directives in the field. The Network's research encouraged litigation of EC law in the national courts, and has been known to impact on national court decisions, and on the revision of national sex equality law (see Cichowski 2004). In particular, the reports examined the comparative advantages and disadvantages of using national courts and Art. 234, and provided best-strategies to potential litigators in specific domains of sex equality law.

By the end of the 1990s, women's rights activists were a highly-organized, taken-for-granted, component of European governance. Their networks were housed in permanent offices. In 1990, the European Women's Lobby (EWL) was established as an umbrella organization that now represents about 250 women's groups throughout the EU. Today, the EWL is the main peak association representing women's interests in Brussels. The Commission depends heavily on their expertise for legislative proposals, and for its help in monitoring Member States' compliance with existing legislation.

The 1990s were a decade of steady expansion in litigation, legislation, and mobilization in the sex equality domain. In the 1990–7 period, the ECJ had already received twice as many preliminary references in the field than it had in the previous decade! As this chapter shows, the diversity of

---

[16] Each *CREW Report* has a section that is specifically dedicated to ECJ case law and then subsequent national-level equality cases (the column "The Verdict").

claims being brought grew as the Court pushed its aggressive rights-based strategy forward.

V Conclusion

In this chapter, we have shown that the sex equality arena in Europe evolved progressively, through (*a*) the ECJ's construction of the Treaty and secondary legislation, and (*b*) the positive feedback of the Court's rulemaking on the activities of workers, national judges, the EC legislator, and interest groups. The Member States could not have anticipated these dynamics. Although they chose not to provide for the direct effect of Treaty provisions or directives in 1957, the Court found that Art. 141 and the core provisions of the foundational directive conferred rights directly on individuals, particularly women suffering discrimination in the workplace. During the proceedings in *Defrenne II*, the UK argued that the equal pay for equal work principle was "incomplete," and it cautioned that legislative—not judicial—authority should have the responsibility to "complete" this area of law, lest the legal system become the sight of continuous litigation. Such fears were realized: in this domain, constitutionalization led to extensive judicialization.

Member State governments have continuously been forced to play catch-up with the legal system. They have revised the Treaty, ratified the Court's policy choices in secondary legislation, and adjusted their own national law, all in response to the Court's evolving jurisprudence. These outcomes conflict with the predictions of Moravcsik (1998) and Tsebelis and Garrett (2001) who claim that European integration, as managed by supranational organizations like the Court and the Commission, *never* produce "unintended consequences." Moravcsik's most straightforward contention—which he packages both as a theoretical prediction and an empirical fact—is that the EU's organizations do not "alter the terms under which governments negotiate new bargains" (1998: 482–90). We submit that Moravcsik's category of "unintended consequences" must—at a minimum—include situations in which the Court's jurisprudence requires or prompts the Member State governments to enact the Court's policy choices in primary and secondary law. Given Tsebelis and Garret's priorities (the impact of changes in the EU's decision rules and organizational capacities on legislative outcomes), the category on "unintended consequences" must include—at the very least—the creation or development of new institutions (rules, procedures, policies) to which Member State governments would not have agreed, at any given moment in time, within then current decision-rules. Both theses are refuted by the evidence.[17] In the sex equality field, "unintended consequences" are a routine feature of institutional development, as every Member State government knows.

As discussed briefly in Chapter 1, case studies such as this one are open to various criticisms to the effect that one has selected off the dependent variable, a point to which we have two responses. First, selecting off the dependent variable provides an appropriate means of testing certain kinds of causal arguments (see Dion 1998), including those stating: that there will never be found an outcome, y, not caused by x. One negative finding invalidates the claim. As important, a case study can also help us to discover *why* the refuted claim—for example that the system of supranational governance created by the Member States *never* produces unintended consequences—does not hold. It may be that the refuted proposition might be restated in probabilistic form, and thereby rescued, but we are not sure how Moravcsik, or Garrett and Tsebelis, could do so.

Second, our analysis of the impact of the legal system on the development of institutions in one legal domain does not provide a proper test of the Court's impact on positive integration more broadly. We claim only that the narrative and the accompanying data analysis (*a*) add support to the theory of judicialization and integration laid out in Chapters 1 and 2; and (*b*) refute hypotheses allegedly derivable from intergovernmentalist integration theory. That said, Chapters 3–5 of this book are purposive case studies designed, in part, to enhance variation on candidate independent variables (see Chapter 1). Our analysis of the evolution of sex equality law, therefore, deserves to be evaluated in the light of how other domains of EC law and politics have developed. Because we have found that the legal system tends to operate in similar and predicted ways across domains that vary on theoretically-relevant dimensions, confidence in our theory is strengthened. Although our findings may help us and others generate new hypotheses about how integration has proceeded, we cannot test these propositions against the same data (Eckstein 1975).

The chapter does not address a host of important questions that we see as being important to the evolution of this domain. Virtually all scholars in

---

[17] See also the contributions to Sandholtz and Stone Sweet (eds.) (1998); Stone Sweet, Sandholtz, and Fligstein (eds.) (2001); and Chapters 2 and 3 of this book.

the field acknowledge that the Court succeeded in placing sex discrimination at the heart of the European agenda, an achievement that no one had predicted in 1960 or 1970. But the best legal scholarship has become increasingly exigent. There now exists a vibrant literature that critiques the Court's jurisprudence from various standpoints, including with respect to contemporary debates in feminist theory and gender studies (e.g. Fredman 1992; Kenney 1995; Senden 1996; Hervey and Shaw 1998; Ellis 2000). This literature shows, among other things, that there are inherent limitations to the capacity of law and courts to eradicate sex discrimination. Some of these limitations are material. Victims of discrimination need money, good lawyers, and a great deal of patience. It took Ms. Defrenne and Ms. Marshall more than a decade to have their cases finally settled. Some limitations are ideational. The law itself tends to reify distinctions between men and women, and their respective places in the economy, and these reifications can affect the development of the law.[18] In the social security field, for example, most pension systems are predicated on the assumption that the main "breadwinner" in any family is male. This assumption influences how judges deal with social security problems (Sohrab 1994; Fredman 1992). There would seem to be no reason to expect that judges are somehow less representative of elite opinion on gender issues than are other governmental elites.

Finally, we remind readers that this book focuses primarily on how European institutions evolve and institutionalize through use. At times, this focus entails searching for, and seeking to explain, feedback effects. *Judicialization* is one type of feedback effect, which has structured and has in turn been impacted by another macro process, the *Europeanization* of national law. We are skeptical of any approach that would portray either of these processes as automatic—or a series of simple mechanical adjustments—of one system, or arena of activity, to another. After all, we view the institutions created through adjudication as being, first and foremost, norm-based parameters that govern choice. We do not see law or precedent as sets of complete or precise commands. Judicial institutions organize argumentation, formally recognizing some kinds of politics and some kinds of arguments, while discouraging others. Doctrinal frameworks can

---

[18] Moreover, since the *Defrenne* cases, scholars and activists have regularly expressed disappointment that the ECJ has not gone far enough. The Court's steadfast refusal to rule that directives can have horizontal direct effects has been heavily criticized, for example, as has its lack of support for aggressive affirmative action programs (see the line of cases beginning with *Kalanke*, ECJ C-450/93, 1995). See also Prechal (1996) and Senden (1996).

help actors decide how to behave in relevant situations. But choice always remains, including with respect to the question of whether and how to pay attention to the Court's pronouncements.

In this regard, we noted that national judges have not always been willing or able to adopt fully the argumentation framework the Court has fashioned for dealing with indirect sex discrimination. We saw, in the *Webb* case, that national judges sometimes may follow the Court only when compelled to do so. And we know that actors—governments, legislators, judges, individuals—may seek to avoid compliance with the Court's ruling, or they may interpret decisions narrowly. In such cases, more (not less) litigation is likely. Although it is not our main focus, we also recognize that one of the most important, and largely uncharted, areas of research on legal integration concerns problems and inconsistencies in national application and adjustment to the Court's case law, which varies across court system, legal domain, and time. These problems have been generated by the Court's sustained commitment to making EC law effective in national legal systems.

5

Environmental Protection

With Markus Gehring

In the two domains of European law and policy examined thus far, judicial lawmaking quickly outpaced the activities of the European Community (EC) legislator and of Member State governments[1] producing, on a nearly continuous basis, the conditions under which EC institutions would subsequently evolve. In the period leading up to the Single European Act (SEA), governments adjusted their interests to the interests of market actors, and to the European Court of Justice's (ECJ's) jurisprudence on trading rules. The Member States did not reverse the *Dassonville/Cassis* line of case law, nor did they succeed in maintaining the Luxembourg compromise. Instead, increasingly cognizant of the mounting costs associated with maintaining disparate national regulatory regimes, they ratified the Court's moves, reducing their own autonomy in the process. In the social provisions field, policy outcomes fixed by directives adopted in the Council of Ministers have not stuck. The ECJ interpreted Art. 141 and the foundational directives broadly, in terms of their effects on individuals, as bearers of rights guaranteed under EC constitutional—not just secondary or national—law. National and intergovernmental interpretations of these provisions, to the extent that they would reduce the effectiveness of individual rights, have been pushed aside. Further, the Court has supplanted the Council as the locus of lawmaking on numerous occasions, enacting legislative provisions that had stalled under unanimity voting. Lacking the consensus necessary to reverse the Court in this area, Member State governments have been forced to adapt to the Court's case law, codifying the ECJ's policy choices in

---

[1] The Court established traders' rights in the very first preliminary reference concerning Art. 28 (*Dassonville*, ECJ 8/74, 1974) following the entry into force of that provision. In the field of sex equality, the ECJ found Art. 141 to be directly effective in the second preliminary reference of that domain (*Defrenne II*, ECJ 43/75); pursuant to the next reference (*Defrenne III*, ECJ 149/1977, 1978), the Court declared a "fundamental right," under EC law, to be free of discrimination based on sex.

Treaty revision, Council legislation, and the amendment of national legal regimes. In both domains, a continuous flow of references enabled the Court to assert and then maintain its control over outcomes.

In this chapter, we examine the emergence and institutionalization of a new policy domain: environmental protection. Prior to the SEA, the Treaty of Rome did not provide for the competence of the EC's legislative organs in this area; indeed, the Treaty made no mention of the environment at all. Nonetheless, in 1983 the Court (*ADBHU*, ECJ 240/1983, 1985) announced that protecting the environment constituted "one of the Community's central objectives." With the Single Act (signed 1985), the Member States formally recognized the EC's legislative authority in the field, competences that were strengthened by the Treaty of European Union (signed 1992) and the Treaty of Amsterdam (signed 1997).

Partly due to lack of Treaty basis, and partly due to factors to be discussed, the legal system's influence on the development of the EC's policy has not been as pervasive as it has been for the main categories of law and policy established under the original Rome Treaty. In the EC, as in national political systems, environmental protection began to emerge as an identifiable policy sector only in the 1970s. At that time, Community measures in the field were treated as regulatory harmonization in the service of market integration. Gradually, litigating in the area became routine, and adjudication became one means of organizing the sector's development. If the Court has not been the crucial policymaker in the field, it has been no less reticent, once activated by litigation, to use its powers to enhance supranational governance in the area. Indeed, as this chapter shows, the outcomes produced by the legal system are patterned in ways that closely resemble those produced in the free movement and sex equality domains.

The chapter proceeds as follows. In Part I, we provide a brief overview of the evolution of environmental protection as a supranational field of governance. Part II focuses on the Court's attempts to manage the relationship between freedom of trade and the EC's environmental policies. This case law served to legitimize the EC's competences in the field prior to the Single Act. In Part III, we assess the Court's interactions with the EC legislator and the Member States, from the perspective of delegation theory (see Chapter 1). The ECJ, when it acts as a *trustee* of the Treaty, determines the constitutional rules governing the field. We also examine what happens when the Court functions as an *agent* of the legislator, that is, when it is asked to resolve disputes about the meaning of provisions contained in EC statutes. We found no evidence that the Court regularly defers to the interests of powerful

Member States; it has, instead, pursued the "Community's interest," broadly conceived, even when engaging in routine statutory interpretation.

I The Policy Domain

In advanced industrial states, environmental protection began to emerge as a field of regulation in its own right only in the 1970s. Indeed, until the mid-1980s, no government of an EC Member State contained an autonomous Ministry of the Environment. Regulatory authority in the domain was typically shared among various ministerial authorities—of the interior, health, and agriculture, and among those responsible for public works, housing, planning, and transport (Weale et al. 2000: 223–5). These arrangements proved to be untenable. As environmental problems became more acute and complex, so did the need for more coherent, coordinated policy (Jänicke and Weidner (eds.) 1997). At the same time, new Green political parties and social movements succeeded in raising the political salience of environmental issues, effectively "mainstreaming" them (Jamison, Eyerman, and Cramer 1990; Dalton 1994; Bowman 1999; Rootes (ed.) 1999). Today, nearly all of the Member States possess a cabinet-level Ministry of the Environment, and most have created new regulatory agencies to deal with specific environmental problems.

The development of the Community's capacities in the domain follows a similar trajectory (Hildebrand 1992; Sbragia 1996; Weale 1996). In the 1970s, the EC became aware of connections between its commitment to economic prosperity through trade liberalization and mounting environmental problems. The Commission produced two *Environmental Action Programmes* (EAPs), in 1973 and 1977, establishing the EC's priorities in the area; and the Council of Ministers began to enact secondary legislation, under general grants of authority provided for by the Rome Treaty. At this time, environmental issues were managed by a small, twenty-person unit in the Commission, a Directorate General (DG) that had been created in 1973 to deal with matters of both consumer protection and the environment. In 1981, DGXI—for environment, nuclear safety, and civil protection—took on the task, and that body's importance has steadily advanced since. In the 1986–95 decade, the number of permanent staff in what is now simply called the "Environment DG" grew tenfold, to more than 500. Today, the DG employs around 600 staff. During this same period, a stable and dense network of NGOs and technical experts has grown to help the Commission draft new legislation and to produce rules under existing "parent" direct-ives. In the 1990s, Demmke (1997) reports, DGXI used more than thirty-five permanent committees in these processes; in 1989, more than 3,000 experts, nearly 1,800 of whom came from the private or NGO sectors, participated in comitology processes. With successive treaty revision, the powers of the European Parliament (EP) also increased dramatically, the result being that the EP's Environment Committee is today a major player in the legislative process (Hubschmid and Moser 1997).

THE TREATY

Until 1987, when the Single Act entered into force, the EC did not possess explicit, Treaty-based authority to take environmental protection meas-ures. In 1971, the Commission suggested that such competence ought to be exercised through what is now Art. 308 (EC), granting residual authority to the Community.[2] Four years later, the EC produced the first legislation in the field, basing it on Art. 308 and Art. 94 (EC): the common market heading.[3] The Single Act provided express Treaty basis for legislating, in what are now Arts. 174–176 (EC).

Beginning with the Single Act, each major revision of the Rome Treaty has established new and reinforced existing rules and principles related to the environment. The Maastricht Treaty of European Union, which entered into force in 1993, placed environmental protection on a par with the other priorities of the EC. Art. 2 (EC) now reads:

The Community shall have as its task, by establishing a common market and an economic and monetary union and by implementing [its] common policies or activities . . . to promote . . . a harmonious, balanced, and sustainable development of economic activities, *sustainable and non-inflationary growth*, a high degree of conver-gence of economic performance, a high level of employment and of social protection,

---

[2] Art. 308 (ex-Art. 235):

If action by the Community should prove necessary to attain, in the course of the operation of the common market, one of the objectives of the Community and this Treaty has not provided the necessary powers, the Council shall, acting unanimously on a proposal from the Commission and after consulting the European Parliament, take the appropriate measures.

[3] Art. 94 (ex-Art. 100):

The Council shall, acting unanimously on a proposal from the Commission and after consult-ing the European Parliament and the Economic and Social Committee, issue directives for the approximation of such laws, regulations or administrative provisions of the Member States as directly affect the establishment or functioning of the common market.

a high level of protection and improvement of the quality of the environment, the raising of the standard of living and quality of life, and economic and social cohesion and solidarity among Member States [emphases added].

This list of objectives is neither judicially-enforceable on its own nor hierarchically organized. The EC is to pursue these priorities simultaneously. The Treaty does not define the term, "sustainable development," nor does it clarify what a "high level of protection" would entail. The Treaty of Amsterdam, which entered into force in 1999, made two important changes. First, it revised Art. 6 (EC), which now reads: "Environmental protection requirements must be integrated into the definition and implementation of Community policies and activities . . . in particular with a view to promoting sustainable development."

Second, it amended Art. 95 (EC), permitting the Member States—with respect to the internal market harmonization measures—to adopt higher levels of environmental protection, relative to EC levels. Thus, the EC is now required to "green" its legislative procedures and outputs, while Member States are allowed to derogate from EC market rules in the environmental protection realm in order to enhance protection.

Several other "principles" of EC law bearing on environmental measures deserve mention. The Single Act introduced the "subsidiarity" principle and the "precautionary principle"; it also mandated that, where possible, the EC should legislate on the presumption that "the polluter pays," and that "environmental damage is to be rectified at its source." Subsidiarity is now found in Art. 5 (EC), but it was originally developed in the Single Act with reference to the EC's environmental measures. For our purposes, the principle permits the EC to legislate when environmental protection measures "can be achieved better at a Community level than at the level of the Member States." Subsidiarity is a binding constitutional rule, although there is no common understanding of how it should be applied in practice. The precautionary principle requires that the Community exercise special care when dealing with substances or activities likely to cause damage to the environment. The EC should act to prevent such damage, even when the science on the substance or activity may not be sufficiently developed to quantify the risk involved in failing to act in a preemptive manner. Nonetheless, the principle, per se, does not tell legislators, regulators, or courts what form precautionary measures ought to take.[4] The presumptions that the polluter should pay, and

---

[4] Invoking the precautionary principle, the ECJ upheld bans on the export of British beef during the "Mad Cow Disease" epidemic (*R. v. Minister of Agriculture,* ECJ C-157/96, 1998; *Commission v. UK,* ECJ C-180/96, 1998).

that environmental damage should be dealt with at its source, are also often difficult to apply in any consistent way. Automobiles are the leading source of air pollution, for example, but it is not obvious who should pay for the damage caused—the driver, the manufacturer, the producer of the fuel, everyone? Such pollution might be dealt with at its source, but only by requiring major changes in the internal combustion engine (Krämer 2003: 23–6).

In summary, the Treaty now requires the EC (*a*) to raise the level of environmental protection in the EC; (*b*) to prevent environmental damage wherever possible; (*c*) to ensure sustainable development; and (*d*) to integrate environmental concerns into its activities outside of the field—all without unnecessarily curtailing Member State autonomy (subsidiarity).

Legal basis of secondary legislation

The evolution of legal basis in the environmental protection field is enormously complex. For our purposes, there are two main sources of complexity. First, to the extent that Community action in the field of environmental protection also affects the operation of the internal market—production, marketing, competition, trade—proposed legislation is often justified under the common market heading. Second, from 1987 to 1999, the procedures for legislating under, respectively, the common market and environment headings differed in important ways.

Prior to 1987, the EC adopted environmental protection measures under (de facto) unanimity voting in the Council of Ministers, pursuant either to Art. 94 (the common market heading), or to Art. 308 (granting residual authority to the EC), or both. The EP was consulted, but its views had no binding force. The Single Act introduced qualified majority voting (QMV) for the adoption of directives designed to complete the internal market—under a new Art. 95. It also expanded the prerogatives of the Parliament. For Art. 95 directives, a new "cooperation procedure" was established, wherein the EP could propose amendments that the Council of Ministers could, nonetheless, override. In 1999, pursuant to the Treaty of Amsterdam, the "co-decision procedure" was established for most harmonization legislation, further enhancing the bargaining powers of the EP within the legislative process.

The SEA expressly provided for the Community's competences in the environmental protection field, through Arts. 174–176 (ex-Arts. 130r, 130s, and 130t). From 1987 to 1993, Arts. 175 and 176 read as follows:

Art. 175: The Council acting unanimously on a proposal from the Commission and after consulting the European Parliament . . . shall decide what action is to be taken by the Community.

Art 176: The protective measures adopted, in common pursuant to Art. [175] shall not prevent any Member State from maintaining or introducing more stringent protective measures compatible with this Treaty.

In 1993, pursuant to the Treaty of European Union, Art. 175 was amended: QMV replaced (de facto) unanimity in the Council. In 1999, after the entry into force of the Treaty of Amsterdam, co-decision became the normal mode of adopting legislation under Art. 175, while Art. 176 remained unchanged.

Thus, between 1987 and 1999, the gap between Art. 95 and Art. 175 (with regard to rules governing voting procedures and the respective powers of the EC's legislative bodies) closed, in stages. Where choices had to be made, the Commission and the Parliament typically preferred to legislate under Art. 95, rather than Art. 175 (majority voting, enhanced EP involvement), while the Council of Ministers typically preferred Art. 175 (de facto unanimity, reduced EP involvement). Not surprisingly, during the 1987–99 period, legal basis conflicts in the field became routine. We examine the Court's activities in this area at several points in this chapter.

LEGISLATING

Figure 5.1 plots annual levels of legislative activity in the environmental protection domain. In the 1970s, the EC produced a handful of important directives: on motor vehicle noise and exhaust, the quality of drinking water, the management of waste and toxic substances, and the protection of natural habitats and endangered birds. By the end of the 1980s, more

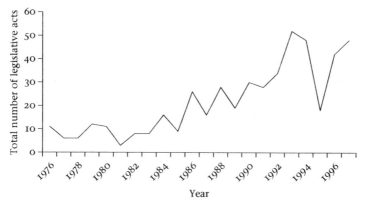

Figure 5.1. Annual Number of EC Legislative Acts Adopted—Environment
Source: Rachel Cichowski (2002).

than 200 pieces of legislation were in place, a number rising to more than 300 a decade later. Legislators regularly revise the most important of these directives, to meet new challenges and circumstances. Today, the EC's role in the field compares favorably to that of most federal states. It regulates across the full-range of issue-areas: nature conservation and habitat protection; air, water, and noise pollution; the composition, packaging, and recycling of retail goods and containers; industrial waste and drainage, including hazardous waste; and so on. In addition, environmental protection measures can be found in legislation produced by the DGs responsible for agriculture, trade, tourism, transport, and energy.

The EC's legislative agenda is organized by the EAP. Six programs have been adopted to date: 1973, 1977, 1983, 1987, 1993, 2002. The evolution of the EAP shows a steady move away from intergovernmental modes of governance. In 1972, the Commission proposed that the EC develop an EAP, not least as a substitute for explicit Treaty basis. France objected, insisting that any collective action in the field must be taken outside of the Rome Treaty, through strictly intergovernmental agreements. In the end, a compromise was reached, and the first Action Programme, elaborated by the Commission, was adopted in a joint declaration issued by the EC and the Member State governments (Krämer 2003: 4). After the Single Act (Art. 175.3), new EAPs are proposed by the Commission and issued through a joint decision of the Council of Ministers and the EP. The instrument is today legally binding.

The Treaty now also provides for strong supranationalism in the field. Co-decision is the normal procedure for adopting environmental legislation; and Arts. 2 and 174 of the Treaty appear to enable the EC to legislate in any area of environmental protection policy presently being made at the national level, notwithstanding the subsidiarity principle. EC measures in the field always constitute at least minimum standards of protection, although Arts. 95 and 176 permit Member States to opt for higher standards, but only in so far as national measures are based on existing EC legislation.

Within these rules, of course, there is wide latitude for developing alternative policy instruments and styles. In all federal systems, the question of which level of government should be responsible for the various aspects of environmental policy mixes with the question of determining how to balance the contending goals of economic growth and environmental protection. The EC has wrestled with these issues over the past twenty-five years, with no more success at finding stable solutions than other federal polities have had. The Commission justifies the EC's role in the field in two main ways.[5] First, many environmental problems are transnational in nature, and therefore must be dealt with at the supranational level; further, the EC itself creates or exacerbates these problems (a negative externality of economic growth), and should therefore be responsible for dealing with them. Second, because national disparities in environmental regulation impose differential costs on producers and traders, thereby distorting markets, harmonized environmental standards are necessary, in order "to level the playing field." In the past decade, lawyers, social scientists, NGOs, and governmental officials (including within the Commission itself) have engaged in a lively, mostly inconclusive, debate on how to determine optimal standards of protection, with what kinds of policy instruments, at what level of government (see Esty and Geradin 1998; Faure 1998; Esty 1999; Revesz 2000). In some areas, at least, the move is away from strict harmonization, and "command and control" instruments, and toward more flexibility and local accountability (see Scott 2000).

LOBBYING

Figure 5.2 charts (*a*) the number of new environmental interest groups registered with the Commission in Brussels, and (*b*) the cumulative number of such groups over the life of the EC. As in other policy sectors, the total

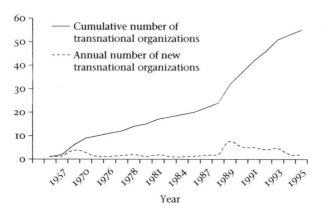

Figure 5.2. Annual Number of Lobby Groups—Environment
Source: Rachel Cichowski (2002).

[5] The Commission also points to the steady growth in the EC's role in environmental (as well as consumer) protection to counter criticism to the effect that European integration is more about liberalizing markets for producers, rather than regulating markets for the common good.

number of groups involved is far higher than Figure 5.2 might suggest, since Brussels lobbying is dominated by what are, in effect, peak associations.

Interest group representation in the sector grew gradually, in symbiosis with the Community's legislative activities (Webster 1998; Cichowski 2002). In 1959, only one NGO, dedicated to the preservation of forests, had a presence in Brussels; the 1960s saw the founding of a handful of public interest and industry groups, mainly concerned with pollution, transportation, and energy policy. In 1970, several NGOs committed to recycling arrived on the scene, and they helped push the EC to adopt the waste directives in 1975. An important turning point came in the mid-1970s, with the founding of the European Environmental Bureau (EEB), the leading peak association in the sector. Today, the EEB represents more than 130 environmental groups from across the EU and the European Free Trade Area. In the 1980s, NGOs with global constituencies, including Friends of the Earth, Climate Network, the World Wildlife Fund, Greenpeace, International Friends of Nature, Earth Action Network, and Birdlife International, set up offices in Brussels. These groups, joined by the European Federation for Transport and Environment, began coordinating their activities under the Green-8 banner in the 1990s.

Environmental groups do not enjoy a monopoly on lobbying in the field. Rather, they compete with producer and other industry groups—which are often better financed and organized—for influence over policy. In the 1970s, the Commission helped to create the EEB with the expectation that it would work to build support for EC environmental initiatives, as well to "offset [the] powerful Brussels based industrial lobby" (Mazey and Richardson 1992: 120; Barnes and Barnes 1999: 116). The bet paid off, as the EEB's influence on policy has steadily increased, often rivaling that of industry groups (Ruzza 1996). Until recently, business groups tended to focus their attentions on DGIII (the internal market). As the center of gravity for such regulation shifted, industry groups began to monitor and participate in the activities of both DGXI and the Environment Committee of the EP, and they have been successful at watering down several important reforms (see Krämer 2003: 48–9). With the so-called Greening of the Treaty, post-Maastricht, industry and environmental groups press their respective cases at every stage of the legislative process to which they have access. The 1994 Packaging Directive (94/62), for example, is reported to be the most heavily lobbied piece of legislation in EU history (Haverland 1998: ch. 8; Weale et al. 2000: 117).

LITIGATING

The disputes coded as "environment" cases in our databases fall into five main categories.[6] First, private parties may challenge the lawfulness of environmental regulation (EU or national) as a hindrance to economic activity, asserting trading rights under the Rome Treaty. Second, private parties may plead, before a national judge, that the government has improperly transposed, interpreted, or applied EC rules. Third, in some countries, NGOs are able to use national courts for what are, in effect, public interest suits against activities alleged to be in violation of EC environmental rules. If and how such suits are brought depends heavily on national standing rules. The Court receives cases in these first three categories through the Art. 234 preliminary reference procedure. Art. 226 infringement proceedings comprise a fourth category: the Commission prosecutes a Member State for a breach of EC law, including failure to implement or enforce an environmental directive. Fifth, the Court resolves legal basis disputes between the EC legislative institutions, and some of the most important of these have involved lawmaking in the environmental field. The Court has never received an Art. 227 submission, whereby one Member State sues another Member State for failure to abide by EU environmental law.

Figure 5.3 plots the annual number of preliminary references and rulings in the domain; we have excluded all references "joined" to the one case that is counted.[7] From 1982 through mid-1998, national judges sent eighty-two references in the field, of which sixteen cases were joined to one another. During this period, the ECJ rendered fifty-one preliminary rulings. In thirty-one of these rulings, the Court gave clear guidance as to whether a particular national rule or practice either was (*a*) a violation of EC law, or (*b*) not invalid under EC law. In each of these rulings, private parties had challenged the validity of a national rule or practice that a representative of the government chose to defend. In 55 percent of the cases ($n = 17$), individuals prevailed over the government.[8]

---

[6] For each of our data-sets, we followed the coding practices of the ECJ and the Commission respectively, although these practices sometimes differ.

[7] We also exclude from the analysis the first ten cases that the ECJ codes as falling within the environment domain. Each of these concerns the Common Fisheries Policy.

[8] In the period for which we have comprehensive data (through 1993), the Commission's briefs to the Court tracked the relevant part of final rulings in this domain in over 90% of the cases; Member State observations were successful in about 60% of the cases. For an analysis, see Cichowski (2002).

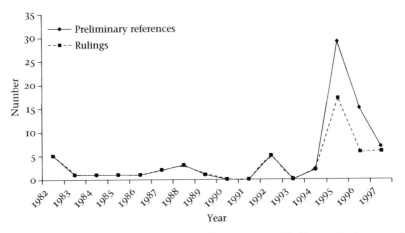

Figure 5.3. Annual Number of Preliminary References and Rulings—Environment
Source: Alec Stone Sweet and Thomas L. Brunell Data Set on Preliminary References in EC Law, 1958–98, Robert Schuman Centre for Advanced Studies, European University Institute (San Domenico di Fiesole, Italy: 1999). See Stone Sweet and Brunell (2002).

In its preliminary rulings, the Court has shown itself to be committed to environmental protection as a policy goal. When a national government wins an interpretive battle, it is typically against private parties who are pleading EC law in order to *weaken* environmental protection rules. To take the most prevalent class of cases, waste disposal and recycling companies have sought to shield themselves from criminal or civil penalties through the claim that national environmental regulations violate the EC's trading rules (e.g. *Gallotti*, ECJ C-58/95, 1996, joined to nine other cases). In the other important class of references, national authorities defend an enhanced level of protection for the environment. As a general rule, the Court will side with the Member State government, so long as the latter's environmental regulations and policy priorities follow from the Community's. Where this is not the case, the Court typically censures it.

Figure 5.4 charts the annual number of infringement proceedings and rulings pursuant to Art. 226 in the environment field (see also Tables 2.2 and 2.3). Since 1985, 12 percent of all Art. 226 actions, and 14 percent of all Art. 226 rulings, concern Member State noncompliance with EC environmental law. The vast majority of these allege improper implementation of EC secondary legislation. Since 1995, one out of every five Art. 226 rulings has been in the field of the environment. Through 1998, 212 proceedings had been brought, leading to 138 rulings. The Court found the defendant

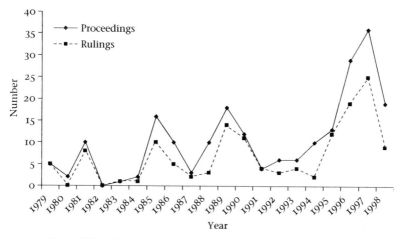

Figure 5.4. Annual Number of Infringement Proceedings and Rulings—Environment
Source: Data compiled by Markus Gehring and Alec Stone Sweet from the *European Court Reports*, the *Official Journal of the EC*, and the *Official Journal of the EU*.

Member State to be in violation of EC law in 122, or 88 percent, of these rulings.

Individuals, business groups, and environmental NGOs help the Commission monitor compliance with EU environmental law, and they continuously lobby the Commission to institute proceedings against Member States they regard as being in noncompliance. In 1982, the Commission received ten formal complaints from such sources; in 1992 the number of complaints rose to 587; and in 2002 it reached 700. Art. 226 proceedings are typically long, drawn out affairs. At present, the average duration between the formal initiation of a proceeding and the rendering of an ECJ judgment is about five years.

In contrast to the situation in free movement of goods and social provisions, infringement proceedings are a far more important source of the Court's caseload than are preliminary references. Relative to trade litigation, for example, some judges have been reticent to make references (see Ward 1993, 1999; Golub 1996), if a reference entails challenging a government's policy determination as to the proper balance between economic development and environmental protection. This reticence has gradually eroded. Traditional standing rules—which make public interest litigation in the national courts difficult or impossible—are another big reason (see Faulks and Rose 1996). Restrictive standing requirements, too, are eroding.

Although there currently exists no EC "right to a clean environment," per se, a series of directives adopted since 1990 have given individuals and NGOs certain procedural rights, including access to information and official documents (Krämer 2003: 136–46). These rights are often used for purposes of litigation and lobbying. In 1991 the ECJ (*Commission* v. *Germany*, C-131/88, 1991) held that directives containing mandatory provisions must be implemented in ways that will enable individuals "to ascertain the full extent of their rights and where appropriate, rely on them before the national courts." Although activists may rightly complain that this ruling has been slow to bear fruit, it is undeniable that national judges have since become much more willing to entertain public interest suits. To take just one important example, citizens groups and NGOs have successfully used national courts to quash planning and development decisions taken by national or local governments in the absence of environmental impact assessments required by EC law (see especially *Kraaijeveld*, ECJ C-72/95, 1996; *Haarlemmerliede*, ECJ C-81/96, 1998; *WWF*, ECJ C-435/97, 1999).

In 2000, the Commission published its *White Paper on Environmental Liability*. Among other things, the Commission proposes what it calls "enhanced access to justice." Although details are still to be worked out, the Commission states:

[I]nterest groups should have the right to ask [a national] court for an injunction . . . in order to make the potential polluter act or abstain from action, to prevent significant damage to the environment. They should be allowed, for this purpose, to sue the polluter, without going to the state first. Injunctive relief could aim at the prohibition of a damaging activity or at ordering the operator to prevent damage before or after an incident, or at making [the operator] take measures of reinstatement.

If adopted as law, the change would explicitly enable an important form of public interest litigation in the field.

II Free Movement of Goods and the Environment

In any new federal polity, the role of the legal system is likely to shift, in so far as market-building progresses and federal regulatory capacities grow. In the 1960s and 1970s, the European Court's primary constitutional tasks were to ensure the supremacy of EC law vis-à-vis national law, thereby helping to resolve the commitment dilemmas associated with federal arrangements

(Chapters 1 and 3). We view this role as a crucial, if primitive, aspect of modern constitutional judicial review. In the last two decades, the Court has increasingly been asked to adjudicate conflicts organized entirely by supranational competences and rules. In performing this latter task, the ECJ resembles, in authority and function, national "constitutional" or "supreme" courts, while retaining its own peculiar "supranational" characteristics. The clearest evidence of the shift occurs when the Court balances the rights of individuals, guaranteed under EC law, against the Community's interest in pursuing its own public policy goals. In performing this role, the Court has been led to construct a much more sophisticated form of constitutionalism. The adjudication of disputes involving alleged conflicts between trading rights and environmental regulation mixes both tasks.

Chapter 3 traced the evolution of one grand constitutional narrative: the development of the EC's trading rules through adjudication. This case law has exhibited enormous capacity to absorb new developments as they occur. One stream of environmental protection litigation comprises a branch of free movement of goods law.[9] Litigating environmental law did not begin until after the consolidation of the *Dassonville–Cassis* framework; and it took place against the backdrop of new, EC-level, market regulation. In its jurisprudence on Art. 28, the ECJ had given strong advantages to traders and the Commission in their efforts to use the courts to open markets. At the same time, the EC and the Member States had come to view environmental hazards as a negative externality of market liberalization, which in turn led them to consider more aggressive measures to protect the environment. Once applied to specific market activities, these two logics inevitably collided with one another, litigation being the result.

BALANCING TRADERS' RIGHTS AGAINST THE GENERAL INTEREST

The first important environmental protection cases were brought by waste management companies, who claimed that their rights under the Treaty of Rome had been violated by national and EC rules regulating waste disposal.

---

[9] In this chapter, we do not discuss an important line of cases that make up this stream: preliminary references involving the prosecution of individuals for trading in wild bird species. In response, the Court developed proportionality tests to resolve disputes that pit the rights of traders against the EC's interest in wild bird conservation. The seminal cases are *Gourmettrie Van den Berg* (ECJ C-169/89, 1990); *Vergy* (ECJ C-149/94, 1996); and *Van der Feesten* (ECJ C-202/94, 1996). For commentary on the early case law, see Freestone (1996) and Wils (1994).

In 1975, the Council adopted Directive 75/439 on waste oils, and framework legislation, and Directive 75/442, on waste disposal more generally. Directive 75/439 required the Member States to "take the necessary measures to ensure the safe collection and disposal of waste oils, preferably by recycling." It further authorized the Member States, when these aims "[could] not otherwise be achieved," to divide their territory into zones of waste recovery, and to certify those companies that would provide services for each zone. Some Member States introduced a permit system that granted exclusive rights to designated companies. Undertakings excluded by the system, and those prosecuted for breaching them, sought to defend their interests in the Courts. Because waste oils constituted an exchangeable "good" and were therefore subject to free movement of goods provisions, they claimed that their rights under EC law had been abridged by these new disposal arrangements. In *Inter-Huiles* (ECJ 172/82, 1983), the Court confronted the French version of the system, a 1979 decree that made it virtually impossible to legally export waste oils to disposal sites in other Member States. The French government sought to justify the decree on environmental protection grounds, a defense the Court rejected. No Member State, it ruled, could organize its disposal system in ways that blocked exports of waste oils to facilities lawfully operating in, and authorized by, other Member States. In a series of subsequent cases involving Directives 75/439 and 75/442, the Court upheld the rights of companies to trade waste across borders (e.g. *Rhônes-Alpes Huiles*, ECJ 295/82; *Vanacker*, ECJ C-37/92, 1993; *Chemische Afvalstoffen*, C-203/96, 1998; *FFAD*, C-209/98, 2000).

In *Inter-Huiles*, the Court engaged in a classic form of review: helping a national judge assess whether a Member State government had properly transposed a directive. The ECJ held, in effect, that the French decree was disproportionate to the purpose of the Directive 75/439 and to the Treaty's free movement of goods provisions. We saw in Chapters 3 and 4 that it has been the Court's policy to tightly control national discretion where that discretion might be used to restrict the exercise of fundamental rights or principles guaranteed by the Treaty. *Inter-Huiles* simply replicates the move in a new legal domain. The Court skirted the much more delicate question of whether the Directive itself might conflict with the Treaty. Two weeks after the ECJ handed down *Inter-Huiles*, a different French court raised just that issue. In *ADBHU* (ECJ 240/83, 1985), the Court, for the first time, considered the rights of traders in light of the Community's interest in protecting the environment.

ADBHU: limits to "Freedom of Trade"

The French decree implementing Directive 75/439 forbade the burning of waste oils as fuel, while providing for the collection, disposal, and recycling of such waste by authorized companies in specified zones of activity. Pursuant to the decree, the French public prosecutor sought to abolish an association (ADBHU), whose purpose was to defend the commercial interests of those who manufactured and used stoves that burned waste oil, on the grounds that the Association's activities comprised an incitement to commit a criminal offense. The Association responded by attacking the French and the EC rules as being invalid under the Treaty (free movement of goods, freedom to provide services, and anti-trust rules), leading the judge to refer the matter to Luxembourg. In hearings, Italy, the Council of Ministers, and the Commission urged the Court to find the Directive compatible with the Treaty. If proportionality principles were respected, they argued, the Directive would not restrict intra-EC trade more than would be necessary to achieve the "general interest"—which they characterized as the duty of public authorities "to ensure that the disposal of waste oils is carried out in a way [that] avoids harm to the environment."

In its decision, the Court stressed that "the principles of free movement of goods and freedom of competition, together with freedom of trade as a fundamental right, are general principles of Community law of which the Court ensures obedience." It then went on to uphold the Directive in the following terms:

[T]he principle of freedom of trade is not to be viewed in absolute terms but is subject to certain limits justified by the objectives of general interest pursued by the Community provided that the rights in question are not substantially impaired.

There is no reason to conclude that the Directive has exceeded those limits. The Directive must be seen in the perspective of environmental protection, which is one of the Community's essential objectives.

It follows from the foregoing that . . . in so far as such measures, in particular the requirement that permits must be obtained in advance, have a restrictive effect on the freedom of trade and of competition, they must nevertheless neither be discriminatory nor go beyond the inevitable restrictions . . . justified by the pursuit of the objective of environmental protection, which is in the general interest.

The ruling thereby secured the Directive's constitutional validity, while mandating strict scrutiny of national implementing measures with regard to free movement rules.

ADBHU is considered a "landmark decision" (Demiray 1994: 83; Krämer 1993: 112): the Court identified environmental protection as an "essential objective" of the Community, thus legitimizing the policy domain in the absence of explicit Treaty basis. The ruling also deserves to be assessed as an important step in the maturation of the system of constitutional judicial review in a quasi-federal EC. Given shared competences and the nature of the preliminary reference system, the legal system will always be asked to review the compatibility of national law with EC law. In activities characterized as "negative integration," the legal system operates to remove national barriers to intra-EC trade and other forms of transnational exchange. In activities typically considered to be "positive integration," the legal system works to ensure that EC law is properly transposed and enforced in national legal systems. In *ADBHU*, the Court is led to manage the relationship between negative and positive integration. Both parties rested their cases on EC norms asserted to be of fundamental—that is, of constitutional—status. When one party attacks the validity or application of an EC statutory rule on the basis of a fundamental freedom (free movement of goods, workers, freedom to provide services, and so on), the defense can only be that the EC legislation constitutes a means to attain a fundamental objective of the Community. As claimed throughout this book, we expect the judicial response to be to erect least-means, proportionality balancing standards. In *ADBHU*, the Commission and the Council of Ministers counseled the Court to do so, thereby enhancing the social legitimacy of what constitutes, in effect, an extension of its authority in a new area of European policymaking.

Today, as Temmink (2000: 63) puts it, the Court "plays a decisive role in locating the balance between free movement of goods and environmental objectives."

TRADERS' RIGHTS, THE COMMUNITY INTEREST, AND MEMBER STATE AUTONOMY

Certain generic problems of how best to regulate to protect the environment in a federal system have not been resolved anywhere, let alone in the EC. Determining which level of government ought to regulate, under what restrictions, is perhaps the most important example. Here we examine two infringement cases that the Commission brought against Member States for having enacted environmental regulations in violation of free movement of goods provisions. The first—*Danish Bottles* (ECJ 302/86, 1988)—concerned a regulatory matter that had not yet been preempted by Community legislation. The second—*Wallonian Waste* (ECJ C-2/90, 1992)—concerned a decree issued by a subnational government that seemed to contravene both Art. 28 and existing EC directives on waste disposal. Although the Court's decisions are not easy to reconcile with one another, both innovated on its *Dassonville–Cassis* jurisprudence in ways that further enhanced the role of the Court.

Commission v. *Denmark: environmental protection as mandatory requirement*

In 1981, Denmark introduced rules requiring all beer and soft drinks marketed on its territory to be sold in returnable, recyclable containers. The government established a procedure for approving containers, to be administered by the National Agency for the Protection of the Environment. The Agency possessed powers to refuse approval of (*a*) containers deemed to be "technically unsuitable" for a deposit-and-return system or reuse, and (*b*) containers for which there existed an "available and suitable" alternative that had been previously approved. In practice, the Agency also sought to limit the number of approved containers to around thirty, on the grounds that retailers should not be made to bear the higher costs of handling and storing multiple formats. Prompted by interest groups representing retail interests in Brussels, the Commission took the view that the mandatory deposit-and-return system and the preapproval procedure were incompatible with Art. 28. After a series of written exchanges, Denmark agreed to soften its rules in 1984. Amendments exempted non-metal bottles from the system of prior approval, for (*a*) imported drinks meant to test the Danish market, and (*b*) yet to be approved containers for quantities not to exceed a maximum of 3,000 hectoliters per year. The Brussels-based groups maintained their opposition to the rules and, in 1986, the Commission decided to refer the matter to the Court.

In the Commission's view, the system failed the test of proportionality established by the ECJ for indistinctly applicable measures (IAMs) having the potential to hinder EC trade. IAMs are national product or marketing standards that apply equally to both domestic and imported goods. In *Cassis de Dijon* (ECJ 120/78, 1979), the Court extended the coverage of Art. 28 and least-means balancing to IAMs, that is, to the whole of national regulatory regimes; it tempered the move by making available to national authorities a new set of justifiable derogations (see Chapter 3). Claimed Art. 28 derogations—the jurisprudence of "mandatory requirements," or the "rule of reason"—are available only for regulatory matters not yet harmonized, subject to the strict proportionality review of the courts. At the time "Danish Bottles" was being heard, the list of headings available for such treatment did not include environmental protection. Nonetheless, the Court's ruling in *ADBHU* gave Denmark a strong basis for its claim that the recycling system could be justified under just such a heading.

In it decision, the Court rehearsed what it called its "established case law," citing *Cassis de Dijon*, before moving on to the Danish government's defense:

The Court has already held in its judgment [in *ADBHU*] that the protection of the environment is "one of the Community's essential objectives," which may justify certain limitations of the principle of free movement of goods. That view is moreover confirmed by the Single European Act.

In view of the foregoing, it must therefore be stated that the protection of the environment is a mandatory requirement [that] may limit the application of Article [28] of the Treaty.

It then turned to assessing the proportionality of the Danish measures. In a series of terse declarations, the Court held that establishing an efficient deposit-and-return system in itself could not be regarded as disproportionate to the goal of environmental protection, even if it did raise importers' costs. However, it viewed a procedure for prior approval of containers to be presumptively unjustified, to the extent that the Agency could refuse authorization "even [where the importer] is prepared to ensure that returned containers are re-used." The Danish solution to the problem—relaxing the preapproval requirement for a limited quantity of containers otherwise subject to the deposit-and-return regime—did not save the system. In the Court's view, even the amended procedures went too far: to ensure an efficient recycling system, Denmark had been led to restrict the rights of traders too much.

Commission v. *Belgium: preemption and mandatory requirements*

In 1983, the Walloon regional government moved to prohibit the dumping or storage of waste from "a foreign state," including any "region of Belgium other than Wallonia." The decree was reissued in 1987. After receiving complaints on the matter from waste disposal businesses in and outside of Belgium, the Commission outlined its objections to the prohibition in letters to the Belgian government sent in 1988 and again in 1990. The Belgian government chose not to respond to the letters, leading the Commission to refer the matter to the ECJ.

The Commission alleged that the Walloon decree violated Council directives on waste and Art. 30 of the Treaty. First, Council Directive 75/442
sought to harmonize market rules, to create a level playing field for traders in
waste while promoting the protection of human health and the environment. The Directive required the Member States to develop arrangements
for the reduction in, and the safe collection and recycling of, waste, in consultation with the Commission. It further required the Member States to certify and supervise waste disposal and recycling concerns, while prohibiting
them from developing a system that would either "obstruct intra-EC trade
[or negatively] affect the conditions of competition." Council Directive
84/631 permitted cross-border movement of hazardous waste, once holders
of such waste had notified the Member States concerned, and had received
approval for shipment. The Commission argued that these directives did not
allow any authority to completely ban the shipment or storage of waste from
another Member State. Second, the Commission argued that the decree violated rules governing the free movement of goods. Given the Court's case
law on Art. 28 (see Chapter 3), the Commission was confident in its assertion
that Belgium could not make claims to derogations under Art. 28 (e.g. under
the headings of public health or environmental protection). Community
legislation had preempted the field, and the measures in question directly
discriminated between "domestic" and "imported" goods, both of which
are conditions that foreclose access to derogations under the *Cassis de Dijon*
line of decisions.

Given the state of the law, Belgium could only mount a weak defense. It
argued that the Walloon government's decree constituted "an exceptional
emergency measure" taken in response to a recent massive "influx of
waste," and that the decree would soon be repealed. The government also
claimed that Art. 28 did not apply, since the decree was aimed at prohibiting
the dumping of non-reuseable and unrecyclable waste. In effect, Belgium
was arguing that when a substance has a negative economic value, as when
one pays a second party to dispose of a hazardous substance, it should not
be considered a "good" from the point of view of Art. 28. In the present case,
the decree at issue was "not aimed at protecting trade in goods of Walloon
origin," but at a substance that "is not capable of being marketed." The
Commission, citing the Court on the matter (discussed further in the next
section), disagreed. In its view, whether waste will be reused depended
heavily on the relative costs of disposal versus recycling, and the relative
costs of reclaimed versus unrecycled products, costs that vary as market
conditions change. The Commission also asked took pains to note that "its

position is consistent with the solution reached by the United States Supreme Court in a case analogous to this [one]."[10]

The Court held that the decree violated Directive 84/631 (but not 75/442): because the Community had preempted the field, Member States had no discretion to ban transborder shipments in hazardous waste. It then rejected Belgium's view that trade in such waste fell outside the coverage of Art. 28:

[O]bjects which are shipped across a frontier for the purposes of commercial transactions are subject to Art. [28], whatever the nature of those transactions.

[W]aste, whether recyclable or not, is to be regarded as "goods" the movement of which, in accordance with Art. [28] of the Treaty, must in principle not be prevented.

To this point, it could only be assumed that the Commission had won its case. Under the *Dassonville–Cassis de Dijon* regime, (*a*) preemption blocked Member States from claiming derogations under Art. 30, and (*b*) Member States had access to derogations under Art. 28 (mandatory requirements) only when the lawfulness of IAMs was at stake.

Curiously, the Court held that the Walloon measures could be justified under its jurisprudence on mandatory requirements, despite the fact that they were not IAMs, and despite openly discriminating against imports:

Imperative requirements can indeed be taken into account only in the case of measures which apply without distinction to both domestic and imported products. However, in assessing whether or not the barrier in question is discriminatory, account must be taken of the particular nature of waste. The principle that environmental damage should as a matter of priority be remedied at source, laid down by Art. 130r (2) of the Treaty . . . entails that it is for each region, municipality or other local authority to take appropriate steps to ensure that its own waste is collected, treated and disposed of; it must accordingly be disposed of as close as possible to the place where it is produced, in order to limit as far as possible the transport of waste.

It follows that having regard to the differences between waste produced in different places and to the connection of the waste with its place of production, the contested waste cannot be regarded as discriminatory.

The ruling creates intractable problems for those who would seek to rationalize this part of the decision with the *Cassis de Dijon* line of case law. Indeed, it has been roundly criticized "by the majority of legal writers" (Krämer 2003: 337–8). The ruling indicates that the Court will not strictly apply *Cassis de Dijon* to the extent that the nature of the traded good poses a

---

[10] *Philadelphia* v. *New Jersey*, 437 US 617 (1978). Waste even of no market value enjoys the constitutional protection afforded to interstate trade.

significant environmental threat. There is additional evidence that the ECJ went to unusual lengths to demonstrate its commitment to environmental protection. It is extremely rare for the Court to base a judgment on grounds that had not been raised by one of the parties in oral or written pleadings. In this instance, the Court chose to reopen arguments not once but twice; yet neither Belgium nor the Commission nor the Advocate General anticipated the Court's reasoning on the compatibility of the Walloon measures with Art. 28.[11]

III The Court and Legislative Authority

When it interprets the Treaty of Rome, the Court acts as a "trustee" of the EC's constitution, exercising broad fiduciary duties to defend the constitution's normative superiority with respect to all other EC norms. As we have seen throughout this book, the rules governing legislating in the Community have been (re)constructed through adjudication, under the Court's trusteeship. When it interprets EC secondary legislation, the Court acts as an "agent" of the EC's legislative bodies. The ECJ's discretionary authority (Chapter 1) vis-à-vis the Community legislator is not solely derivable from legislative procedures (legal basis, voting rules, the relative prerogatives of the Commission, Council, and EP). It will be enhanced in so far as litigated provisions of secondary legislation are "incomplete", and to the extent that the EC lawmakers, a composite rather than a unified "principle," have policy disagreements relative to those statutory provisions the Court interprets. In this section, we briefly examine the Court's activities as trustee and agent in the domain of environmental protection.

THE COURT AS TRUSTEE

In Part II, we saw that the Court has used its constitutional authority to develop balancing tests to resolve tensions between the EC's commitments

---

[11] As noted, the Court introduced uncertainty as to the relationship between Arts. 28–30 and local restrictions on trade in waste products, leading national judges to probe this relationship further. In a 2000 preliminary ruling (*Entreprenoerforeningens Affalds/Miljoesektion/FFAD*, ECJ C-209/98), the Court persisted in analyzing local restrictions under Arts. 28–30, although the pertinent EC secondary legislation would normally have been expected to control the question at hand.

to free trade and environmental protection. Here we look at two additional constitutional tasks of the Court in the domain. First, the ECJ resolves disputes between the Community's legislative bodies, supervising the choice of legal basis. The Single Act made such choices complex and politically delicate. The second type of dispute concerns national implementation failures; we focus on the case of Germany, clearly a high-standard Member State when it comes to environmental regulation.

Determining legal basis

The complexity of the market–environmental protection nexus, as it related to legal basis determinations, complicated the ECJ's attempt to build a simple, comprehensive doctrinal structure to organize these decisions. In 1987 (*Commission* v. *Council*, ECJ 45/86), the ECJ held that "the choice of legal basis . . . must be made on objective factors which are amenable to judicial review." In 1988 (*Commission* v. *Council*, ECJ 165/87), the Court ruled that such choices must be made with respect to the "principal" purpose and field of action of the legislation at hand, whereas the "incidental" effects that the legislation might register in other areas of the Treaty must be ignored. Where two areas of the treaty were directly implicated, the Court ruled, the legislation should be adopted on both legal bases.

This solution, however, was not easily adapted to the Community's environmental measures, since these typically blend the aims of market perfection and environmental protection. During the post-SEA/pre-TEU period, the choice of legal basis for environmental regulation became a matter of high politics, determining, among other things, legislative procedures. Simplifying, if the main objective—or "center of gravity"—of a proposed directive was taken to be harmonization of market rules, then Art. 95 (ex-Art. 100a) would be the appropriate procedure: the directive would be adopted by qualified majority voting, and the EP would exercise its powers under the cooperation procedure. But if a proposed directive was considered to fall primarily under the environmental protection heading, then Art. 175 (ex-Art. 130s) governed: the Council would adopt the measure under unanimity voting, and the EP would possess only the right to be consulted.

The *Titanium Dioxide* case is the most important early decision on legal basis. The case involved a failed attempt, made by the Commission in 1988, to induce the Council of Ministers to adopt—under Art. 95—a directive on waste produced by the titanium dioxide industry. The roots of the dispute go back much further. In 1978 (on the basis of ex-Arts. 100 and 235), the Council had adopted Directive 78/176; among other things, the legislation directed the Commission to draft a proposal to harmonize waste management for the industry, within six months of receiving certain information from the Member States. In 1983, the Commission finally submitted the proposal to the Council, where it languished until the German government decided to make it a priority, in 1988. In the meantime, following the entry into force of the SEA, the Commission had changed the legal basis of the measure, from ex-Arts. 100 and 235 (i.e. unanimity voting in the Council) to Art. 95 (qualified majority voting and the cooperation procedure). The Council, anxious to preserve unanimity, took the view that the directive should be based on Art. 175 (ex-Art. 130s); and in June 1989, despite the formal opposition of the Commission and the Parliament to this decision, the Council adopted Directive 89/428 under Art. 175. Three months later, the Commission asked the ECJ to annul the legislation on the grounds that it lacked valid legal basis.

The ECJ (*Commission* v. *Council*, ECJ C-300/89, 1991) sided with the Commission and the Parliament, annulling the directive. The Court began by noting that "the directive is concerned, indissociably, with both the protection of the environmental and the elimination of disparities in conditions of competition." It then turned to the procedural issue, implying that the choice of legal basis must be conditioned by respect for what it called a "fundamental democratic principle": that "the peoples [of Europe] should take part in the exercise of power through the intermediary of a representative assembly." If ex-Art. 130s were to be used as the legal basis for the directive, the Court declared, then "the very purpose of the cooperation procedure, which is to increase the involvement of the European Parliament in the legislative process of the Community, would . . . be jeopardized." It then held that ex-Art. 100a (Art. 95) was in any case the appropriate legal basis for the measure, not least because:

Art. 100a requires the Commission, in its proposals for measures for the approximation of the laws of the Member States which have as their object the establishment and functioning of the internal market, to take as a base a high level of protection in matters of environmental protection. That provision thus expressly indicates that the objectives of environmental protection . . . may be effectively pursued by means of harmonizing measures adopted on the basis of Art. 100a.

The decision, Krämer (2002: 27) reports, "was heavily criticized by the Member States as shifting the balance of power in waste management" from intergovernmental to supranational authority.

The Court's rulings on legal basis disputes have favored majoritarian voting procedures and, thus, supranational modes of governance (this chapter's conclusion). That said, the Council has also won some disputes, the most important of which concerned the adoption of the 1991 framework directive on waste (Council Directive 91/156). In that case (*Commission* v. *Council*, ECJ C-155/91, 1993), the ECJ upheld the Council's decision to enact the Waste Directive under Art. 175 (ex-Art. 130s), in the face of objections by the Commission and Parliament. The Court took pains to distinguish this situation from that of *Titanium Dioxide*, probably because the two disputes otherwise looked similar. While the *Waste Directive* case was being argued, however, the state of the law changed. In the Court's *Walloon Waste* ruling (discussed above), the Court held that governmental interests in the protection of the environment could justify exceptions to the principle of freedom of trade. In *Waste Directive*, the Court explicitly employs the analysis in *Walloon Waste* for the purposes of determining the main object of the directive. In the Court's view, the importance of creating effective systems for waste management— located "as close as possible to the place where [such waste] is produced"— comprised the measure's overriding purpose, whereas the harmonization of market rules in the area could have "only ancillary effects on the conditions of competition and trade." In such cases, however, the Court only guesses as to a measure's impact on market conditions, since its assessment proceeds entirely in the abstract. We are left to conclude that the Court, in both *Walloon Waste* and *Waste Directive*, has expressed an overriding policy interest in carving out a special rationale for environmental protection measures.

Once an important element of everyday legislative politics in the environmental field, legal basis disputes of the kind that pitted Art. 95 and Art. 175 against one another have all but disappeared. The co-decision procedure now applies to both. The general rule is that Art. 175 covers most environmental protection legislation, excepting standards for product composition and labeling, and for regulating noise and air pollution, which are covered by Art. 95.

Transposition failures[12]

According to Art. 249 of the Rome Treaty, directives are "binding, as to the result to be achieved," but "leave to national authorities the choice of form

---

[12] The implementation and enforcement of EC directives in national legal orders are vast topics not sufficiently addressed in this book (see Prechal 1995), let alone in this chapter. Since 1999, the Commission has issued an *Annual Survey on the Implementation and Enforcement of Community Environmental Law*, available on the European Environmental Law Homepage (www.eel.nl). In this domain, there exists a growing literature (reviewed by Haverland 2003) on the linked topics of transposition (García Ureta (ed.) 1998; Scott 2000), national enforcement (Somsen (ed.) 1996; Knill and Lenschow 1998; Jordan 1999), and the Europeanization of administrative practices (Weal et al. 1996; Holder (ed.) 1997; Demmke (ed.) 1997; Jordan 2001).

and method." In the environmental protection field, directives typically mandate substantive outcomes (e.g. minimum levels of air or water quality; the establishment of nature reserves), and procedures (e.g. reporting and monitoring requirements). The Member States are legally required to trans-pose directives into national law by specified deadlines, but Art. 249 grants discretion as to the means of doing so. After the SEA, the Commission began to use Art. 226 infringement proceedings more aggressively, in particular, to expose Member States for failing to transpose environment directives properly. The Commission also hoped to induce the Court to constrain Member State discretion under Art. 249.

The strategy paid off. The Court made it clear that any "environmental directive [containing] mandatory requirements" could not be imple-mented through "non-binding national measures, in particular by admin-istrative provisions" (Krämer 2003: 375). Even strict, de facto compliance with such requirements does not relieve the Member States of the duty to formally transpose the mandatory provisions of a directive into national law. Thus, the Court held that the Member States were required to ensure the "practical application of EC environmental law," not least through making that law directly effective in national courts where appropriate. In what remains good—if underexploited—law, the Court held (*Commission v. Germany*, C-131/88, 1991) that:

The transposition of a directive into domestic law does not necessarily require that its provisions be incorporated formally and verbatim in express, specific legislation; a general legal context may, depending on the content of the directive, be adequate for the purpose provided that it does indeed guarantee the full application of the direc-tive in a sufficiently clear and precise manner so that where the directive is intended to create rights for individuals, the persons concerned can ascertain the full extent of their rights and where appropriate, rely on them before the national courts.

Further, the Court has held that the national rules implementing any bind-ing rules of environmental directives must cover the entire territory of the Member State in the same transparent, enforceable way.

From the point of view of supranational governance, this case law appears sensible, even innocuous. When we look more closely at its effects on national governance, however, we see that it has subverted deep-rooted administrative practices, and generated anxiety about the absence of limits to an expanding "Europeanization" of administration. Prior to 1990, for example, some Member States transposed specific mandatory requirements in the environment field through administrative decrees, regulations, and other instruments issued by the government or a ministry. Often the pertinent, enabling statute did not state the EC rule at all; rather it delegated to executive authority the power to make the rule. In federal and quasi-federal Member States (Austria, Germany, Italy, Spain) and even in unitary states like the United Kingdom (Gibraltar) and France (overseas territories), jurisdiction in the field may be divided between the national government, federated states, and regional and local authorities. In Germany, the *Länder* are charged with monitoring and enforcing federal environmental rules, over which the *Bundesrat* (the federal "senate," composed of representatives of the governments of the *Länder*) has a veto.

Although Germany is clearly a "high-standard" Member State in environmental protection, it has been the defendant in more enforcement actions than all but Belgium and Italy. The reason has more to do with its comparative difficulty in adjusting to implementation requirements, than to any systematic failure to meet substantive targets contained in environmental directives. Indeed, the Court built it case law on proper implementation largely through confronting German practices.

To take one important example, in December 1988 the Commission initiated infringement proceedings against Germany for inadequately transposing Directive 80/779 on smog. The directive established maximum levels of air pollution (the concentration of "sulphur dioxide and suspended particulates") for various periods and conditions. The Commission alleged that Germany had failed to adopt clear, mandatory rules, including penalties for noncompliance, and thus had failed to render the directive effective. In response, Germany noted that none of the relevant provisions of the smog directive went beyond the 1974 German statute that governed the same problem. Indeed, Germany itself had sought to impose its own rules on the EC as a whole, through Directive 80/779. Moreover, it protested, the complaint was "pure formalism," in that the Commission had not showed that the smog levels fixed by the directive had been exceeded. The Commission agreed that Germany was in broad compliance with the levels.

The Germans were correct: formal distinctions between different types of legal rules and administrative practices lay at the core of the Commission's complaint. In transposing the smog directive, Germany had left intact its own 1974 statute on air pollution, and the standard administrative practices it used for regulating in the area. The German statute required the government, upon the consent of the *Bundesrat*, to issue "administrative provisions" to give effect to the law. The government had done so through administrative circulars. Both sides agreed that the provisions of the circular precisely reproduced EC smog limits. In the Commission's view, however, it was unclear if the provisions of German administrative circulars constituted "mandatory" legal norms. Germany argued that the smog circulars contained, in fact, binding law leaving "no discretion to the administration." A long argument ensued as to whether such circulars could create rights that could be invoked by individuals before a judge. The views of scholars and the jurisprudence of the courts could not resolve the question, since there was a great deal of variance across different policy sectors. In support of the German position, the fact remained that the smog circulars were virtually unique: in so far as they had to be approved by the *Bundesrat*, they bound administrators as much as any other form of delegated legislation or, for that matter, federal statute. The Commission, however, considered the circular to be an inappropriate means of transposing mandatory EC rules per se.

In it ruling (*Commission* v. *Germany*, ECJ C-361/88, 1991), the Court began by restating what it characterized as "established" precedent: Member States possessed meaningful discretion over modes of transposition, subject to the principles of effectiveness and legal certainty. It then sided with the Commission:

It must be stated that . . . Germany has not pointed to any national judicial decision explicitly recognizing that [the smog] circular, apart from being binding on the administration, has direct effect *vis-à-vis* third parties. It cannot be claimed, therefore, that individuals are in a position to know with certainty the full extent of their rights in order to rely on them, where appropriate, before the national courts, or that those whose activities are liable to give rise to [air pollution] nuisances are adequately informed of their obligations.

The Court then went on to restate its prior holding that EC directives containing binding rules must be implemented that satisfy the requirements of normative "specificity, precision, and clarity," so as to render the rights and duties created by EC law enforceable by national judges. Two years later, the German government replaced the circular with a Federal *regulation*, thereby satisfying the Commission.

The Court has since reiterated the main features of this judgment in a series of subsequent infringement proceedings: on various forms of air pollution, such as lead (*Commission* v. *Germany*, ECJ C-59/89, 1991); on the quality of surface water for extraction of drinking water (*Commission* v. *Germany*, ECJ C-58/89, 1991); and on the designation of wildlife protection reserves (*Commission* v. *Italy*, ECJ C-334/89, 1991; *Commission* v. *Spain*, ECJ C-242/94, 1995; *Commission* v. *Germany*, ECJ C-83/97, 1997). The Court has also refused to take into account the nature of German federalism in evaluating that state's implementation failures (e.g. *Commission* v. *Germany*, ECJ C-58/89, 1991).

The German government expressed its displeasure with the ruling, but nevertheless promised to adopt laws that would fulfill the "formal critique" of the ECJ. Doctrinal authorities were almost evenly split. Those who condemned the ruling supported the position taken by the German government in the case. A former president of the Federal Administrative Court (*Bundesverwaltungsgericht*), Horst Sendler (1993), went so far as to declare that the ECJ had begun to destroy the delicate, underlying structures of German administrative law. Others (e.g. Steiling 1992) supported the Court, for having helped to resolve internal debates about the effects of technical regulations in the area of environmental law. In effect, the ECJ pushed the German government to modernize the legal instruments it uses in the domain (Koch 1991). Today, there appears to be wide agreement that the effectiveness of environmental regulations depends critically on their capacity to generate judicially enforceable rights, and the Court's influence in helping to reform the German situation is favorably noted (Jarras 1999: 48).

THE COURT AS AGENT: INTERPRETING THE DIRECTIVES

The expansion of European environmental regulation has meant that the Court is increasingly involved in interpreting statutes for the purpose of helping national judges to apply them in national legal orders. Indeed, statutory review of EC environmental legislation is today one of the ECJ's primary tasks. Although routine, the interpretation of EC secondary legislation is also statutory construction, that is, judicial lawmaking. In the area of waste management, for example, a long series of preliminary references have asked the Court to clarify the notion of waste in the various EC statutes. The central question in these cases is whether the heading of "waste" covers goods capable of being reutilized, and therefore of economic value. Many business concerns in the waste management and recycling industries, as well as some of the "greener" Member States, would prefer to distinguish "waste" from "secondary raw materials," or "reuseable by-products." The EC has struggled with this problem without much success. When litigation on the issue comes to the ECJ via Art. 234, it is not uncommon for multiple (as many as five) governments to file briefs (e.g. *Tombesi*, ECJ C-304/94 [joined], 1997; *Inter-Environnement Wallonie*, ECJ C-129/96, 1997; *Arco Chemie*, ECJ C418/97 [joined], 2000; *Mayer Perry*, ECJ C-444/00, 2003). Each government defends its own interpretation of the definition of "waste," and the Court decides. The Court's dominance over legislative interpretation, made possible by Art. 234 caseload, is secured by the lack of consensus on the part of the Member States themselves. Further, Art. 226 infringement proceedings can enable the Court to impose its preferred interpretation on governments that hold a different view. In 1995, for example, the ECJ (*Commission v. Germany*, C-422/92, 1995) censured Germany for having adopted legislation that "excluded certain categories of recyclable waste" from the EC-governed regime, which admits only one category, "waste." Among other things, the decision made it clear that the EC enjoyed exclusive competence over the matter.

Statutory review of EC directives typically serves to reduce national autonomy in the domain. In *Lappel Bank* (ECJ C-44/95, 1996), the Court imposed its interpretation of secondary legislation over the objections of a consortium of powerful Member States. The Court did so even after the legislation had been revised to "reverse" a prior ECJ ruling.

Lappel Bank: balancing ecological and economic interests

Since the mid-1980s, the Court has confronted a common if delicate problem faced by high constitutional and administrative courts in all advanced industrial states: how to balance ecological conservation objectives with pressures for economic development.

The most important line of decisions concern the 1979 Bird Directive (79/409) and the 1992 Habitats Directive (92/43). Among other things, the 1979 legislation required the Member States to protect the EC's population of wild birds and to guard against the "deterioration" of their habitats "while taking account of economic and recreational requirements." They do so by designating and maintaining "special preservation areas" (SPAs) for endangered species. In *Leybucht Dykes* (*Commission v. Germany*, ECJ C-57/89, 1991), the Court ruled that:

the power of the Member States to reduce the extent of a special protection area can be justified only on exceptional grounds.

Those grounds must correspond to a general interest which is superior to the general interest represented by the ecological objective of the directive. In that context, the interests referred to in Art. 2 of the directive, namely, economic and recreational requirements, do not enter into consideration. As the Court pointed out in its judgments in Case 247/85 (*Commission v. Belgium*) and Case 262/85 (*Commission v. Italy*), that provision does not constitute an autonomous derogation from the general system of protection established by the directive.

At the time of the decision, Germany had nearly completed the disputed works: the construction of new dikes and a reservoir adjacent to an SPA. The

Court found that these projects were justified on public interest grounds, in so far as they were more likely to improve than to worsen the situation for the wild bird population in the area. "[T]he danger of flooding and the protection of the coast constitute sufficiently serious reasons to justify" the project, the Court held, "as long as those measures are confined to a strict minimum and involve only the smallest possible reduction of the special protection area." Least-means testing was thereby brought to bear on the question of how SPAs, once designated, were to be maintained. Although it was found that the new dike would benefit local fishermen, the Court ruled that for government "to take account of such an interest is in principle incompatible with the requirements of the provision." The doctrine developed in *Leybucht Dykes* was soon thereafter applied in the *Santoña Marshes* case (*Commission* v. *Spain*, ECJ C-355/90, 1993), an area that Spain had not designated as an SPA, but should have under the Birds Directive. The case law was confirmed and generalized in *Commission* v. *Netherlands* (ECJ C-3/96, 1998).

Immediately following the *Leybucht Dykes* decision, the UK and other governments began to press the Commission to amend the Birds Directive, in order to recalibrate the balance between ecological and economic considerations in governmental decisions. The UK's view was that the whole of the Birds Directive had to be understood in both its economic and ornithological context, whereas the Court had given far too much weight to the latter. The Council of Ministers decided to use the Habitats Directive, then under its consideration, to amend the Birds Directive and, in effect, reverse the Court (Holder 1997: 1479; Cichowski 2002: 233). As adopted, the 1992 Habitats Directive revised the Birds Directive to permit a derogation from the general Member State obligation to maintain the integrity of protected zones. Development in SPAs could take place "for imperative reasons of overriding public interest, including those of a social or economic nature."

At the time *Leybucht Dykes* was being decided, the saga of the Lappell Bank's status as an SPA was heading for the courts. The Lappell Bank was an inter-tidal mudflat on the north coast of Kent. Part of the Medway Estuary and Marshes system, it was also an important feeding, nesting, and staging ground for a broad population of migratory birds, including some endangered species. In 1986, the government made the Medway system a candidate for SPA status. Unfortunately for the birds, the mudflat was also adjacent to the Port of Sheerness, one of the few ports in southeast England that could accommodate deep-sea vessels, and the fifth largest cargo port in the United Kingdom. In 1989, a local authority gave the Port authority to expand into the Lappel Bank; the Secretary of State for the Environment quashed the decision in 1991, partly on the grounds that the project would violate the Birds Directive. Two years later, after intense lobbying on both sides of the issue, the Medway system was classified as an SPA. The Lappell Bank, however, was excluded from the designation, the Secretary of State having determined that the economic benefits of the Port's expansion outweighed the value of bird conservation.

The Royal Society for the Protection of Birds challenged this decision, arguing that the Secretary of State had given too much weight to economic interests. The group's application for judicial review was rejected by successive courts, before reaching the House of Lords in 1995. Although the port expansion was well underway and could not be stopped, it was clear that the case carried important implications for future planning and decision-making. Pressed by the Royal Society, the House of Lords sent two questions to the ECJ. First, in deciding whether to designate an SPA, was a Member State allowed to consider the economic and recreational requirements mentioned in Art. 2 of the Birds Directive? Second, "if the answer to Question 1 is 'no,'" does either the ECJ's decision in *Leybucht Dykes*, or the 1992 amendment to the Birds Directive, provide justification for taking into account, respectively, "superior" or "overriding" public interests of an economic kind? The key problem was that these two latter, permissible derogations to the Birds Directive related to the obligation of the Member States "to avoid pollution and deterioration of habitats or any disturbances affecting birds" in SPAs—that is, to maintaining the integrity of SPAs—not to establishing the SPA in the first place.

The Commission sided with the Royal Society, arguing that economic interests could only be "ancillary" to "ornithological criteria" in any decision to classify an area as a protected zone. In their view, "superior interests" of the kind recognized by the Court in *Leybucht Dykes* could never include "economic and social interests." The United Kingdom, supported by France, reasoned that it made little sense for Member States to possess more discretion to take measures that would weaken an existing conservation scheme, than they had to take decisions to create an SPA in the first place. France argued that the "economic and recreational requirements" mentioned in Art. 2 constituted general provisions that infuse the directive as a whole; consequently, Member States "must be guided by considerations of an economic nature in carrying out their obligations to create SPAs." If it were otherwise, a Member State could classify an area as protected and then proceed to develop it under the new 1992 derogation.

The Court, after summarizing the arguments of the United Kingdom and France, bluntly rejected them: "a Member State is not authorized to take account of the economic requirements mentioned in Art. 2 thereof when designating an SPA and defining its boundaries." The Court treated the second question as if it had been already decided by existing case law. Following *Leybucht Dykes* and *Santoña Marshes*, it held that economic requirements could never rise to "a general interest superior to that represented by the ecological objective" of the Birds Directive, and that the 1992 amendment did not apply to "the initial stage of classification of an area as an SPA":

> Economic requirements, as an imperative reason of overriding public interest allowing a derogation from the obligation to classify a site according to its ecological value, cannot enter into consideration at that stage. But that does not . . . mean that they cannot be taken into account as a later stage under the procedure provided for by . . . the Habitats Directive.

Establishing modes of judicial control for permissible derogations to obligations to maintain SPAs will be an important area for litigating in the future.

IV   Conclusion

When we examine adjudication in the environmental protection domain, we encounter some of the same basic themes that emerged in earlier chapters. The Court treats EC law as conferring judicially-enforceable rights on private parties, and has produced least-means, proportionality standards for balancing rights against the public interest. Through its rulings, it has acted—relatively systematically—to reduce the domain of national autonomy, to expand supranational modes of governance to the detriment of intergovernmental modes, and to create conditions for the gradual Europeanization of national administration and judging. Trusteeship begets judicial supremacy over institutional evolution. As important, even when the Court acts as an agent of the EC legislator, it does not seem to fear legislative reversal.

These empirical observations have theoretical implications. According to the "unified model of EU politics" proclaimed by Tsebelis and Garrett (2001), for example, supranational institutions like the Court never produce "unintended consequences." The burden of the argument largely rests on Member

State governments' control of legislative procedures. In this chapter, we briefly discussed the adjudication of legal basis disputes in the environment field. When the Court rejects the Council of Ministers' chosen procedures, governments lose control; the "unified model" disintegrates (see also Stone Sweet and Sandholtz 2002; Farrell and Héritier 2003). The point is not merely a formality. As Tsebelis and Garrett argue, we should expect different legislative procedures to generate different substantive outcomes, unless there are no differences in the policy preferences of the EC's legislative organs.

Legal basis disputes have been the subject of high quality, systematic research. Joseph Jupille (2000, extended by 2004) analyzed every such dispute brought to the Court during the 1987–2000 period ($n = 34$). He was particularly interested in testing hypotheses derived from what he calls the "strategic model." The strategic model focuses on the conditions under which the Court is most likely to constrain itself, with respect to the preferences of Member State governments. Jupille found no support for the models that, like Tsebelis and Garrett's, assume that the Court fears reversal. "[T]he data," he writes (2000: 14), "strongly disconfirm the strategic view of Court behavior as operationalized here. Quite simply, the Court appears totally unconcerned to insulate its ... judgments from legislative override. [It] appears dedicated throughout the period to the extension of 'integration,' defined as majoritarian decisionmaking in the Council and the attendant increase in legislative output." Margaret McCown (2001, 2004) also examined outcomes in every legal basis dispute. She confirmed Jupille's findings. Moreover, she found that the Court had produced an intricate, precedent-based doctrinal framework to which governments adapted. The process through which the EC's organs determine the legal basis of legislation has been fully judicialized.

Finally, as in any federal polity, ensuring the "practical application" of EC environmental law is a far more difficult task than inducing governmental officials to put the right words on the right piece of paper. In the face of opposition, and without the support of other public authorities, judges are not particularly well positioned to accomplish the broad objectives of EC environmental protection policies. Local governments and administrations may balk at enforcing regulations against powerful business concerns that would be adversely affected. And concerned citizens and interest groups may face obstacles in the courts, such as standing doctrines that may exclude public interest litigation. Expanding standing in the field is now on the agenda, but opening the legal system up to public interest litigation still faces resistance. These points accepted, the future of environmental governance in the EU will rely more, not less, on courts.

6

Conclusion

In this book, I have pursued two main objectives. First, I have sought to demonstrate that the course of European integration has been profoundly shaped by a system of adjudication managed by the Court of Justice. As argued in Chapter 2, market integration and the construction of supranational governance proceeded symbiotically,[1] through a set of self-reinforcing processes that linked activities in economic, political, and judicial arenas of decisionmaking. Judicial authority over the institutional evolution of the Rome Treaty constituted a necessary causal condition for the development of these linkages. Second, I have sought to test a range of propositions about how the legal system operates, and to trace the effects of the ECJ's case law on policy outcomes, and on the policy-relevant behavior of nonjudicial actors. In some areas, including free movement of goods (Chapter 3) and sex equality (Chapter 4), judges—not governments or legislatures or the Member States—have broadly determined the paths along which institutions[2] evolved. Judicial supremacy partly inheres in the ECJ's status as trustee (Chapter 1), partly in the dynamics of the constitutionalization process provoked by the Court in the mid-1960s (Chapter 2), and partly by the propagation and diffusion of specific techniques of judicial governance, such as those associated with precedent-based balancing standards (Chapters 3, 4, and 5). Every chapter of the book presents evidence refuting claims that the Court and the national courts operate as relatively perfect "agents" of the Member States or national governments. And every chapter shows that the activities of supranational organizations, such as the European Court, routinely produce "unintended consequences," from the perspective of those who have designed and redesigned the EC.[3] Indeed, I do

---

[1] Based on Stone Sweet and Brunell (1998a) and Fligstein and Stone Sweet (2002).

[2] By "institutions," I mean rule systems, normative stuctures, law.

[3] The production, through adjudication, of new rules and procedures governing the decisionmaking of the Member States and national governments, which the latter would not have adopted on their own, given decision rules then in place.

not see how theories that make predictions about how integration has proceeded from institutional design—including those of Garrett (1993, 1995), Moravcsik (1998), and Tsebelis and Garrett (2001)—can be rescued.

INTEGRATION, CONSTITUTIONALIZATION, EUROPEANIZATION

Integration under the Treaty of Rome has proceeded now for more than four decades. The process has been punctuated by discrete events registered in political, economic, and legal domains of action. But these events have been embedded in a larger flow. European integration is fundamentally about how a large number of actors, operating in relatively separate arenas, were able to produce new forms of exchange and collective governance for themselves. Market actors, interest groups, national governments and administrators, the EU's organs, technical experts, the legal profession, and the courts have found themselves having to confront one another. It is remarkable how successful they have been in building new institutions, organizational capacity, and means of coordinating activities across fields and domains. The institutionalization of supranational governance has, in turn, pushed for more, not less, integration.

Today, national economies are highly integrated; market regulation reflects European rules; EC law holds sway over national law and adminis-tration; and interested parties continue to push for institutional innovation in Brussels and Luxembourg. Strikingly, half of world trade occurs within the borders of the EC, a share that will rise sharply with enlargement. Transnational networks of producers and public interest groups have oriented their activities toward Brussels. The EC's political organizations govern by making, applying, and interpreting rules that are authoritative throughout the territory of the EC. National courts routinely enforce European law and coordinate EC and national regulatory regimes; and national parliaments and bureaucracies incorporate EC legislation into their procedures and practices. Member State governments have facilitated integration, at times proactively, but often only by being dragged along. Integration has been a powerful force because it has served to embed inter-ests, investments, and identities, in a dynamic, expansionary way. It has done so by connecting arenas for economic, political, and legal decision-making (Stone Sweet and Brunell 1998*a*; Fligstein and Stone Sweet 2002), giving the system strength and resilience.

The analysis raises a critical question: to what extent did European integration have to proceed as it did? It might be possible to read this account in a primitive, "functionalist,"[4] way: a preexisting configuration of actors and their preferences mixed with the Treaty of Rome and EC organs to produce, teleologically as it were, the main outcomes described. I would reject such an interpretation. European integration has been structured by crucial events that were not predictable from any *ex ante* historical moment. There is simply no good reason why the constitutionalization of the Treaty of Rome, or many other crucial events, had to happen. If national judges had ignored or rejected the Court's moves in the 1960s, the EC project would have floundered. If, in the 1980s, the Member States had refused to recommit to collective governance, based on enhanced supranationalism, the Single European Act would not have been negotiated and ratified. Traders and other organized interest groups played important roles in these transitions, not least by litigating and lobbying. But political actors, operating in the EC's legislative and judicial organs, ultimately produced the broader institutional terrain of the EC. If my collaborators and I have elaborated a dynamic causal account of integration, the theory is nonetheless a probabilistic one.[5] Although we claim to have explained some of the most important features of European integration over time, we deny that these outcomes were predetermined in any theoretically meaningful way.

Skeptics might still ask: what is the natural limit to this process? Is there a way in which national governments would choose to roll back integration?

I would respond with a question: has there ever been a period, in the history of the EC/EU, wherein politicians, scholars, journalists, and interested groups have *not* been engaged in anxious hand-wringing and lamentation about "crisis" in Europe, or its counterpart, *malaise*. Yet integration has steadily proceeded; indeed, the rhetoric of "crisis" has been the catalysts for its widening and deepening (Sandholtz and Zysman 1989). As in all federal polities, the instruments of market regulation have evolved. In many policy domains, regulatory styles are today more "flexible" than they were in earlier decades; and subsidiarity could come to mean something other than a polite bow to local sensibilities (Wyatt 2000; Von Bogdandy and Bast 2002). Yet it is the EC's legislative and judicial organs that determine, in

---

[4] See Chapter 1, footnote 9.

[5] The statistical tests of our propositions were sensitive to necessary but not sufficient conditions, and relationships among variables are always expressed as contingencies ("to the extent that"). See Stone Sweet and Brunell (1998a); Fligstein and Stone Sweet (2002).

a formal sense, the degree of flexibility and decentralized governance there will be in the Union. Regulatory styles may change, but I know of no important example of roll back.

Some potential limits might issue from the very success of integration. As the Treaty system has evolved, as judicialization has proceeded, so have the webs of constraints that all actors face in seeking to pursue their interests. The complexity of the legislative process, given the hybrid nature of the EC legislator and the multiplicity of interests represented, may slow the production of legislation. Some lobbying groups, such as certain producers, have already attained their main ends, and now may act mostly to block new regulation that would negatively impact them. There will always be some governments seeking to reassert dominance lost. The European Commission is a relatively small organization: it is underfunded, stretched thin, and under recurrent attack for being too technocratic, unwieldy, and sometimes corrupt (Craig 2000). As in the late 1970s, the limits of the current institutions have already been reached. With enlargement, all of these problems may be exacerbated, slowing progress on important issues. And it is always possible that militantly anti-European governments could come to power across Europe.

Yet there are countervailing forces. European economies are highly integrated, and exports are critical to economic growth. The EU, for all intents and purposes, is a single economy. The most powerful firms are typically those that have most heavily invested in the European market. They lobby at both the national and supranational levels for EU institutions that promote economic growth and work for them. And they have been joined by groups who act in the name of consumers, environmental protection, and other "diffuse" public interests. The governments of the Member States listen to these people. Today, national administrative and judicial systems are increasingly integrated. It would take a series of cataclysmic economic or political events for all of these actors to want to extricate themselves from the project. Far more likely, when limits are reached, then creative institutional solutions to problems will be found once more.

The legal system has provided some—but by no means all—of the institutional underpinnings for what has happened. It has done so by engaging the decisionmaking of other actors, including governments, the Commission, and a growing variety of litigating parties.

There are a number of reasons why the constitutionalization of the Rome Treaty generated an expansive logic of its own, entailing an increasing demand for law, rule clarification, and capacities for monitoring and enforcement. From the beginning, the central mission of the EC was to create the conditions for the development of the Common Market. Yet impersonal exchange, across jurisdictional boundaries, is problematic for reasons that social scientists have explored at some length (see Greif 1989, 1993; North 1990; Fligstein and Stone Sweet 2002). As elsewhere, the success of integration has depended heavily on the extent to which the EC could develop effective organizational capacities: to guarantee property rights, to enforce competition rules, to adjudicate legal claims, to build a European framework for regulating market activities, and so on. At the very least, constitutionalization accelerated this process. In my view, one can go further: the ECJ authoritatively reconstituted the Community in ways that linked the demand for and supply of European law and courts to the activities of market actors, and then to all activities governed by EC law. Constitutionalization not only positioned the courts as primary arenas for negative integration; it made them supervisors of positive integration, and curators of a growing corpus of rights which the Court found in the Treaty itself.

In addition, the EC governs principally through making rules (directives, regulations, decisions), drawing affected groups into deliberative procedures (comitology and other modes of consultation); it has little capacity to govern through taxation, redistribution, and direct enforcement. The EC has weak coercive capacities; the Commission succeeds by brokering interests, and arbitraging across domains and organizations; the administration and enforcement of EC law is typically left to national authorities. In consequence, modes of supranational governance tend to be heavily norm-based: legalistic but incomplete. To be effective, EC policies must be implemented and "completed," which requires high levels of coordination across multiple levels of government. Judges are necessarily implicated in such a political system. With constitutionalization, the national courts, too, developed into privileged sites for deliberation and rulemaking, not least because they are charged with supervising the transposition and implementation of EC law by national authorities. It is hardly surprising that, with the expansion of supranational governance and the consolidation of supremacy and direct effect, national administrative autonomy has been undermined, and judicial discretion enhanced. Subversion of national ways of doing things is not the whole story, however. As the scope of supranational governance has widened and deepened, government official operating at regional, national, and subnational levels have themselves been led to adopt the kinds of rulemaking practices and discourses under way in European policy arenas (Le Galès 2001; Radaelli and Featherstone 2001; Stone Sweet, Sandholtz, and Fligstein (eds.) 2001).

The recitation is not meant to imply that the Europeanization of national law and politics has proceeded mechanically, or without friction. If integration provokes Europeanization, the latter process has proceeded according to its own quite different logics.[6] One important indicator of the success of the integration project is that scholars are now earnestly studying the *Europeanization* of national politics.

One can, of course, conceptualize *Europeanization* in different ways. For our purposes, we can define it as the impact of social and market integration (the development of transnational society) and supranational governance (EU rules, procedures, and the activities of EU organizations) on processes and outcomes taking place at the national level. The research is organized through specifying the dependent variable: impact will vary across time, policy domains, national organizations (or arenas), and across Member States or jurisdictions within states. The assertion is that the dependent variable of integration studies becomes the independent variable of Europeanization studies. Europeanization has partly been provoked by how the various modes of supranational governance have actually been *institutionalized* over time (Stone Sweet, Sandholtz, and Fligstein (eds.) 2001). But we have only just begun thinking about how—through what social mechanisms or processes—such impact is registered (see Héritier, Knill, and Mingers 1996; Le Galès 2001; Radaelli and Featherstone (eds.) 2001). With constitutionalization, the judiciary has gradually evolved into a kind of central nervous system for the EU. It helps to regulate Europeanization in diverse ways, but there is nothing simple, "natural," or robotic about how it does so. European legal integration—which is itself the first important form of Europeanization—has been and will always be a complex, messy process (Conant 2002).

In the past decade, academic lawyers and social scientists have produced an impressive stack of studies documenting how individuals and groups have used EC law in the courts of the Member States in order to change local laws, administrative practices, and workplace rules. Yet little progress has been made in elaborating testable theory of such politics. Under what conditions does policy reform through litigation succeed? How much

---

[6] It is a fact, rather serious criticism, that theories of integration are not designed to explain the mechanisms of Europeanization; they seek to explain the evolution of supranational governance.

variation—across policy domains and court systems—in success rates exist, and what factors best explain that variation? Strikingly, there is no systematic research on a host of variables that one would think might be important, including differences in: national rules governing standing; discretion to send preliminary references to the ECJ; local settlement regimes; provision of remedies; etc. No one has yet charted the growth of law firms specializing in litigating European law, or examined how such growth has impacted legal integration. Social scientists have given more attention to various "extra-legal" factors, such as the relative capacities of potential litigants to organize themselves, differences in levels of resources that interest groups command, the openness of non-judicial state structures to process social demands, and the "fit" between supranational and national modes of governance (e.g. Tesoka 1999; Green Cowles, Caporaso, and Risse (eds.) 2001; Börzel 2002; Cichowski 2002). But this research typically examines only a small number of national cases, in just one or two policy areas. We still desperately need comparative, contextually-rich case studies that blend the lawyer's concern with doctrinal evolution, and the social scientist's concern with explanation, in a sustained way.

THE CONSTITUTION AND JUDICIAL MODES OF GOVERNANCE

The rhetoric of constitutionalization has been at the heart of discourse on legal integration for more than thirty years. The discourse implies that a constitution has been constructed out of a treaty. I find the various arguments associated with this rhetoric theoretically defensible, and empirically useful. In my view, it would be an artificial, tortuous, but not impossible (e.g. Schilling 1996) exercise to define the term, "constitution," so as to exclude the Rome Treaty, while including most constitutions of established nation states. My preference would be start with a generic conception of the words, *constitution* and *constitutionalism*, and then to situate the EC's particular experience comparatively, relative to that of other polities. By constitution, I mean a body of meta-rules: normative statements that govern how all other rules are to be made, applied, and interpreted (Stone 1994). Robust constitutionalism—the norm that the exercise of public authority must conform to constitutional norms or be invalid juridically—is rare in the world. Wherever constitutionalism presently exists, it has emerged through a combination of practice and design. The paradigmatic cases are those that have been produced through the gradual consolidation of the power of judges to review the legality of the acts of legislatures, executives and in federal politics, the acts of federated states and their courts. The Community experienced this same process.

Ultimately, the EC experience—the "Treaty-as-Constitution," the "Constitution-as-Process"—created the conditions for its own demise. Europe is presently experiencing a "constitutional moment," the result of which is known: the Union will soon have a "real" Constitution, properly signed and stamped in all of the right places. Scholars have already produced a small mountain of material analyzing the constitution-making process, which I will not comment upon here. Instead, I will briefly address the relationship between European integration and constitutionalization, on the one hand, and the present proceedings on the other.

First, it should be obvious that the move to produce a formal constitution cannot be dissociated from the overall process of integration. The so-called democratic deficit and the various "legitimacy gaps" that allegedly afflict the EC took on salience with the broad expansion of supranational govern-ance. If EC programs had not become meaningful to the lives of more and more people, the democratic legitimacy of the European political system would have remained a rather distant question debated, if at all, by the same elites who have always dominated EC politics. Scholars and judges have long argued (e.g., Mancini 1991; Weiler 1986), and compellingly so, that the Court's commitment to a rights-based jurisprudence of the Treaty had bol-stered the democratic legitimacy of the Community. The present reflects the legacy of the past in an even more profound way. It is clear that much of what the constitutional convention has done is to codify what had been institutionalized over the course of decades.[7] As Lenaerts and Desomer (2002) showed, the "essential bricks" and mortar for a "constitutional treaty" of the EU had hardened over four decades, under the ECJ's tutelage. The most striking—and, to my mind, most important—examples are the codification of a charter of rights (Di Fabio 2001), and the consecration of proportionality as a general norm of government.

Second, one of the purest measures of the success of the Court's bid to constitutionalize the treaty system in the 1960s is the overloading of the preliminary reference procedure. In the 1980s, the Court was still able to process references in less than a year; today, the average delay from date of reference to date of decision is more than three years. The Commission's

---

[7] There are, of course, important exceptions that have claimed a disproportionate share of attention (e.g. voting rights in the Council of Ministers).

more aggressive use of enforcement actions has also increased the burden on the Court (Chapter 2). In 1970, the ECJ rendered 64 rulings; it issued 132 in 1980, and 275 in 2000. According to Turner and Munoz (2000), the number of cases pending before the ECJ and the Court of First Instance "increased from 238 in 1980 to 1,233 in 1998." Given that the demand for more adjudication of EC law will only grow, the system is already in deep crisis. Reforms have been proposed, by scholars (Arnull 1999, 2000; Rasmussen 2000; Turner and Munoz 2000), governments (Wooldrige 1996), the Commission, past judges, and the present Court itself (see the summaries and analyses of Craig and de Burca [2003: 473–9]). Recent discussions include: transforming the legal system into a hierarchically-organized appellate system, with the ECJ at its apex; creating lower level EU courts of referral—a kind of "circuit court" system to help process references—which would refer to the ECJ the most important questions of law; and expanding the jurisdiction of the Court of First Instance to deal with disputes related to the interpretation of EC secondary legislation, especially in more technical areas of EC law. Little progress has been made, while the need for fundamental reforms becomes even more acute.

Third, the European Court governs primarily through precedent, through propagating doctrinal frameworks that guide the argumentation and decisionmaking of lawyers, judges, and governmental officials.[8] Had the Court wavered in its commitment to building precedent, there would have been no constitutionalization of the Treaty, no steady judicialization of EC policymaking, no Europeanization of national law. Precedent, quite literally, embodies the past, and the past that matters in judicial politics is path dependent (Chapter 1). At the same time, it is a potent instrument of organizing the future, normatively. The Court has been extraordinarily successful at inducing legal and political elites to reproduce the modes of reasoning it had applied, on a step-by-step basis in the past, to the problems of the present.

Last, without precedent, there is no proportionality. In my view, with the exception of the diffusion of the Court's constitutional doctrines (Chapter 2), the most transformative institutional innovation in the history of legal integration will be the emergence of proportionality balancing as a master technique of judicial governance in the EU.[9] For more than three decades

---

[8] That is, actors who do not otherwise interact with one another on a continuous basis and are, indeed, widely dispersed across the breadth of the Union.

[9] If direct effect and supremacy make up the necessary "hardware" for the adjudication of EC law, proportionality appears to be evolving into its basic "operating system."

now, the Court has consciously embraced, and sought to extend, proportionality standards. They now permeate virtually every domain of European law. In 1990, with the Treaty of European Union, the Member States ratified the Court's commitment to the principle. As revised, the Treaty of Rome now reads (Art. 5.3): "Any action by the Community shall not go beyond what is necessary to achieve the objectives of this Treaty." Further, as we have seen, the Court also requires all judges in the Union to deploy least-means tests to control the measures taken by the Member States in areas governed by EC law. The institutionalization of such control judicializes the European polity in a profound, and unusually formal, sense.[10] If proportionality is to be at the core of European governance, then the judicial (re)construction of Europe has barely begun.

[10] Perhaps the greatest weakness of this book is the absence of sustained analysis of the effects of proportionality-based judicial reasoning on integration and supranational governance. It seems to me that a proper conclusion to this book would emphasize other flaws, including: the absence of serious discussion of the Court of First Instance, and of the legal system's relationship to the European Court of Human Rights, and the appellate body of the WTO; the deleterious consequences of adhering to initial choices of domains of analysis meant excluding research on other important domains (e.g. competition law, intellectual property, free movement of workers, capital, and services, the evolution of European citizenship); the willful ignorance of issues related to the coming enlargement; the concern for testing social scientists' propositions about how the EC has evolved, but not hypotheses suggested by legal scholarship. I trust readers to add to this list.

References

Judicial Decisions

European Court of Justice

Stork, ECJ 1/58 [1959] ECR 17.
Van Gend en Loos, ECJ 26/62 [1963] ECR 1.
Costa, ECJ 6/64 [1964] ECR 585.
Stauder, ECJ 29/69 [1969] ECR 419.
Internationale Handelsgesellschaft, ECJ 11/70 [1970] ECR 1125.
Defrenne I, ECJ 80/70 [1971] ECR 445.
Nold, ECJ 4/73 [1974] ECR 491.
Van Duyn, ECJ 41/74 [1974] ECR 1337.
Dassonville, ECJ 8/74 [1974] ECR 837.
Rutili, ECJ 36/75 [1975] ECR 1219.
Defrenne II, ECJ 43/75 [1976] ECR 455.
De Peijper. ECJ 104/75, [1976] ECR 613.
Kramer, ECJ 3/76 [1976] ECR 1279.
Rewe-Zentralfinanz, ECJ 33/76 [1976] ECR 1989.
Comet, ECJ 45/76 [1976] ECR 2043.
Simmenthal, ECJ 35/76 [1976] ECR 1871.
Simmenthal, ECJ 106/77 [1978] ECR 629.
Defrenne III, ECJ 149/77 [1978] ECR 1365.
Cassis de Dijon, ECJ 120/78 [1979] ECR 649.
Macarthy's, ECJ 129/79 [1980] ECR 1275.
Jenkins, ECJ 96/80 [1981] ECR 911.
Rewe-Handelsgesellschaft Nord, ECJ 158/80 [1981] ECR 1805.
Commission v. Luxembourg, ECJ 58/81 [1982] 2175.
Commission v. UK, ECJ 61/81 [1982] ECR 2601.
Oosthoek, ECJ 286/81 [1982] ECR 4575.
Inter-Huiles, ECJ 172/82 [1983] ECR 555.
Rhônes-Alpes Huiles, ECJ 295/82 [1984] 575.
Von Colson, ECJ 14/83 [1984] ECR 1891.
Commission v. Denmark, ECJ 143/83 [1985] ECR 427.
ADBHU, ECJ 240/83 [1985] ECR 531.
Marshall I, ECJ 152/84 [1986] ECR 723.
Bilka, ECJ 170/84 [1986] ECR 1607.
Commission v. Belgium, ECJ 247/85 [1989] ECR 3071.
Commission v. Italy, ECJ 262/85 [1987] ECR 3073.
Foto Frost, ECJ 314/85 [1987] ECR 4199.

Commission v. Council, ECJ 45/86 [1987] ECR 1493.

Smanor, ECJ 298/87 [1988] ECR 4489.

Commission v. Denmark (Danish Bottles), ECJ 302/86 [1988] ECR 4607.

Buet, ECJ 382/87 [1989] ECR 1235.

Wachauf, ECJ 5/88 [1989] ECR 2609.

Commission v. Council, ECJ 165/87 [1988] ECR 5545.

Danfoss, ECJ 109/88 [1989] ECR 3199.

Commission v. Germany, ECJ C-131/88 [1991] ECR I-825.

Rinner-Kühn, ECJ 171/88 [1989] ECR 2743.

Dekker, ECJ C-177/88 [1990] ECR I-3941.

Hertz, C-179/88 [1990] ECR I-3979.

Barber, ECJ C-262/88 [1990] ECR I-1889.

Bonfait, ECJ C-269/89 [1990] ECR I-4169.

Commission v. Germany, ECJ C-361/88 and C-59/89 [1991] ECR I-2567.

GB INNO BM, ECJ 362/88 [1990] ECR I-557.

Kowalska, ECJ C-33/89 [1990] I-2591.

Commission v. Germany (Leybucht Dykes), ECJ C-57/89 [1991] ECR 2849.

Commission v. Germany, ECJ C-57/89 [1991] ECR 2849.

Commission v. Germany, ECJ C-58/89 [1991] ECR I-4983.

Marleasing, Case C-106/89 [1990] ECR I-4135.

Gourmettrie Van den Berg, ECJ C-169/89 [1990] ECR I-2143.

Nimz, ECJ C-184/89 [1991] ECR I-297.

SARPP, ECJ 241/89 [1990] ECR I-4695.

Commission v. Council (Titanium Dioxide), ECJ C-300/89 [1991] ECR I-2687.

Commission v. Italy, ECJ C-334/89 [1991] ECR I- 93.

Commission v. Netherlands, ECJ C-353/89 [1991] ECR I-4069.

Francovich, Case C-6 & 9/90 [1991] ECR I-5357.

Commission v. Belgium (Walloon Waste), ECJ C-2/90 [1992] ECR I-4431.

Commission v. Spain (Santoña Marshes), ECJ C-355/90 [1993] ECR I-4221.

Bötel, ECJ C-360/90 [1992] ECR I-3589.

Ten Oever, ECJ C-109, 110, 152, and 200/91 [1993] ECR I-4879.

Commission v. Council (Waste Directive), ECJ C-155/91 [1993] ECR I-939.

Keck, ECJ C-267 and C-268/91 [1993] ECR I-6097.

Marshall II, ECJ C-271/91 [1993] ECR I-4367.

Vanacker, ECJ C-37/92 [1993] ECR I-4947.

Enderby, ECJ C-127/92 [1993] ECR I-5535.

Dori, ECJ C-91/92 [1994] ECR I-3325.

Hünermund, ECJ C-292/92 [1993] I-6787.

Stadt Lengervich, ECJ C-399, 409, 425/92, and C-34, 50, and 78/93 [1994] ECR I-5727.

Tankstation, ECJ C-401/92 [1994] ECR I-2199.

Commission v. Germany, ECJ C-422/92 [1995] ECR I-1097.

Webb, ECJ C-32/93 [1994] ECR I-3567.

Brasserie du Pecheur, Case C-46/93 [1996] ECR I-1029.

Vroege, ECJ C-57/93 [1994] ECR I-4541.

Punto Casa, ECJ C-69 and 258/93 [1994] ECR I-2355.

Fisscher, ECJ C-128/93 [1994] ECR I-4583.

Gillespie, ECJ C-342/93 [1996] ECR I-475.

Leclerc-Siplec, ECJ C-412/93 [1995] ECR I-179.

Kalanke, ECJ C-450/93 [1995] ECR I-3051.

Lewark, ECJ C-457/93 [1996] ECR I-243.

Mars, ECJ 470/93 [1995] I-1923.

P v. S, ECJ C-13/94 [1996] ECR I-2143.

Belgapom, ECJ C-63/94 [1995] ECR I-2467.

Vergy, ECJ C-149/94 [1996] ECR I-299.

Van der Feesten, ECJ C-202/94 [1996] ECR I-355.

Commission v. Spain, ECJ C-242/94 [1995] ECR I-303.

Tombesi, ECJ C-304/94, C-330/94, C-342/94, and C-224/95 [1997] ECR I-3561.

Gallotti, ECJ C-58/95 [1996] ECR I-4345.

Lappel Bank, ECJ C-44/95 [1996] ECR I-3805.

Kraaijeveld, ECJ C-72/95 [1996] ECR I-5403.

Familiapress, ECJ 368/95 [1997] ECR I-3689.

Commission v. Netherlands, ECJ C-3/96 [1998] ECR I-3031.

Schröder, ECJ C-50/96 [2000] ECR I-743.

Haarlemmerliede, ECJ C-81/96 [1998] ECR I-3923.

Inter-Environnement Wallonie, ECJ C-129/96 [1997] ECR I-7411.

R. v. Minister of Agriculture, ECJ C-157/96 [1998] ECR I-2211.

Commission v. UK, ECJ C-180/96 [1998] ECR I-2265.

Chemische Afvalstoffen Dusseldorp, ECJ C-203/96 [1998] ECR I-4075.

IN.CO.GE'90, ECJ C-10 and C-22/97 [1998] ECR I-6307.

Commission v. Greece, ECJ C-387/97 [2000] ECR I-5047.

Commission v. Germany, ECJ C-83/97 [1997] ECR I-7191.

Arco Chemie, ECJ C418/97 and C-419/97 [2000] ECR I-4475.

WWF, ECJ C-435/97 [1999] ECR I-5613.

Entreprenoerforeningens Affalds/Miljoesektion/FFAD, ECJ C-209/98 [2000] ECR I-4313.

KO, ECJ 405/98 [2001] ECR I-1795.

Mayer Perry, ECJ C-444/00 [2003] ECR I-6163.

French Constitutional Council

Constitutional Council 1975. Decision 74/54 [1975] *Recueil des Décisions du C.C* 19.

French Council of State

Conseil d'État 1989. *Nicolo* [1990] Dalloz 136.

French Cour de Cassation

Cour de Cassation 1975. *Jacques Vabre* [1975] Dalloz 497.

German Federal Constitutional Court

GFCC 1974. *Solange I*, BVerfGE [1974] 34: 269.
GFCC 1987. *Solange II*, BVerfGE [1987] 73: 339.
GFCC 1993. *Maastricht Treaty*, BVerfGE [1993] 89: 155.

Italian Constitutional Court

ICC 1964/14. *Costa*, 1964 I Foro It. 465.
ICC 1984/170. *Granital* [1984] Giurisprudenza Costituzionale 1098.
ICC 1989/232. *Fragd*, 1990 I Foro It. 1855.

United States Supreme Court

Griggs v. *Duke Power Co.*, 401 US 424 (1970).
Philadelphia v. *New Jersey*, 437 US 617 (1978).

General

Alexy, Robert. (2002). *A Theory of Constitutional Rights*. Oxford: Oxford University Press.
Allott, Philip. (1997). 'The Crisis of European Constitutionalism', *Common Market Law Review* 34: 439.
Alter, Karen. (2001). *Establishing the Supremacy of European Law*. Oxford: Oxford University Press.
—— and Sophie Meunier-Aitshalia. (1994). 'Judicial Politics in the European Community: European Integration and the Pathbreaking *Cassis de Dijon* Decision', *Comparative Political Studies* 26: 535.
—— and Jeannette Vargas. (2000). 'Explaining Variation in the Use of European Litigation Strategies: EC Law and British Gender Equality', *Comparative Political Studies* 33: 452.
Anagnostaras, Giorios. (2001). 'The Principle of State Liability for Judicial Breaches: The Impact of EC Law', *European Public Law* 7: 281.
Anderson, Svein, and Kjell Eliasson. (1991). 'European Community Lobbying', *European Journal of Political Research* 20: 173.
Arnull, Anthony. (1989). 'The Use and Abuse of Article 177 EC', *Modern Law Review* 52: 622.
—— (1999). 'Judicial Architecture or Judicial Folly? The Challenge Facing the EU', *European Law Review* 24: 516.
—— (2000). 'Modernising the Community Courts', *Cambridge Yearbook of European Legal Studies* 3: 37.
Arthur, W. Brian. (1994). *Increasing Returns and Path Dependence in the Economy*. Ann Arbor, MI: University of Michigan Press.
Balla, Steven J. (1998). 'Administrative Procedures and Political Control of the Bureaucracy', *American Political Science Review* 92: 663.

Balkin, Jack. (1987). 'Deconstructive Practice and Legal Theory', *Yale Law Journal* 96: 743.

—— (1990). 'Nested Oppositions', *Yale Law Journal* 99: 1669.

Barav, Ami. (1985). 'Cour Constitutionnelle Italienne et Droit Communautaire: Le Fantôme de Simmenthal', *Revue Triméstérielle de Droit Européen* 21: 313.

Barnes, Pamela, and Ian Barnes. (1999). *Environmental Policy in the EU*. Cheltenham: Elgar.

Bates Robert, Avner Greif, Margaret Levi, Jean-Laurent Rosenthal, and Barry Weingast. (1998). *Analytic Narratives*. Princeton, NJ: Princeton University Press.

Bengoetxea, Joxe. (2003). 'The Scope for Discretion, Coherence, and Citizenship', in O. Wiklund (ed.), *Judicial Discretion in European Perspective*. Stockholm: Kluwer Law International.

Bergman, Torbjörn, Wolfgang C. Müller, and Kaare Strøm (eds.) (2000). 'Parliamentary Democracy and the Chain of Delegation', Special Issue of *European Journal of Political Research* 37: 255.

Berlin, Dominique. (1992). 'Interactions between the Lawmaker and the Judiciary within the EC', *Legal Issues of European Integration* 1992: 17.

Börzel, Tanja. (2001). 'Non-Compliance in the European Union. Pathology or Statistical Artefact', *Journal of European Public Policy* 8: 803.

—— (2002). *States and Regions in the European Union. Institutional Adaptation in Germany and Spain*. Cambridge: Cambridge University Press.

—— (2003). 'Guarding the Treaty: The Compliance Strategies of the European Commission', *The State of the European Union: Law, Politics, and Society* 6: 197.

—— and Rachel Cichowski (eds.) (2003). *The State of the European Union*. Oxford: Oxford University Press.

Bowman, Michael J. (1999). 'International Treaties and the Global Protection of Birds: Part I', *Journal of Environmental Law* 11: 87.

Brennan, Geoffrey and James M. Buchanan. (1985). *The Reason of Rules: Constitutional Political Economy*. Cambridge: Cambridge University Press.

Burley, Anne-Marie and Walter Mattli. (1993). 'Europe Before the Court: A Political Theory of Legal Integration', *International Organization* 47: 41.

Cameron, David. (1998). 'Creating Supranational Authority in Monetary and Exchange Rate Policy: The Sources and Effects of EMU', in W. Sandholtz and A. Stone Sweet (ed.), *European Integration and Supranational Governance*. Oxford: Oxford University Press.

Caporaso, James. (1996). 'The European Community and Forms of State: Westphalian, Regulatory, or Post-Modern', *Journal of Common Market Studies* 34: 29.

—— and John Keeler. (1995). 'The European Union and Regional Integration Theory', in C. Rhodes and S. Mazey (eds.), *The State of the European Union: Building a European Polity?* Boulder, CO: Lynne Rienner.

—— and Alec Stone Sweet. (2001). 'Institutional Logics of European Integration', in A. Stone Sweet, W. Sandholtz, and N. Fligstein (eds.), *The Institutionalization of Europe*. Oxford: Oxford University Press.

Cappelletti, Mauro, Monica Seccombe, and Joseph Weiler (eds.) (1986). *Integration through Law: Europe and the American Federal Experience. Vol. 1, Methods, Tools and Institutions*. Berlin: De Gruyter.

Caranta, Roberto. (1995). 'Judicial Protection Against Member States: A New Jus Commune Takes Shape', *Common Market Law Review* 32: 703.

Christiansen, Thomas Erik, Knud Jørgensen, and Antje Wiener (eds.) (2001). *The Social Construction of Europe*. Thousand Oaks, CA: Sage.

Cichowski, Rachel. (1998). 'Integrating the Environment: The European Court and the Construction of Supranational Policy', *Journal of European Public Policy* 5: 387.

—— (2001). 'Judicial Rulemaking and the Institutionalization of EU Sex Equality Policy', in A. Stone Sweet, W. Sandholtz, and N. Fligstein (eds.), *The Institutionalization of Europe*. Oxford: Oxford University Press.

—— (2002). *Litigation, Mobilization, and Governance: The European Court and Transnational Activists*. Doctoral Dissertation, Department of Political Science, University of California-Irvine.

—— (2004). 'Women's Rights, the European Court and Supranational Constitutionalism', *Law and Society Review*, 38(3), September 2004.

Claes, Monica, and Bruno deWitte. (1998). 'Report on the Netherlands', in A-M. Slaughter, J. H. H. Weiler, and A. Stone Sweet (eds.), *The European Courts and National Courts: Doctrine and Jurisprudence*. Oxford: Hart Publishing.

Clinton-Davis, Stanley. (1996). 'Enforcing EC Environmental Law', in H. Somsen (ed.), *Protecting the European Environment: Enforcing European Environmental Law*. London: Blackstone Press.

Collier, Jane F. (1973). *Law and Social Change in Zinacantan*. Stanford, CA: Stanford University Press.

Collins, Doreen (1975). *The European Communities: The Social Policy of the First Phase: Vol. II, The European Economic Community 1958–1972*. London: Martin Robertson.

Conant, Lisa. (2002). *Justice Contained: Law and Politics in the EU*. Ithaca, NY: Cornell University Press.

Craig, Paul. (1991). 'Sovereignty of the UK Parliament After Factortame', *Yearbook of European Law* 11: 221.

—— (1997). 'Once More unto the Breach: The Community, the State, and Damages Liability', *Law Quarterly Review* 113: 67.

—— (1998). 'Report on the United Kingdom', in A-M. Slaughter, J. H. H. Weiler, and A. Stone Sweet (eds.), *The European Courts and National Courts: Doctrine and Jurisprudence*. Oxford: Hart Publishing.

—— (2000). 'The Fall and Renewal of the Commission: Acountability, Contract, and Administrative Organization', *European Law Journal* 6: 98.

—— and Gráinne de Burca. (1998). *EU Law*, 2nd edn. Oxford: Oxford University Press.

——, —— (eds.) (1999). *The Evolution of EU Law*. Oxford: Oxford University Press.

——, —— (2003). *EU Law*, 3rd edn. Oxford: Oxford University Press.

Center for Research on European Women (CREW). (1985). *CREW Reports* 5. No. 2. Brussels: CREW Publications.

—— (1993). *CREW Reports* 1993/3, no. 8/9. Brussels: CREW Publications.

European Women's Lobby. 1996. *EWL Newsletter*, Vol. 10. Brussels: EWL.

Current Survey. (1994). *European Law Review* 15: 195.

Curtin, Deirdre. (1990). 'Scalping the Community Legislator: Occupational Pensions and "Barber" ', *Common Market Law Review* 27: 475.

—— (1993). 'The Constitutional Structure of the Union: A Europe of Bits and Pieces', *Common Market Law Review* 30: 17.

Dalton, Russell. (1994). *The Green Rainbow*. New Haven, CT: Yale University Press.

David, Paul. (1992). 'Path-Dependence and Predictability in Dynamic Systems with Local Network Externalities: A Paradigm for Historical Economics', in D. Foray and H. Freeman (eds), *Technology and the Wealth of Nations*. London: Pinter.

—— (1993). 'Historical Economics in the Long Run: Some Implications of Path Dependence', in G. Snacks (ed.), *Historical Analysis in Economics*. London: Routledge.

—— (1994). 'Why are Institutions the Carriers of History? Path Dependence and the Evolution of Conventions, Organizations, and Institutions', *Structural Change and Economic Dynamics* 5: 205.

De Burca, Gráinne. (2001). 'The Drafting of the EU Charter of Fundamental Rights', *European Law Review* 26: 126.

Dehousse, Renaud. (1994). *La Cour de Justice des Communautés Européennes*. Paris: Montchrestien.

—— (1988). 'Completing the Internal Market: Institutional Constraints and Challenges', in R. Bieber (ed.), *1992: One Europe?* Baden-Baden: Nomos.

Demiray, David. (1994). 'The Movement of Goods in a Green Market', *Legal Issues of European Integration* 1994: 73.

Demmke, Christoph. (1997). 'National Officials and their Role in the Executive Process: "Comitology" and European Environmental Policy', in C. Demmke (ed.), *Managing European Environmental Policy: The Role of the Member States in the Process*. Maastricht: European Institute of Public Administration.

—— (ed.) (1997). *Managing European Environmental Policy: The Role of the Member States in the Process*. Maastricht: European Institute of Public Administration.

Deshormes, Fausta. (1992). 'Women of Europe', *Women's Studies International Forum* 15: 51.

Di Fabio, Udo. (2001). 'A European Charter: Towards a Constitution for the Union', *Columbia Journal of European Law* 7: 159.

Dion, Douglas. (1998). 'Evidence and Inference in the Comparative Case Study', *Comparative Politics* 30: 127.

Dogan, Rhys. (1997). 'Comitology: Little Processes with Big Implications', *West European Politics* 20: 31.

Dougan, Michael. (2004). *National Remedies Before the European Court of Justice*. Oxford: Hart Publishing.

Durkheim, Emile. (1947). *The Division of Labor in Society*. New York: Free Press.

Dyson, Kenneth (ed.) (1992). *The Politics of German Regulation*. Aldershot and Brookfield, VT: Dartmouth Press.

Eckstein, Harry. (1975). 'Case Studies and Theory in Political Science', in F. Greenstein and N. Polsby (eds.), *Handbook of Political Science*, vii. Reading, MA: Addison-Wesley.

—— (1988). 'A Culturalist Theory of Political Change', *American Political Science Review* 82: 789.

Egan, Michelle. (2001). *Constructing a European Market: Standards, Regulations, and Governance*. Oxford: Oxford University Press.

Ellis, Evelyn. (1996). 'Equal Pay for Work of Equal Value: the UK's Legislation in Light of Community Law', in T. Hervey and D. O'Keefe (eds.), *Sex Equality Law in the EU*. Chichester: Wiley.

—— (1998). *European Community Sex Equality Law*. Oxford: Oxford University Press.

—— (2000). 'The Recent Jurisprudence of the Court of Justice in the Field of Sex Equality', *Common Market Law Review* 27: 1403.

Ellickson, Robert C. (1991). *Order Without Law: How Neighbors Settle Disputes*. Cambridge, MA: Harvard University Press.

Empel, Martijn Van. (1992). 'The 1992 Programme: Interaction Between Legislator And Judiciary', *Legal Issues of European Integration* 1992: 1.

Epstein, David and Sharyn O'Halloran. (1999). *Delegating Powers: A Transaction Cost Politics Approach to Policy Making under Separation of Powers*. Cambridge: Cambridge University Press.

Esty, Daniel. (1999). 'Economic Integration and the Environment', in N. Vig and R. Axelrod (eds.), *The Global Environment: Institutions, Law, and Policy*. Washington, DC: CQ Press.

—— and Damien Geradin. (1998). 'Environmental Protection and International Competitiveness: A Conceptual Framework', *Journal of World Trade* 32: 5.

Etzioni, Amitai. (2001). *Political Unification Revisited: On Building Supranational Communities*. Lanham, MD, Oxford, New York: Lexington.

Faulks, J., and L. Rose. (1996). 'Common Interest Groups and the Enforcement of European Environmental Law', in H. Somsen (ed.) *Protecting the European Environment: Enforcing European Environmental Law*. London: Blackstone.

Fama, Eugene F. and Michael C. Jensen. (1983). 'The Separation of Ownership from Control', *Journal of Law and Economics* 26: 301.

Farrell, Henry, and Adrienne Héritier. (2003). 'Formal and Informal Institutions Under Codecision: Continuous Constitution-Building in Europe', *Governance* 16: 577.

Faure, Michael. (1998). 'Harmonisation of Environmental Law and Market Integration: Harmonising for the Wrong Reasons?', *European Environmental Law Review* 1998: 169.

Fernandez Esteban, Maria Luisa. (1994). 'La Noción de Constitución Europea en la Jurisprudecia del Tribunal de Justicia de las Comunidas Europeas', *Revista Española de Derecho Constitucional* 14: 241.

Fligstein, Neil. (2001). *The Architecture of Markets: An Economic Sociology of Twenty-First-Century Capitalist Societies*. Princeton, NJ: Princeton University Press.

—— and Peter Brantley. (1995). 'The Single Market Program and the Interests of Business', in B. Eichengreen and J. Frieden (eds.), *Politics and Institutions in an Integrated Europe*. Berlin: Verlag-Springer.

—— and Iona Mara Drita. (1996). 'How to Make a Market: Reflections on the European Union's Single Market Program', *American Journal of Sociology* 102: 1.

—— and Jason McNichol. (1998). 'The Institutional Terrain of the European Union', in W. Sandholtz and A. Stone Sweet (eds.), *European Integration and Supranational Governance*. Oxford: Oxford University Press.

—— and Alec Stone Sweet. (2002). 'Of Polities and Markets: An Institutionalist Account of European Integration', *American Journal of Sociology* 107: 1206.

Fredman, Sandra. (1992). 'EC Discrimination Law: A Critique', *Industrial Law Journal* 21: 119.

Freestone, David. (1996). 'The Enforcement of the Wild Birds Directive', in H. Somsen (ed.), *Protecting the European Environment: Enforcing EC Environmental Law*. London: Blackstone Press.

García Ureta, A. (ed.). (1998). *Transposición y control de la normative ambiental comunitaria*. Oñati: Basauri.

Garrett, Geoffrey. (1992). 'International Cooperation and Institutional Choice: The EC's Internal Market', *International Organization* 46: 533.

—— 1995). 'The Politics of Legal Integration in the European Union', *International Organization* 49: 171.

—— R. Dan Kelemen, and Heiner Schulz. (1998). 'The European Court of Justice, National Governments and Legal Integration in the European Union', *International Organization* 52: 149.

Goldstein, Leslie Friedman. (2001). *Constituting Federal Sovereignty: The European Union in Comparative Context*. Baltimore: Johns Hopkins.

Goldstone, Jack. (1998). 'Initial Conditions, General Laws, Path Dependence and Explanation in Historical Sociology'. *American Journal of Sociology* 104: 829.

Goldthorpe, John H. (ed.). (1997). Special Issue 'Current Issues in Comparative Macrosociology: A Debate on Methodological Issues,' *Comparative Social Research* 16.

Golub, Jonathan. (1996). 'The Politics of Judicial Discretion: Rethinking the Interaction between National Courts and the ECJ', *West European Politics* 19: 360.

Greaves, Rosa. (1998). 'Advertising Restrictions and the Free Movement of Goods and Services', *European Law Review* 23: 305.

Green Cowles, Maria, James Caporaso, and Thomas Risse (eds.) (2001). *Transforming Europe: Europeanization and Domestic Change*. Ithaca, NY: Cornell University Press.

Greenwood, Justin and Mark Aspinwall (eds.) (1998). *Collective Action in the European Union: Interests and the New Politics of Associability*. London and New York: Routledge.

Greif, Avner. (1989). 'Reputation and Coalitions in Medieval Trade: Evidence on the Maghribi Traders', *Journal of Economic History* 49: 857.

—— (1993). 'Contract Enforceability and Economic Institutions in early Trade: The Maghribi Trader's Coalition', *American Economic Review* 83: 425.

Haas, Ernst. (1958). *The Uniting of Europe: Political, Social, and Economic Forces, 1950–57*. Stanford, CA: Stanford University Press.

—— (1961). 'International Integration: The European and the Universal Process', *International Organization* 15: 366.

—— (1975). 'Obsolescence of Regional Integration Theory', *Research series No. 25*. Berkeley: University of California Center for International Studies.

—— (2001). 'Does Constructivism Subsume Neo-Functionalism?', in T. Christiansen, K. E. Jørgensen, and A. Wiener (eds.), *The Social Construction of Europe*. Thousand Oaks, CA: Sage.

Habermas, Jurgen. (1995). 'Remarks on Dieter Grimm's "Does Europe Need a Constitution"', *European Law Journal* 1: 303.

Hall, Peter and Rosemary Taylor. (1996). 'Political Science and the Three Institutionalisms', *Political Studies* 44: 936.

Harlow, Carol. (1992). 'A Community of Interests?: Making the Most of European Law', *Modern Law Review* 55: 331.

Hart, Herbert Lionel Adolphus (1994). *The Concept of Law*. Oxford: Clarendon Press.

Hartley, Trevor. (2001). 'The Constitutional Foundations of the European Union', *Law Quarterly Review* 117: 225.

Haverland, Markus. (1998). *National Autonomy, European Integration, and the Politics of Packaging Waste*. Doctoral Thesis, Netherlands School for Social and Economic Policy Research.

—— (2003). 'The Impact of the EU on Environmental Policies', in C. Radaelli and K. Featherstone (eds.), *The Politics of Europeanization*. Oxford, Oxford University Press.

Héritier, Adrienne. (1999). *Policy-Making and Diversity in Europe: Escaping Deadlock*. Cambridge: Cambridge University Press.

—— (2001). 'Overt and Covert Institutionalization in Europe', in A. Stone Sweet, W. Sandholtz, and N. Fligstein (eds.), *The Institutionalization of Europe*. Oxford: Oxford University Press.

—— Christoph Knill and Susanne Mingers. (1996). *Ringing the Changes in Europe: Regulatory Competition and the Transformation of the State: Britain, France, Germany*. Berlin, New York: De Gruyter.

Hervey, Tamara, and Jo Shaw. (1998). 'Women, Work, and Care. Women's Dual Role and Double Burden in Sex Equality Law', *Journal of European Social Policy* 8: 43.

Hildebrand, Philipp M. (1992). 'The European Community's Environmental Policy, 1957 to "1992"', *Environmental Politics* 3: 14.

Hobhouse, L. T. (1906). *Morals in Evolution: A Study in Comparative Ethics*. New York: Holt (Reprint: New York: Johnson, 1968).

Høege, Katja. (1998). 'The Danish Maastricht Judgment', *European Law Review* 24: 80.

Holder, Jane. (1997). 'Case Law: Case C-44/95', *Common Market Law Review* 34: 1469.

—— (ed.). (1997). *The Impact of EC Environmental Law in the UK*. Chichester: Wiley.

Holyoak, Keith, and Paul Thagard. (1995). *Mental Leaps: Analogy in Creative Thought*. Cambridge, MA: MIT Press.

—— —— (1997). 'The Analogical Mind', *American Psychologist* 52: 35.

Honeyball, Simon and Jo Shaw. (1991). 'Sex, Law, and the Retiring Man', *European Law Review* 16: 47.

Hoskins, Mark. (1996). 'Tilting the Balance: Supremacy and National Procedural Rules', *European Law Review* 21: 365.

Hoskyns, Catherine. (1996). *Integrating Gender*. London: Verso.

Huber, John and Charles Shipan. (2000). 'The Costs of Control: Legislators, Agencies, and Transaction Costs', *Legislative Studies Quarterly* 25: 25.

Hubschmid, Claudia, and Peter Moser. (1997). 'The Cooperation Procedure in the EU: Why was the European Parliament Influential in the Decision on Car Emissions', *Journal of Common Market Studies* 35: 225.

Jamison, Andrew, Ron Eyerman, and Jacqueline Cramer. (1990). *The Making of the New Environmental Consciousness*. Edinburgh: Edinburgh University Press.

Jänicke, Martin and Helmut Weidner. (eds.) (1997). *National Environmental Policies: A Comparative Study of Capacity Building*. Berlin: Springer.

Jarras, Hans. (1999). *Bundesimmissionsschutzgesetz Kommentar*. Munich: Beck.

Jarvis, Malcolm. (1998). *The Application of EC Law by National Courts*. Oxford: Oxford University Press.

Jepperson, Ronald L. (2001). *The Development and Application of Sociological Neo-Institutionalism* (Robert Schuman Centre Working Paper 2001/5). San Domenico di Fiesole: European University Institute.

Joerges, Christian, and Jurgen Neyer. (1997). 'From Intergovernmental Bargaining to Deliberative Political Processes: The Constitutionalisation of Comitology', *European Law Journal* 3: 272.

Jordan, Andrew. (1999). 'The Implementation of EU Environmental Policy: A Problem without a Political Solution', *Environment and Planning C: Government and Policy* 17: 69.

—— (2001). 'National Environmental Ministries: Managers or Ciphers of EU Environmental Policy?', *Public Administration* 79: 643.

Jupille, Joseph. (2000). 'Power, Preferences, and Procedural Choice in the European Court of Justice', paper presented at the Annual Meeting of the American Political Science Association, 2000.

—— (2004). *Procedural Politics: Influence and Institutional Choice in the European Union*. New York: Cambridge University Press.

Keane, Mark. (1988). *Analogical Problem Solving*. Chichester: Ellis Horwood.

Kenney, Sally. (1992). *For Whose Protection? Reproductive Hazards and Exclusionary Policies in the United States and Britain*. Ann Arbor, MI: University of Michigan Press.

—— (1994). 'Pregnancy and Disability: Comparing the United States and the European Community', *Disability Law Reporter Service* 3: 8.

—— (1996). 'Pregnancy Discrimination: Toward Substantive Equality', *Wisconsin Women's Law Journal* 10: 351.

—— (1999). 'Beyond Principals and Agents: Seeing Courts as Organizations by Comparing Référendaires at the European Court of Justice and Law Clerks at the U.S. Supreme Court', *Comparative Political Studies* 33: 593.

Keohane, Robert (1984). *After Hegemony: Cooperation and Discord in the World Political Economy*. Princeton, NJ: Princeton University Press.

—— and Stanley Hoffman. (1991). 'Institutional change in Europe in the 1980s', in R. Keohane and S. Hoffman (eds.), *The New European Community*. Boulder, CO: Westview Press.

Kiewiet, Roderick, and Matthew D. McCubbins. (1991). *The Logic of Delegation: Congressional Parties and the Appropriations Process*. Chicago: University of Chicago Press.

Kilpatrick, Claire, Tonia Novitz, Paul Skidmore, and Paula Skidmore. (2001). *The Future of Remedies in Europe*. Oxford: Hart Publishing.

Kilroy, Bernadette A. (1996). 'Member State Control or Judicial Independence?: The Integrative Role of the European Court of Justice, 1958–1994'. Unpublished manuscript.

Knill, C. and Andrea Lenschow. (1998). 'Coping with Europe: The Impact of British and German Administration on the Implementation of EU Environmental Policy', *Journal of European Public Policy* 5: 595.

Kornhauser, Lewis. (1992). 'Modeling Collegial Courts I: Path-Dependence,' *International Review of Law and Economics* 12: 169.

Krämer, Ludwig. (1993). 'Environmental Protection and Article 30 EEC Treaty', *Common Market Law Review* 30: 111.

—— (2002). *Casebook on EU Environmental Law*. Oxford: Hart Publishing.

—— (2003). *EC Environmental Law*. London: Sweet and Maxwell.

Le Galès, Patrick. (2001). 'When National and European Policy Domains Collide', in A. Stone Sweet, W. Sandholtz, and N. Fligstein (eds.), *The Institutionalization of Europe*. Oxford: Oxford University Press.

Lenaerts, Koen. (1990). 'Constitutionalism and the Many Faces of Federalism'. *American Journal of Comparative Law* 38: 205.

—— and Marlies Desomer. (2002). 'Brick for a Constitutional Treaty of the European Union', *European Law Review* 27: 377.

Levitsky, Jonathan. (1994). 'The Europeanization of the British Style', *American Journal of Comparative Law* 42: 347.

MacCormick, Neil. (1978). *Legal Reasoning and Legal Theory*. Oxford: Clarendon Press.

Maher, Imelda. (1994). 'National Courts as European Community Courts', *Legal Studies* 14: 226.

Majone, Giandomenico. (2001). 'Two Logics of Delegation: Agency and Fiduciary Relations in EU Governance', *European Union Politics* 2: 103.

Malinowski, Bronislaw. (1932). *Crime and Custom in Savage Society*. London: Paul, Trench, and Trubner.

Mancini, Federico G. (1991). 'The Making of a Constitution for Europe', in R. Keohane and S. Hoffman (eds.), *The New European Community*. Boulder, CO: Westview Press.

—— and David Keeling. (1994). 'Democracy and the European Court of Justice', *Modern Law Review* 57: 175.

March, James G. and Johan P. Olsen. (1989). *Rediscovering Institutions*. New York: Free Press.

Marks, Gary, Lisbet Hooghe, and Kermit Blank. (1996). 'European Integration from the 1980s: State Centric vs. Multilevel Governance', *Journal of Common Market Studies* 34: 341.

Mattli, Walter. (1999). *The Logic of Regional Integration: Europe and Beyond*. New York: Cambridge University Press.

—— and Anne-Marie Slaughter. (1998). 'Revisiting the European Court of Justice', *International Organization* 52: 177.

Maurer, Andreas, and Wolfgang Wessels. (2003). 'The European Union Matters: Structuring Self-Made Offers and Demands', in W. Wolfgang Wessels, A. Maurer, and J. Mittag (eds.), *Fifteen into One? The European Union and Its Member States*. Manchester: Manchester University Press.

Mazey, Sonia. (1998). 'The European Union and Women's Rights', *Journal of European Public Policy* 5: 131.

—— and Jeremy Richardson. (2001). 'Institutionalizing Promiscuity: Commission-Interest Group Relations in the EU', in A. Stone Sweet, W. Sandholtz, and N. Fligstein (eds.), *The Institutionalization of Europe*. Oxford: Oxford University Press.

—— —— (eds.), (1993). *Lobbying in the European Union*. Oxford: Oxford University Press.

—— —— (1992). 'Environmental Groups and the EC', *Environmental Politics* 1: 109.

McCown, Margaret. (2001). 'The Use of Judge Made Law in European Judicial Integration: Precedent Based Argumentation in EU Inter-Institutional Disputes', Paper presented at the Conference of the European Community Studies Association, Madison, WI.

—— *Drafting a Constitution Case by Case: Precedent and the Judicial Integration of the European Union*. Doctorial Dissertation, Department of Politics and International Relations, University of Oxford.

McNamara, Katherine. (2001). 'Where Do Rules Come From? The Creation of the European Central Bank', in A. Stone Sweet, W. Sandholtz, and N. Fligstein (eds.), *The Institutionalization of Europe*. Oxford: Oxford University Press.

Milgrom, Paul and John Roberts. (1992). *Economics, Organization and Management*. Englewood Cliffs, NJ: Prentice Hall International.

Mitrany, David. (1947). 'The International Consequences of National Planning', *Yale Review* 37: 18.

—— (1966). *A Working Peace System*. Chicago: Quadrangle.

Moe, Terry. (1987). 'An Assessment of the Positive Theory of Congressional Dominance', *Legislative Studies Quarterly* 12: 475.

—— (1990). 'Political Institutions: The Neglected Side of the Story', *Journal of Law, Economics, and Organisation* 6: 213.

Moravscik, Andrew. (1991). 'Negotiating the Single European Act: National interests and Conventional Statecraft in the European Community'. *International Organization* 45: 19.

Moravscik, Andrew. (1993). 'Preferences and Power in the European Community: A Liberal Intergovernmentalist Approach', *Journal of Common Market Studies* 31: 473.

—— (1995). 'Liberal Intergovernmentalism and Integration: A Rejoinder', *Journal of Common Market Studies* 33: 611.

—— (1998). *The Choice for Europe: Social Purpose and State Power from Messina to Maastricht*. Ithaca, NY: Cornell University Press.

Mortelmans, Kamiel. (1991). 'Article 30 of the EEC Treaty and Legislation Relating to Market Circumstances: Time to Consider a New Definition?', *Common Market Law Review* 28: 115.

—— (1996). 'Community Law: More than a Functional Area of Law, Less than a Legal System', *Legal Issues of European Integration* 1996: 23.

North, Douglass R. (1990). *Institutions, Institutional Change, and Economic Performance*. Cambridge: Cambridge University Press.

Nyikos, Stacy. (2000). *The European Court of Justice and the National Courts: Strategic Interaction within the EU Judicial Process*. Doctoral Dissertation, Department of Government and Foreign Affairs, University of Virginia.

Oliver, Peter. (1996). *Free Movement of Goods in the European Community*. London: Sweet and Maxwell.

O'Reilly, Dolores and Alec Stone Sweet. (1998). 'The Liberalization and European Reregulation of Air Transport', in W. Sandholtz and A. Stone Sweet (eds.), *European Integration and Supranational Governance*. Oxford: Oxford University Press.

Page, Edward and Dionyssis Dimitrakopoulos. (1997). 'The Dynamics of EU Growth: A Cross-Time Analysis', *Journal of Theoretical Politics* 3: 365.

Parsons, Talcott and Edward A. Shils (eds.) (1951). *A General Theory of Action*. Cambridge, MA: Harvard University Press.

Pierson, Paul. (1998). 'The Path to European Integration: A Historical-Institutionalist Analysis', in W. Sandholtz and A. Stone Sweet (eds.), *European Integration and Supranational Governance*. Oxford: Oxford University Press.

Pillinger, Jane. (1992). *Feminising the Market*. London: Macmillan.

Pitarkis, Jean-Yves and George Tridimas. (2003). 'Joint Dynamics of Legal and Economic Integration in the European Union', *European Journal of Law and Economics* 16: 357.

Poiares-Maduro, Miguel. (1998). *We, the Court: The European Court of Justice and the European Economic Constitution*. Oxford: Hart Publishing.

Pollack, Mark. (1994). 'Creeping Competence: The Expanding Agenda of the European Community', *Journal of Public Policy* 14: 95.

—— (1997). 'Representing Diffuse Interests in EC Policy-Making', *Journal of European Public Policy* 4: 572.

—— (1998). 'Engines of Integration?: Supranational Autonomy and Influence in the EU', in W. Sandholtz and A. Stone Sweet (eds.). *European Integration and Supranational Governance*. Oxford: Oxford University Press.

—— (2003). *The Engines of Integration: Delegation, Agency, and Agency Setting in the European Union*. Oxford: Oxford University Press.

Prechal, Sacha. (1995). *Directives in European Law*. Oxford: Oxford University Press.

—— (1996). 'Case Law: Kalanke', *Common Market Law Review* 33: 45.

Radaelli, Claudio, and Kevin Featherstone (eds.). (2002). *The Politics of Europeanization*. Oxford: Oxford University Press.

Rasmussen, Hjalte. (2000). 'Remedying the Crumbling EC Judicial System', *Common Market Law Review* 37: 1071.

Rawlings, Richard. (1993). 'The Eurolaw Game: Some Deductions from a Saga', *Journal of Law and Society* 20: 309.

Revesz, Richard. (2000). 'Environmental Regulation in Federal Systems', *Yearbook of Environmental Law* I: 1.

Rootes, Christopher (ed.). (1999). *Environmental Movements: Local, National, and Global*. London: Frank Cass.

Ruzza, Carlo. (1996). 'Inter-Organization Negotiation in Political Decision-Making: EC Bureaucrats and the Environment', in C. Samson and N. South (eds.), *The Social Construction of Social Policy*. London: Macmillan.

Sandholtz, Wayne. (1992). *High-Tech Europe: The Politics of International Cooperation*. Berkeley: University of California Press.

—— (1993). 'Choosing Union: Monetary Politics and Maastricht', *International Organization* 47: 1.

—— (1996). 'Membership Matters: Limits of the Functional Approach to European Institutions', *Journal of Common Market Studies* 34: 403.

—— (1998). 'The Emergence of a Supranational Telecommunications Regime', in W. Sandholtz and A. Stone Sweet (eds.), *European Integration and Supranational Governance*. Oxford: Oxford University Press.

—— and Alec Stone Sweet. (eds.) (1998). *European Integration and Supranational Governance*. Oxford: Oxford University Press.

—— and John Zysman. (1989). '1992: Recasting the European Bargain', *World Politics* 42: 95.

Sartor, Giovanni. (1994). 'A Formal Model of Legal Argumentation', *Ratio Juris*, 7: 177.

Sbragia, Alberta. (1993). 'The European Community: A Balancing Act', *Publius* 23: 23.

—— (1996). 'Environmental Policy: The Push-Pull of Policy-Making', in H. Wallace and W. Wallace (eds.), *Policy-Making in the European Union*. Oxford: Oxford University Press.

—— (1998). 'Institution-Building from Below and Above: The European Community in Global Environmental Politics', in W. Sandholtz and A. Stone Sweet (eds.), *European Integration and Supranational Governance*. Oxford: Oxford University Press.

Scharpf, Fritz W. (1988). 'The Joint–Decision Trap: Lessons from German Federalism and European Integration', *Public Administration* 66: 239.

—— (1996). 'Negative and Positive Integration in the Political Economy of European Welfare States', in G. Marks, F. Scharpf, P. Schmitter, and W. Streeck (eds.), *Governance in the European Union*. Thousand Oaks, CA: Sage.

Scharpf, Fritz W. (1999). *Governing in Europe: Effective and Democratic?* Oxford: Oxford University Press.

Schilling, Theodor. (1996). 'The Autonomy of the Community Legal Order: An Analysis of Possible Foundations', *Harvard Law Review* 37: 389.

Schlucter, Wolfgang. (2003). 'The Sociology of Law as an Empirical Theory of Validity', *European Sociological Review* 19: 537.

Schmitter, Phillippe and Wolfgang Streeck. (1991). 'From National Corporatism to Transnational Pluralism', *Politics and Society* 19: 133.

Scott, Joanne. (2000). 'Flexibility in the Implementation of EC Environmental Law', *Yearbook of European Environmental Law* 1: 37.

Senden, Linda. (1996). 'Positive Action in the EU Put to the Test: A Negative Score?', *Maastricht Journal of European and Comparative Law* 3: 146.

Sendler, Horst, (1999). 'Normkonkretisierende Verwaltungsvorschriften im Umweltrecht Aufsatz' *Umwelt-und Planungsrecht – Zeitschrift für Wissenschaft und Praxis*, 321.

Shapiro, Martin. (1981). *Courts: A Comparative and Political Analysis.* Chicago: University of Chicago Press.

—— (1992). 'The European Court of Justice', in A. Sbragia (ed.), *Euro-Politics.* Washington, DC: Brookings Institution.

—— (1999). 'The European Court of Justice', in P. Craig and G. de Burca (eds.), *The Evolution of EU Law.* Oxford: Oxford University Press.

—— (2001). The Institutionalization of European Administrative Space', in W. Sandholtz, A. Stone Sweet and N. Fligstein (eds.) The Institutionalization of Europe. Oxford: Oxford University Press.

—— and Alec Stone Sweet. (2002). *On Law, Politics, and Judicialization.* Oxford: Oxford University Press.

Slaughter, Anne-Marie, Alec Stone Sweet, and Joseph H. H. Weiler (eds.). (1998). *The European Court and the National Courts—Doctrine and Jurisprudence: Legal Change in its Social Context.* Oxford and Evanston, IL: Hart Publishing and Northwestern University Press.

Smith, Michael. (1998). 'Rules, Transgovernmentalism, and the Expansion of European Political Cooperation', in W. Sandholtz and A. Stone Sweet (eds.), *European Integration and Supranational Governance.* Oxford: Oxford University Press.

—— (2001). 'The Quest for Coherence: Institutional Dilemmas of External Action from Maastricht to Amsterdam', in A. Stone Sweet, W. Sandholtz, and N. Fligstein (eds.), *The Institutionalization of Europe.* Oxford: Oxford University Press.

Snyder, Francis. (1996). 'The Effectiveness of European Law', *Modern Law Review* 56: 19.

Somsen, Han. (ed.) (1996). *Protecting the European Environment: Enforcing European Environmental Law.* London: Blackstone Press.

Spellman, Barbara and Keith Holyoak. (1992). 'If Saddam is Hitler then Who is George Bush?: Analogical Mapping Between Systems of Social Roles', *Journal of Personality and Social Psychology* 62: 913.

Stein, Eric. (1981). 'Lawyers, Judges, and the Making of a Transnational Constitution', *American Journal of International Law* 75: 1.

Steiner, Josephine. (1992). 'Drawing the Line: Uses and Abuses of Article 30 EEC', *Common Market Law Review* 29: 749.

—— and Lorna Woods. (2003). *Textbook on EC Law*. Oxford: Oxford University Press.

Stone, Alec. (1989). 'In the Shadow of the Constitutional Council: The "Juridicisation" of the Legislative Process in France', *West European Politics* 12: 12.

—— (1992). 'Where Judicial Politics Are Legislative Politics: The Impact of the French Constitutional Council', *West European Politics* 15: 29.

—— (1994). 'What is a Supranational Constitution?: An Essay in International Relations Theory', *Review of Politics* 56: 441.

Stone Sweet, Alec. (1997). 'The New GATT: Dispute Resolution and the Judicialization of the Trade Regime', in M. Volcansek (ed.), *Law Above Nations: Supranational Courts and the Legalization of Politics*. Gainesville, FA: University of Florida Press.

—— (1998a). 'Constitutional Dialogues in European Community'. In A.-M. Slaughter, A. Stone Sweet, and J. Weiler, (eds.), *The European Court and the National Courts: Legal Change in its Social, Political, and Economic Context*. Oxford: Hart Publishing.

—— (1998b). 'Rules, Dispute Resolution, and Strategic Behavior: Reply to Vanberg', *Journal of Theoretical Politics* 10: 327–38.

—— (1999). 'Judicialization and the Construction of Governance', *Comparative Political Studies* 32: 147–84.

—— (2000). *Governing with Judges: Constitutional Politics in Europe*. Oxford: Oxford University Press.

—— (2002). 'Constitutional Courts and Parliamentary Democracy', *West European Politics* 25: 77.

—— (2003). 'European Integration and the Legal System', in T. Börzel and R. Cichowski, *The State of the European Union: Law, Politics, and Society*. Oxford: Oxford University Press.

—— and Thomas Brunell. (2002). 'The European Court, National Judges and Legal Integration: A Researcher's Guide to the Data Base on Preliminary References in European Law, 1958–98', *European Law Journal* 6: 117–127.

—— —— (1998a). 'Constructing a Supranational Constitution: Dispute Resolution and Governance in the European Community', *American Political Science Review* 92: 63.

—— —— (1998b). 'The European Court and the National Courts: A Statistical Analysis of Preliminary References, 1961–95', *Journal of European Public Policy* 5: 66.

—— and James Caporaso. (1998a). 'La Cour européenne et l'intégration', *Revue Française de Science Politique* 48: 195.

—— —— (1998b). 'From Free Trade to Supranational Polity: The European Court and Integration', in W. Sandholtz and A. Stone Sweet (eds.), *European Integration and Supranational Governance*. Oxford: Oxford University Press.

—— and Margaret McCown. (2003). 'Discretion and Precedent in European Law', in O. Wiklund (ed.), *Judicial Discretion in European Perspective*. Stockholm: Kluwer Law International.

Stone Sweet, Alec. and Wayne Sandholtz. (1997). 'European Integration and Supranational Governance'. *Journal of European Public Policy*, 4: 297.

—— —— 'Integration, Supranational Governance, and the Institutionalization of the European Polity', in W. Sandholtz and A. Stone Sweet (eds.), *European Integration and Supranational Governance*. Oxford: Oxford University Press.

Stone Sweet, Alec and Wayne Sandholtz. (1999). 'European Integration and Supranational Governance Revisted: Rejoinder to Branch and Øhrgaard.' *Journal of European Public Policy* 6: 144.

—— and Wayne Sandholtz. (2002). 'Response to George Tsebelis and Geoffrey Garrett', online at www.nuff.ox.ac.uk/Users/Sweet/index.html.

—— —— and Neil Fligstein. (2001). 'The Institutionalization of European Space', in A. Stone Sweet, W. Sandholtz, and N. Fligstein (eds.), *The Institutionalization of Europe*. Oxford: Oxford University Press.

—— —— —— (eds.). (2001). *The Institutionalization of Europe*. Oxford: Oxford University Press.

Streeck, Wolfgang. (1995). 'From Market-Making to State-building? Reflections on the Political Economy of European Social Policy', in S. Leibfried and P. Pierson (eds.), *European Social Policy: Between Fragmentation and Integration*. Washington, DC: Brookings Institution.

Tallberg, Jonas. (2002). 'Delegation to Supranational Institutions: Why, How, and with What Consequences?', *West European Politics* 25: 23.

Temmink, Harrie. (2000). 'From Danish Bottles to Danish Bees: The Dynamics of Free Movement of Goods and Environmental Protection', in H. Somsen (ed.), *Yearbook of European Environmental Law* 1. Oxford: Oxford University Press, 61.

Tesoka, Sabrina. (1999). 'Judicial Politics in the European Union: Its Impact on National Opportunity Structures for Gender Equality', *Max Planck Institute for the Study of Societies Working Paper 99/2*. Cologne: Max Planck Institute.

Thatcher, Mark and Alec Stone Sweet. (2002). 'Theory and Practice of Delegation to Non-Majoritarian Institutions', *West European Politics*, 25: 1.

—— —— (eds.) (2002). Special Issue: The Politics of Delegation: Non-Majoritarian Institutions in Europe, *West European Politics* 25 (1).

Timmermans, Christiaan. (2002). 'The Constitutionalization of the European Union', *Yearbook of European Law* 22: 1.

Tridimas, Takis. (1994). 'Horizontal Direct Effect of Directives: A Missed Opportunity?', *European Law Review* 19: 620.

Tsebelis, George. (1994). 'The Power of the European Parliament as a Conditional Agenda Setter', *American Political Science Review* 88: 128.

—— and Geoffrey Garrett. (2001). 'The Institutional Foundations of Intergovernmentalism and Supranationalism in the European Union', *International Organization* 55: 357.

Turnbull, Penelope and Wayne Sandholtz. (2001). 'Policing and Immigration: The Creation of New Social Spaces', in A. Stone Sweet, W. Sandholtz, and N. Fligstein (eds.), *The Institutionalization of Europe*. Oxford: Oxford University Press.

Turner, Catherine and Rodolphe Muñoz. (2000). 'Revising the Judicial Architecture of the European Union', *Yearbook of European Law* 19: 1.

Vanberg, Georg. (1998). 'Abstract Judicial Review, Legislative Bargaining, and Policy Compromise', *Journal of Theoretical Politics* 10: 299.

Vegter, Marlies and Sacha Prechal. (1992). 'On Indirect Discrimination and Discrimination on the Grounds of Pregnancy/Maternity', *Report of the Network of Experts on the Implementation of the Equality Directives*.

Von Bogdandy, A. and J. Bast. (2002). 'The EU's Vertical Order of Competences: The Current Law and Proposal for its Reform', *Common Market Law Review* 39: 227.

Vosniadou, S. and A. Ortony (eds.). (1989). *Similarity and Analogical Reasoning*. Cambridge: Cambridge University Press.

Waltz, Kenneth. (1979). *Theory of International Politics*. New York: McGraw–Hill.

Ward, Angela. (1993). 'The Right to an Effective remedy in EC Law and Environmental Protection', *Journal of Environmental Law* 5: 221.

—— (2000a). *Judicial Review and the Rights of Private Parties in EC Law*. Oxford: Oxford University Press.

—— (2000b). 'Litigating Environmental Wrongs in the EC: Problems, Prospects, and Strategies', in H. Somsen (ed.), *Yearbook of European Environmental Law 1*. Oxford: Oxford University Press.

Warner, Harriet. (1984). 'EC Social Policy in Practice: Community Action on Behalf of Women and its Impact in the Member States', *Journal of Common Market Studies* 23: 141.

Weale, Albert. (1996). 'Environmental Rules and Rulemaking in the EU', *Journal of European Public Policy* 3: 594.

—— Geoffrey Pridham, Andrea Williams, and Martin Porter. (1996). 'Environmental Administration in Six Countries', *Public Administration* 74: 255.

—— —— Michelle Cini, Dimitrios Konstadakopulos, Martin Porter, and Brendan Flynn. (2000). *Environmental Governance in Europe*. Oxford: Oxford University Press.

Weatherhill, Stephen. (2003). *Cases and Materials on EU Law*. Oxford: Oxford University Press.

Weatherill, Stephan. (1996). 'After Keck: Some Thoughts on How to Clarify the Clarification', *Common Market Law Review* 33: 886.

Webster, Ruth. (1998). 'Environmental Collective Action: Stable Patterns of Cooperation and Issue Alliances at the European Level', in J. Greenwood and M. Aspinwall (eds.), *Collective Action in the European Union*. London: Routledge.

Weber, Max. (1978). *Economy and Society*. Berkeley: University of California Press.

Weiler, Joseph H. H. (1981). 'The Community System: The Dual Character of Supranationalism', *Yearbook of European Law* 1: 268.

—— (1986). 'Eurocracy and Distrust'. *Washington Law Review*, 61: 1131.

—— (1991). 'The Transformation of Europe', *Yale Law Journal* 100: 2403.

—— (1994). 'A Quiet Revolution: The European Court and Its Interlocutors', *Comparative Political Studies* 26: 510.

Weiler, Joseph H. H. (1995). 'The State "über alles": Demos, Telos and the German Maastricht Decision', in O. Due, M. Lutter, and J. Schwarze (eds.), *Festschrift für Ulrich Everling*. Baden-Baden: Nomos.

—— (1999*a*). *The Constitution of Europe: 'Do the New Clothes Have an Emperor?' and Other Essays on European Integration*. Cambridge: Cambridge University Press.

—— (1999*b*). 'The Constitution of the Common Marketplace: Text and Context in the Evolution of the Free Movement of Goods', in P. Craig and G. de Burca (eds.), *The Evolution of EU Law*. Oxford: Oxford University Press.

—— and Nicolas J. S. Lockhart. (1995*a*). 'Taking Rights Seriously" Seriously: The European Court and its Fundamental Rights Jurisprudence—Part I', *Common Market Law Review* 32: 51.

—— —— (1995*b*). ' "Taking Rights Seriously" Seriously: The European Court and its Fundamental Rights Jurisprudence—Part II', *Common Market Law Review* 32: 579.

Wessels, Wolfgang. (1997). 'An Ever Closer Fusion?', *Journal of Common Market Studies* 35: 267–99.

White, Eric L. (1989). 'In Search of the Limits to Article 30 of the EEC Treaty', *Common Market Law* Review 26: 235.

Whiteford, Elaine A. (1996). 'Occupational Pensions and European Law: Clarity at Last?', in T. Hervey and D. O'Keefe (eds.), *Sex Equality Law in the European Union*. New York, Wiley.

Wiener, Antje and Jo Shaw (eds.) (2003), Special Issue: 'The Evolving Norms of Constitutionlism', *European Law Journal*, 9:

Wiklund, Ola. (2003). 'Taking the World View of the European Judge Seriously: Some Reflections on the Role of Ideology in Adjudication', in O. Wiklund (ed.), *Judicial Discretion in European Perspective*. Stockholm: Kluwer Law International, 29.

—— (ed.) (2003). *Judicial Discretion in European Perspective*. Stockholm: Kluwer Law International.

Williamson, Oliver. (1985). *The Economic Institutions of Capitalism*. New York: Free Press.

Wils, Wouter. (1994). 'The Birds Directive Fifteen Years Later: A Survey of the Case Law and a Comparison with the Habitats Directive', *Journal of Environmental Law* 6: 219.

Wind, Marlene. (2001). *Sovereignty and European Integration: Towards a Post-Hobbesian Order*. Houndmills, New York: Palgrave.

Witte, Bruno de. (1998). 'The Pillar Structure and the Nature of the EU: Greek Temple or French Gothic Cathedral?', in T. Heukels, N. Blokker, and M. Brus (eds.), *The European Union after Amsterdam*. Leiden: Europa Institute of Leiden University.

Wooldridge, Frank. (1996). 'The United Kingdom Memorandum on the European Court of Justice', *European Business Law Review* 7: 279.

Wyatt, Derrick. (2000). 'Is Subsidiarity Justiciable?', in D. O'Keefe (ed.), *Liber Amoricum Gordon Slynn*. The Hague: Kluwer.

Young, Lorna, Miriam Lenz, and Dóra Sif Tynes. (2000). 'Horizontal What? Back to Basics', *European Law Review* 25: 502.

Index of Cases

Index